Tax Power

for the

Self-Employed

Straightforward Advice from an Expert

James O. Parker

Attorney at Law

D1501183

SPHINX® PUBLISHING

AN IMPRINT OF SOURCEBOOKS, INC.®
NAPERVILLE, ILLINOIS
www.SphinxLegal.com

First Edition: 2005

Published by: **Sphinx® Publishing, An Imprint of Sourcebooks, Inc.®**

Naperville Office
P.O. Box 4410
Naperville, Illinois 60567-4410
630-961-3900
Fax: 630-961-2168
www.sourcebooks.com
www.SphinxLegal.com

This publication is designed to provide accurate and authoritative information in regard to the subject matter covered. It is sold with the understanding that the publisher is not engaged in rendering legal, accounting, or other professional service. If legal advice or other expert assistance is required, the services of a competent professional person should be sought.

From a Declaration of Principles Jointly Adopted by a Committee of the American Bar Association and a Committee of Publishers and Associations

This product is not a substitute for legal advice.

Disclaimer required by Texas statutes.

Library of Congress Cataloging-in-Publication Data
Parker, James O., 1948-
  Tax power for the self-employed : straightforward advice from an expert /
by James O. Parker.-- 1st ed.
      p. cm.
  Includes index.
  ISBN 1-57248-457-8 (pbk. : alk. paper)
  1. Self-employed--Taxation--Law and legislation--United States--Popular
works. 2. Income tax--Law and legislation--United States--Popular works.
I. Title.

KF6369.6.P37 2004
343.7305'26--dc22
                                                     2005022524

Printed and bound in the United States of America.

BG — 10 9 8 7 6 5 4 3 2 1

Contents

Introduction

Most people who work for others or work for companies have no problems concerning tax delinquencies, since their employers simply withhold taxes from their wages and pay them to the U.S. Treasury. However, in the twenty-five years that I have practiced law, I have encountered a number of small business owners and self-employed individuals who were faced with serious tax deficiencies. Even those who have managed to pay their taxes on a timely basis have often expressed the feeling that they were not taking advantage of every opportunity to minimize their tax burdens. Most of the individuals with tax troubles were addressing the problems after they had arisen, and there was usually little that could be done to help. The best approach to solving tax problems is to prevent them. The best way to do that is through informed planning.

After showing clients the mistakes they have made, they often ask about books they can turn to in order to avoid future problems. The marketplace offers a large number of books on how to prepare tax returns and a sizable number of tax publications aimed at tax professionals, but very little has been written expressly for owners of small businesses and self-employed individuals. Therefore, I decided to address this need myself. My first effort was *Tax Smarts for Small Business*, which became available in early 2004. Although it offered some guidance for self-employed individuals, it was geared primarily for small business entities. This book, *Tax Power for the Self-Employed,* is aimed exclusively at tax issues affecting those who earn part, if not all, of their income from some form of self-employment.

I conduct my law practice as a self-employed individual and have previously spent a number of years as a self-employed independent contractor, buying and reselling consumer goods and providing remodeling services. This personal experience with self-employment tax issues, coupled with an advanced law degree in taxation, twenty-nine years of teaching various business courses (including tax) at the college level, and the experience of representing numerous clients while working through their tax problems, (whew!) gives me a first-hand perspective of the type of tax information that the typical self-employed individual needs. I have incorporated that knowledge into *Tax Power for the Self-Employed.*

The book begins with a section on what constitutes self-employment income for purposes of U.S. federal income tax laws. In addition to a chapter on the concept of self-employment income, there is a chapter distinguishing hobby income and losses from self-employment income and losses. Another chapter explores circumstances in which a taxpayer may have realized income for tax purposes but does not have the actual receipts—a phenomenon known as *phantom income.*

The second section of the book is concerned with the steps necessary from determining earnings to calculating the tax liability on those earnings. Special attention is given to techniques available to legally minimizing tax liabilities for self-employed taxpayers. The section begins with a chapter on the general business deductions available to the self-employed, and is followed by chapters on the specific deductions available to the self-employed for in-home office expenses and for the cost of goods sold. Non-business deductions for the self-employed are covered next in this segment, with subsequent chapters devoted to issues that are pertinent not only to self-employed workers, but to taxpayers in general. Entire chapters are devoted to deductions from adjusted gross income, exemptions, federal income taxes, and common credits available to offset those taxes. The second section of the book concludes with a chapter on the various retirement plan options that offer either tax deferral or tax exclusion to self-employed taxpayers on some of their earnings.

The final section of the book, which consists of a single chapter, offers guidance to self-employed taxpayers in fulfilling the duties in order to comply with U.S. tax laws. Among the duties discussed are the requirement to make estimated tax payments, the requirement to withhold taxes from the earnings of employees and pay those taxes to the U.S. Treasury, and the requirement of filing various returns. There is also a brief discussion of the most common tax crimes that self-employed taxpayers may inadvertently commit.

Although a single volume cannot possibly cover all of the aspects of the extremely complex U.S. tax laws, this book does offer self-employed taxpayers basic guidance for understanding the fundamental tax issues that they face. Even those who are able to avail themselves of the services of tax professionals should be able to better and more quickly understand their advisors by having spent a few hours acquainting themselves with the issues addressed in *Tax Power for the Self-Employed.*

Great effort has been expended to insure the accuracy of the material in this book. However, tax laws are open to interpretation and are subject to constant change. Therefore, it is advisable to confirm the continued accuracy of materials contained in this book before relying on them.

SECTION 1:
MAKING MONEY

Chapter 1

Self-Employment Income

There are few things that the typical person encounters on a regular basis that are more misunderstood than taxes. Most people simply leave it to their employers to withhold and pay the necessary taxes from their earnings, and then they pay a tax return preparer at the end of the year to tell them whether they owe some more taxes or will be getting a refund. But since self-employed taxpayers are their own employers, they must also take responsibility for making sure that they fulfill their obligations to pay their own taxes, withhold and pay taxes from the earnings of any employees that they may have, and file returns in support of those payments. Therefore, it is advisable for self-employed taxpayers to become familiar with the fundamental concepts of U.S. tax law.

Since the starting point in determining any taxpayer's income-based tax liability begins with ascertaining the party's income, it is only appropriate that this initial chapter be concerned with the concept of income. Furthermore, since this book is designed specifically for self-employed individuals, the concept of self-employment income is given particular attention.

It is essential for self-employed taxpayers to understand that, at least for tax purposes, calculating income is not merely a matter of adding up receipts. Some receipts are not counted as income for tax purposes, and conversely, sometimes taxpayers are considered to have earned income despite the fact that they do not have receipts to show for it. Failure to understand the difference between receipts and income could cause some taxpayers to overstate their incomes and pay taxes they do not owe, while causing other taxpayers to understate their incomes and eventually be assessed unexpected tax deficiencies along with penalties and interest. Because of this, a substantial part of this chapter is devoted to explaining the concept of determining income for tax purposes.

Income determination is only the first step in the calculation of a self-employed taxpayer's tax liability. Most workers who earn their livelihoods as some other party's employee have only a limited number of deductions available to them that they can use to reduce their taxes. Many such taxpayers simply take the familiar *standard deduction* based on marital status and adjusted annually for inflation. Even those who itemize deductions generally deduct little more than the taxes and interest that they pay on their homes.

By contrast, self-employed taxpayers not only have the standard and personal itemized deductions available, but they also have a myriad of business deductions available to them by virtue of being in business for themselves. They also have several deductions that have been granted to them by specific legislation. Failure to take full advantage of these available deductions will result in self-employed taxpayers paying taxes they could legitimately avoid. It is for this reason that several subsequent chapters address, in detail, the various types of deductions that are available to self-employed taxpayers.

In order to detail the opportunities to minimize tax liabilities and meet duties regarding taxes for the self-employed taxpayers, future chapters are devoted to deductions available for exemptions, the types of federal taxes that self-employed workers must usually pay, retirement plans that offer the potential for some tax relief, and the payment and reporting duties that they face. Typically, self-employed workers struggle to raise enough capital to stay in business and generate a livable amount of income. Few self-employed taxpayers can afford to waste money paying more taxes than they are required to pay. Those who are confronted with unexpected tax liabilities, interest, and penalties may be forced out of their self-employment trades and businesses altogether.

It is not uncommon for those who have engaged in some form of money-making activity on a limited basis to be surprised to learn that they are considered to have earned self-employment income that must be reported on Schedule C of Form 1040 and that they must pay taxes, accordingly. Much of their earnings may be offset by their business deductions, but the fact remains that their net earnings will be subject to federal income taxation unless the income is offset by exemptions and personal deductions.

An even bigger surprise for many taxpayers is that engaging in such trivial activities as babysitting, cleaning houses for elderly neighbors on weekends, or keeping a set of books for a small business from their home can subject them to self-employment income. The money they earn will be subject to self-employment tax when the self-employment income from all such activities together exceeds a mere $400 for the year. Business deductions will offset the amount of self-employment earnings that are subject to federal income tax. However, the exemptions and personal deductions that often enable parties to escape federal income taxes on their self-employment income cannot be used to offset the amount of income that is subject to self-employment taxes. This surprise occurs most often because people do not realize what the self-employment tax is and what serves as the basis for it. Understanding these core concepts is step one in learning what you can do to minimize this additional tax burden.

SELF-EMPLOYMENT TAX VS. FICA

Employees are required to pay FICA taxes under provisions of the *Federal Insurance Contributions Act* (FICA). It is comprised of two parts. The first is payment for *Old Age, Survivors, and Disability Insurance* (OASDI), generally referred to as Social Security tax, which is 6.2% of the income subject to the tax. The second is hospital insurance, known as Medicare, which is 1.45% of the income subject to the tax. The portion of the tax that goes to OASDI is used to fund Social Security programs, such as retirement benefits and disability benefits. It is also used to provide benefits for eligible spouses and dependent children of qualified deceased, disabled, or retired taxpayers. The Medicare portion of the FICA tax is used to finance health-care benefits, primarily for elderly retirees.

The OASDI portion of FICA taxes is imposed on only a specified amount of a taxpayer's income. In 2004, the amount was $87,900. The amount of income on which the OASDI portion of FICA taxes is levied is indexed such that it changes each year to the percentage the average income in the U.S. changes. There is no cap on the amount of a taxpayer's earnings that are subject to the Medicare portion of FICA taxes.

Employers are required to pay FICA taxes on behalf of their employees in an amount equal what their employees must pay. As a result, both the employer and employee are each required to pay a total of 7.65% on the amount of the employee's earnings that are subject to both the OASDI and Medicare components of FICA taxes, for a combined total of 15.3%. The combined Medicare tax payments on income in excess of the earnings subject to OASDI is 2.9%.

Self-employed taxpayers are required to pay self-employment taxes in lieu of FICA taxes. Since there is no employer to pay a matching share, the nominal rate for self-employment taxes is set at 15.3%—the total of the combined employer's and employee's share of FICA taxes. Rather than being a progressive tax—such as the U.S. income tax, which starts out at low rates and increases as taxable income increases—it starts out at the highest rate on the very first dollar that is subject to the tax. This can make FICA tax especially burdensome. In fact, the tax is actually a regressive tax, since it drops dramatically once a self-employed taxpayer's self-employment income reaches a relatively high level.

There are many other factors that make self-employment taxes a burden, such as the lack of non-business deductions. These include the itemized or standard deduction allowed in calculating taxable income for income tax purposes, and the lack of any allowance for exemptions for dependents, to reduce the amount of earnings to which the tax rate is applied. However, self-employed taxpayers are allowed to use business-related deductions to reduce their self-employment incomes and thereby reduce their self-employment tax liability. It is for this reason that self-employed taxpayers usually find it important to qualify as many of their deductions as they can for treatment as business deductions. This excludes the amount of the deduction from self-employment tax, whereas non-business deductions will not offset earnings subject to self-employment tax.

EXAMPLE: Phyllis is a self-employed custom cabinetmaker. She received so many orders for cabinets that she bought $75,000 worth of new equipment in order to increase her productive capacity. In order to pay for the equipment, she obtained a second mortgage on her house. The interest payments on the second mortgage qualify for deduction as a personal home mortgage interest deduction on Schedule A of Form 1040. However, since Phyllis used the proceeds of the loan to acquire equipment for business use, Phyllis will be allowed to take a business deduction for the interest on her second mortgage as an alternative to taking a personal itemized deduction for it.

If Phyllis takes a business deduction for her second mortgage interest, it will reduce her business income, which will then reduce the amount of her earnings that are subject to both federal income tax and self-employment taxes. If Phyllis were to take her second mortgage interest expense as a personal itemized deduction on Schedule A, it would not affect the level of her income subject to self-employment taxes. It would not even reduce her federal income tax liability if her total itemized deductions, including her second mortgage interest, failed to exceed her allowable standard deduction.

Many self-employed taxpayers pay larger amounts of self-employment taxes than income taxes. This is attributable to the fact that, although income tax rates reach a much larger maximum of 35% (compared to the 15.3% maximum self-employment tax rate), unlike self-employment taxes, much of the typical taxpayer's earnings are excluded from income taxation due to deductions and exemptions. Also, once a party's taxable income is determined, part of it is taxed in a 10% income tax bracket—followed by a 15% bracket—before rates in excess of the self-employment tax rate are applied.

EXAMPLE: Chauncey is a self-employed rodeo bull rider. He travels to various rodeos competing for prize money. In 2004, he took in $87,000 in winnings. Travel costs, rodeo entry fees, and other business-related expenses ran $47,000, leaving Chauncey with a net operating profit of $40,000 for the year. If Chauncey were married and filed a joint return on which he claimed himself, his wife (who is not employed), and their two children as dependents, his income tax liability would be only about $2,000. This is because about $22,000 of his net income from bull riding would not be subject to federal income taxation due to his exemptions and his standard deduction. Most of the $18,000 balance would be taxed at only a 10% rate for federal income taxes. Also, Chauncey would be entitled to take $2,000 in Child Tax Credit, which would offset virtually his entire federal income tax liability. On the other hand, Chauncey's self-employment tax liability would be $5,651.82. (The calculation of self-employment tax liability is discussed in great detail throughout the book.)

If Chauncey (in the previous example) was required to pay a straight 15.3% of his net earnings in self-employment taxes, his liability for those taxes would be $6,120. Realizing what a burden self-employment taxes have become for self-employed taxpayers—who constitute over two-thirds of the small businesses in the U.S. (according to the Small Business Administration)—Congress has enacted measures that soften the blow of these taxes.

Taxpayers who are regarded as employees have the benefit of an employer paying half of their FICA taxes. They also enjoy the advantage of not having to pay income tax or FICA taxes on the employer's matching share paid on their earnings. Some relief from this inequity has been provided for on line 4 of Schedule SE of Form 1040, which is the schedule for calculating self-employment taxes. This allows taxpayers to reduce the amount of their self-employment income that is subject to self-employment taxes by 7.65%.

This reduction is equivalent to an employer's share of FICA taxes to the extent that the taxpayer's self-employment income does not exceed the maximum amount of income subject to the Social Security portion of FICA taxes. This is accomplished by multiplying the self-employment income by 92.35% (.9235) before applying the self-employment tax rate. The impact of this adjustment is the same as if 92.35% of 15.3% were applied to the full taxable self-employment income. This yields an effective tax rate of 14.13% rather than 15.3%, as long as the total of the taxpayer's income subject to FICA taxes combined with the party's income subject to self-employment taxes does not exceed the maximum amount of income that is subject to the Social Security portion of FICA taxes.

EXAMPLE: Boxcar Yanni works as a self-employed musician playing country music on the pan flute. His net income for 2004, which is subject to self-employment tax, was $55,000. He earned no income as an employee or from other self-employment. In calculating his self-employment taxes, he will multiply his $55,000 self-employment earnings by .9235, leaving a balance of $50,792.50, which will be subject to the 15.3% tax. His self-employment tax liability, calculated by multiplying .153 times $50,792.50, would be $7,771.25. This total self-employment tax liability, when divided by his $55,000 net self-employment income, works out to an effective rate of approximately 14.13%.

In addition to the adjustment in the amount of self-employment income to which self-employment tax rates are applied, taxpayers who pay self-employment taxes are also permitted to deduct one-half of their self-employment tax liability from their total income in order to calculate their adjusted gross income. This way, they avoid paying income tax on that amount of their income. Although this adjustment reduces part of the self-employed party's income that is subject to federal income tax, it does not reduce any part of the individual's income that is subject to self-employment taxes.

However, since most taxpayers are in the 25% marginal tax bracket, the net effect of this adjustment is a savings of 25% of one-half of the effective self-employment tax rate. Since the effective self-employment tax rate for most tax payers is 14.13%, one-half of that is .07065, and 25% of that is approximately 1.77%. This further adjustment reduces the effective self-employment tax rate to 12.36%. However, even with these adjustments, a taxpayer with $85,000 in self-employment income that is fully taxable at the maximum rate will still pay in excess of $10,500 in net self-employment tax alone on that income. This would be more than the income tax liability on that level of income for a married couple filing jointly with two dependent children.

Since a number of self-employed taxpayers work as employees in addition to their self-employed activities, a number of self-employed people benefit from the fact that the tax laws regard FICA taxes and self-employment taxes as components of a single program. Therefore, rather than impose self-employment taxes on a taxpayer's self-employment income independent of income that the party also earns as an employee, the specified base amount of earned income from all sources combined for the tax year is all that will be subject to the full FICA tax rates. If a taxpayer has salary or wages from a source that was not self-employment income and that had already been subjected to FICA taxes—half of which were paid by the employer—then the amount of those earnings will be deducted from the base amount of earnings subject to the Social Security part of FICA taxes. Only the balance will be subject to the full self-employment tax.

EXAMPLE: Butch is a carpenter who works for a construction company. His earnings from that company in 2004 were $70,000, which was subject to FICA taxes. His part was withheld from his paycheck and his employer paid a matching share. On weekends, Butch did carpentry work as a self-employed independent contractor. He earned $30,000 in self-employment income from his weekend work. The amount of self-employment income subject to Social Security tax in 2004 was $87,900. However, since Butch also had earnings of $70,000 as an employee, which had already been subject to Social Security tax, he is allowed to subtract the $70,000 from the earnings limit for self-employment income subject to Social Security tax. This leaves only $17,900 that will be taxed at the full self-employment tax rate. The remaining part of his self-employment income that is subject to self-employment taxes will be subject only to the Medicare portion of self-employment taxes.

It should now be obvious that regardless of the various deductions and exemptions that may be available to a self-employed taxpayer, the most fundamental element in calculating taxable income is the determination of the party's income in general. The larger the income level that a taxpayer starts his or her calculations at, the larger will the party's taxable income generally be once the exemptions and deductions are taken. It is essential that taxpayers are careful not to overstate their incomes, but it is just as important that they do not understate their incomes in order to avoid unexpected tax liabilities, as well as the penalties and interest that go with them.

As previously stated, the concept of income for purposes of determining federal income tax liability is not a simple matter of tallying up receipts. The IRS relies on some very definitive statutes, regulations, and other guidelines in making the determination of what it considers to be income.

INCOME

There are various approaches to determining what constitutes income. Economists are likely to view any increase in wealth as a form of income. A student who receives an allowance from his or her parents while away at college would likely view the allowance as income. However, the Internal Revenue Service (IRS) has its own concept of what constitutes income, which ultimately determines the tax liabilities of those who are subject to its jurisdiction.

At the heart of income determination is the concept of *realization*. Under U.S. tax law, some event must occur that converts potential income—such as appreciation in the value of an asset—into actual gain. It is at that moment that the income resulting from the occurrence is considered to be realized and the tax consequences will result. Among the events that can result in realization of income are sale or exchange of an asset, destruction or theft of an asset, or completion of work to the degree necessary to entitle a worker to be paid.

EXAMPLE: Linda bought a piece of real estate for $190,000. The property was located on a major highway and within three years, development in the area pushed prices up to the point that she had an offer from a developer to buy the property for $550,000. She refused to sell the property. Despite the fact that she had a *bona fide* offer from a ready, willing, and able buyer, which clearly established that the property had appreciated $360,000, she will have no taxable income. Absent an actual sale of the property, she will not have access to the gain, and therefore, the gain will not be considered *realized*.

There are instances in which actual payments are received, but the receipts are not regarded as income under U.S. tax law. The student who receives an allowance from his or her parents, if the payment was a gift, will have no income tax imposed. Conversely, there are also instances in which a party will be considered to have earned income that he or she has not actually received. Once a taxpayer has done everything necessary in order to be entitled to payment for work performed—and the payment is available—the income is considered to have been realized. This makes the payment subject to taxation, even though the party may have decided to postpone receipt of the payment in order to cause the income to be taxed in a later year.

EXAMPLE: During the course of the year, Paul—a self-employed graphic artist—had completed and been paid his fee for an unusually involved project. Fearing that another sizable fee payment would push him into a higher tax bracket, when another client presented him with a check at the conclusion of a project in late December, Paul refused to take the check and told the client to mail it to him on the 31st of December. Although Paul will not actually take physical possession of the check until January of the following year, he will be considered to have realized the income when it became available to him in the preceding December. If he is taxed on a calendar year basis, he will be required to report the income in the year in which he *realized* it, rather than in the year in which he actually *received* it.

Regarding a party as having received income when it becomes available—even though it has not actually been received—is known as *constructive receipt*. However, delaying the receipt of earned income in an effort to postpone the incidence of taxation is not the only form of constructive receipt of income, as you will learn in later chapters.

Taxable Income Sources

- ◆ Wages and salaries
- ◆ Gains from the sale of assets
    - If held as inventory—gain is ordinary income
    - If held for investment—gain is capital gain
        - ▲ If held one year or less—gain is short-term capital gain
        - ▲ If held over one year—gain is long-term capital gain
- ◆ Dividends
- ◆ Interest
- ◆ Tax refunds from state and local governments
- ◆ Alimony received
- ◆ Business income from self-employment
- ◆ Distributions from IRAs
- ◆ Pension and annuity income in excess of contributions by recipient
- ◆ Rental income
- ◆ Farm income
- ◆ Unemployment compensation
- ◆ Social Security benefits
    (may be exempt depending on recipient's income)
- ◆ Insurance proceeds that replace lost earnings or exceed taxpayer's basis in stolen, destroyed, or damaged property
- ◆ Royalties

Nontaxable Income Sources

- ◆ Gifts
- ◆ Inheritances (unless they consist of untaxed decedent's income, such as accrued wages or IRA)
- ◆ Recovery of basis in investments
- ◆ Proceeds from loans
- ◆ Amount of pension or IRA that represents return of taxpayer's previously taxed payments
- ◆ Qualifying proceeds from sale of a qualified residence
- ◆ Interest from certain tax-exempt municipal bonds

Chapter 2
Hobby Income and Loss

Self-employment income includes net income from self-employment derived from carrying on a trade or business as a sole proprietor or as a partner in a partnership. In addition to this traditional source of self-employment income, U.S. tax law also includes compensation for being a director of a corporation and money received from a taxable research grant in the definition of self-employment income.

This is a fairly simple concept of what constitutes self-employment income, but it is not always simple to apply the concept to a given situation. The most troublesome aspect in applying this definition of self-employment income is determining whether a taxpayer is *carrying on a trade* or *business*.

Among the issues that give rise to disputes between the IRS and taxpayers is whether profits or losses that appear to be the result of self-employment business activity are actually the result of a hobby of the taxpayer. Should the IRS determine that previously reported income or losses were actually from a hobby rather than a business, it will recharacterize the income or loss as *hobby income* or *hobby loss*, as the case may be. This can have a significant impact on the taxpayer's tax liability.

DEDUCTIONS AVAILABLE FOR ACTIVITIES NOT ENGAGED IN FOR A PROFIT

The Internal Revenue Code in Section 183 specifically addresses *activities not engaged in for a profit*. Among the significant provisions of that code section is the limitation on deductions allowed for tax purposes that can be used to offset revenue generated from an activity that was not engaged in for a profit. The deductions that are permitted in arriving at taxable income and deductible losses associated with activities that are engaged in for a profit are rather liberal under the provisions of I.R.C. Sec. 162. It permits the deduction of all ordinary and necessary business expenses—unless there is a specific limitation in some other code section. However, if it is determined that an activity was *not* engaged in for a profit, Sec. 183 limits a taxpayer's right to take a deduction for expenses associated with that activity.

If an individual is permitted to take a tax deduction for an expense regardless of whether it was incurred in connection with an activity engaged in for a profit (such as those personal deductions commonly taken on Schedule A of Form 1040), Section 183 makes it clear that such deductions are still permitted. This is true even if the deductible expense is somehow connected with a hobby of the taxpayer.

EXAMPLE: Bob collects stamps for a hobby. He uses one entire room of his house to store stamps and supplies and otherwise pursue his stamp collecting hobby. Bob had to get a mortgage in order to purchase his residence. He is entitled to take a deduction for his entire interest expense for that mortgage on Schedule A of Form 1040. The fact that he devotes a part of his resident to his hobby will not affect his right to take the interest deduction.

However, that deduction is taken against any income from the hobby activity before expenses will be used to reduce your taxable income. Expenses can be deducted if the expense would be deductible as a business expense for an activity engaged in for profit, with certain limitations. First, the expense must be used to offset income from the hobby activity. Second, the deduction cannot exceed the income from the activity, and therefore, cannot be used to generate a loss for the taxpayer that could be used to offset other taxable income.

Business expense deductions (I.R.C. Sec. 212) are those associated with *production or collection of income* or *expenses associated with property held for production of income*, such as an allowance for depreciation on machinery or structures. They are subject to limitations by I.R.C. Sec. 183(b)(2). As a result, deductions provided for by I.R.C. Sec. 212 are available to offset income from an activity not engaged in for a profit only to the extent that such income exceeds both the expenses that the taxpayer could deduct. This is true regardless of whether or not the activity that generated the income is considered to have been engaged in for a profit and the expenses that would be deductible under I.R.C. Sec. 162 had the activity been considered to have been engaged in for profit.

EXAMPLE: Leonardo is an electrical engineer and is employed by a large manufacturing plant. His hobby is painting, and he devotes 1/8 of the space in his home to his hobby. He even frames his own paintings. He occasionally sets up at local festivals and attempts to sell some of his work and is often approached by people seeking to buy some of his paintings. Last year he took in a total of $4,200 from the sale of his paintings, and the expenses he incurred were the following:

⅛ of the property taxes on his home	$ 600
⅛ of the interest on his home mortgage	$1,700
⅛ of the insurance premium on his home	$ 300
Art supplies	$1,000
Framing supplies	$ 500
Allowable depreciation on framing equipment	$ 600

Since the $600 in property taxes and $1,700 in interest on the part of his home attributable to his hobby would have been deductible regardless of whether or not his activity as a painter was engaged in for profit, Leonardo must use those $2,300 of expenses first to offset his income from his painting hobby. Since the cost of insurance on the part of his home used for his hobby and the cost of art supplies and framing supplies would have been deductible as I.R.C. Sec. 162 expenses (had he been engaged in the activity of painting for a profit), that $2,300 should be deducted against his painting income next, to the extent of that income. Since the $4,100 total of those deductions is $100 less than his $4,200 in proceeds from the sale of his paintings, he will be permitted to use $100 of his allowable depreciation on his framing equipment as provided by I.R.C. Sec. 212, to offset that remaining $100 of income from the sale of his paintings. He will not be allowed to use the remaining $500 of allowable depreciation to generate a loss that he could use to offset his income as an engineer, since his painting is a hobby, rather than an activity engaged in for a profit.

ACTIVITIES THAT ARE PRESUMED TO BE ENGAGED IN FOR A PROFIT

It should be readily apparent that, in many cases, it would be far preferable for a taxpayer's activities to be considered to have been engaged in for a profit rather than a hobby. Since conflicts often arise between taxpayers and IRS auditors over this issue, Congress has attempted to resolve the matter to some degree by including a *safe harbor* presumption in I.R.C. Sec. 183(d). If the gross income from an activity exceeds the deductions attributable to it for three or more of the taxable years of five consecutive taxable years ending with the year in question, Sec. 183(d) provides that it shall be presumed that the activity was engaged in for a profit.

When it is presumed that an activity is engaged in for a profit under the provisions of I.R.C. Sec. 183(d), that presumption shall apply to all of the years for the five-year period involved. At the inception of an activity, it may be presumed by a party that the activity will generate income in excess of expenses for at least three of the first five years of the activity, resulting in the taxpayer using losses in the first year or two of the activity to offset other income. However, if the taxpayer ultimately fails to realize the anticipated profits from the activity, he or she will not meet the criteria of Sec. 183(d) necessary to be presumed to be engaged in an activity for profit.

Normally, I.R.C. Sec. 6501 requires that the IRS assess any tax to be imposed on a taxpayer within three years of the later of the due date for which a timely return was filed, or the actual filing date for a return that was filed late. (Provided that the return was not a fraudulent return or one that omitted more than 25% of the taxpayer's properly includible gross income.) However, Sec. 183(e)(4) extends the time for the IRS to make assessments to two years after the due date of the return for the last year in the relevant five-year period. This is the time allowed for making the presumption as to whether an activity of a taxpayer was engaged in for profit, when the taxpayer had income or losses from activities that bring that issue into question.

EXAMPLE: Betsy loves to sew. She made some flags and banners for use as holiday decorations and to display in support of her favorites sports teams and schools. A friend suggested that she should sell some of her flags and banners at a local flea market. She suffered a loss of $4,300 for the first year of her flag and banner selling, and used the loss to offset income that she earned from her regular job as a welder at a local shipyard. She made a small profit from her flag and banner sales the next year, which she reported as self-employment income on her tax return. She had a loss the next year, which she used to offset some of her income as a welder, and made a small profit that she reported as self-employment income for the fourth year of her activity.

If Betsy makes a profit during the fifth year of her activity of selling flags and banners, she will have met the requirements of Sec. 183(d) for presumption that she had engaged in the activity for a profit. However, if Betsy fails to make a profit during the fifth year of her activity of selling flags and banners, she will have made a profit from the activity in only two of the five consecutive preceding years.

Therefore, she will fail to meet the test set forth in Sec. 183(d) for presumption that she had engaged in the activity for a profit.

As a result, unless Betsy can otherwise establish that her flag and banner sales activity was engaged in for a profit, using the losses from that activity to offset ordinary income earned from her employment as a welder was wrongful. The IRS will be allowed to go back and disallow the losses that she took for her first and third years of her flag and banner sales and assess additional taxes and interest. This, despite that the fact that the tax year in which the first loss was taken was more than three years prior to the year her activities were determined not to have been engaged in for a profit.

COMBINING ACTIVITIES IN ORDER TO QUALIFY FOR THE PRESUMPTION

There is a common device used by taxpayers to avoid having an activity that generates losses from being categorized as a hobby and also avoid losing the opportunity to use those losses to offset other income. The trick is to lump those activities together with other activities that generate sufficient profit to more than offset the losses, thus treating the combined activities as a single activity. This is generally allowed, as long as the characterization is not artificial and can reasonably be supported under the facts and circumstances of the case. In making the determination of whether a taxpayer has properly combined several activities into a single activity to show a profit, Regulation Sec. 1.183-1(d)(1) requires that *all the facts and circumstances of the case must be taken into account*, and states that the most significant among them are the following:

♦ the degree of organizational and economic relationship of various undertakings;

♦ the business purpose that is (or might be) served by carrying on the various undertakings separately or together in a trade, business, or investment setting; or,

♦ the similarity of various undertakings.

In applying the factors set forth in Regulation Sec. 1.183-1(d)(1), the courts are particularly interested in whether there is some sort of interrelationship between the different undertakings. Factors such as common management of the various activities and conducting them from a single business entity (rather than separate businesses), and using the same accountant to prepare shared books and records for the various undertakings all support a taxpayer's position that those undertakings constitute a single activity. The fact that a taxpayer's business undertakings benefit from each other by promoting one another also supports the position that the undertakings are a single activity, as does the use of the same accountant to prepare shared books and records for the various undertakings.

PROVING A PROFIT MOTIVE
WHEN THE PRESUMPTION DOES NOT APPLY

For those who fail to meet the *safe harbor* test of Sec. 183(d), it will be necessary to offer sufficient proof that the activity in question was engaged in for a profit, should the IRS question their classification of that activity as such. The Internal Revenue Code does not offer an abundance of guidance to taxpayers who do not meet the requirements of Sec. 183(d) and must prove that an activity was engaged in for profit. Section 183(c) defines an *activity not engaged in for a profit* merely as one for which a taxpayer will not be allowed to take either:

- ◆ deductions for ordinary, necessary business expenses, as provided for in I.R.C. Sec. 162;
- ◆ deductions for expenses incurred in connection with activities engaged in for production or collection of income; or,
- ◆ the management, conservation, or maintenance of property held for the production of income, as provided for in I.R.C. Sec. 212.

This *definition* of an activity that was not engaged in for a profit is actually more of a description of the consequences of such a classification, rather than a definition of it. There is no provision, beyond the presumption provided for in Sec. 182(d), as to what determines whether or not an activity was engaged in for a profit. Undoubtedly, it was this lack of detail in the Code that has caused the Treasury to issue detailed guidance for making such a determination in Treasury Regulation Sec. 1.183-2.

There are a number of factors set forth in Regulation Sec. 1.183-2(b)(1) through (9) for use in determining whether a taxpayer engaged in an activity for the purpose of making a profit. However, the Regulation acknowledges that the list is not exhaustive and specifically provides in Sec. 1.183(b) that factors other than those listed may be considered in making the determination. In applying those factors, the Regulation calls for a simple score-keeping approach. In this approach, the determination of whether or not an activity is considered to have been engaged in for a profit will depend on the objectives that indicate a profit motive for an activity and if they exceed the factors that indicate that the activity was not engaged in for a profit. The nine specific factors contained as subparagraphs in Regulation Sec. 1.183(b) are as follows.

The manner in which the taxpayer carries on the activity. An activity is likely to be considered to have a profit objective due to the manner in which it is carried on, if:

- the taxpayer carries on the activity in a business-like manner;
- the taxpayer maintains complete and accurate books and records;
- the activity is conducted in a manner that is substantially similar to profitable activities of a similar kind; and,
- the taxpayer makes changes in conducting the activity that would be consistent with efforts to improve the activity's profitability, such as changing methods of operation, adopting new techniques, or discontinuing unprofitable aspects of the activity.

The expertise of the taxpayer or his or her advisors. If a taxpayer prepares for a business activity by extensively studying the accepted business, economic, or scientific practices that are commonly used in conducting the activity in question, and then applies the practices in carrying on the activity, it is indicative of an intent to carry on the activity for a profit. The same holds true if the taxpayer engages the services of a consultant with expertise in that field to advise him or her of those practices. However, if, after studying the generally accepted operating techniques, the taxpayer fails to apply those techniques in conducting the activity, it is an indication that the party does not have a profit motive in conducting the activity. This is true unless it can be shown that the taxpayer is attempting to develop a new technique or practice for conducting the activity for a profit.

The time and effort expended by the taxpayer in carrying on the activity. It is an indication that an activity is being conducted for a profit if:

- ◆ the taxpayer devotes substantial personal time and effort to conducting the activity;
- ◆ the activity offers little or no personal pleasure or recreational value to the taxpayer;
- ◆ the taxpayer reduces the time that he or she spends in some other occupation in order to devote time to the activity; and,
- ◆ even if the taxpayer is able to devote only limited time to this activity, he or she hires competent qualified parties to conduct the activity.

The expectation that assets used in the activity may appreciate in value. Taxpayers who do not realize an operating profit from the conduction of an activity may still be able to demonstrate a profit motive in connection with the activity. This may work if it can be shown that there is an expectation that assets used in connection with the activity, such as land, will appreciate sufficiently to more than overcome operating losses and yield a net *profit*. However, Treasury Regulation Sec. 1.183(d)(1) specifically addresses the situation in which a party holds land and uses it for farming. It provides that the investment in the land and the farming of that land will be considered a single activity only if the income from the farming activity exceeds the expenses that are directly attributable to the farming.

The success of the taxpayer in carrying on other similar or dissimilar activities. The explanation accompanying this factor in the Regulation stresses the approach that a taxpayer who is engaged in an unprofitable activity can still show that he or she engaged in the activity with the objective of making a profit. The taxpayer will be successful in this if it can be shown that the party has been involved in similar activities in the past and was able to transform those activities that were unprofitable into profitable ones.

The taxpayer's history of income or losses with respect to the activity. Even activities that are clearly profit-motivated commonly generate losses in their formative years. The Regulation takes notice of that fact in its explanation of the application of this factor. It states that losses from the conduct of an activity will not be considered to be an indication that the activity was not engaged in for a profit unless the *losses continue to be sustained beyond the period which customarily is necessary to bring the operation to profitable status.* However, even if losses continue beyond the normal start-up period for that activity, it will still not be considered as having not been engaged in for a profit if the continued losses are explainable. Among the acceptable explanations that are specifically provided for in Regulation Sec. 1.183-2(6) are:

- customary business risks or reverses;
- drought;
- fire;
- disease;
- theft;
- weather damage;
- involuntary conversions (such as forced sale to a government entity under its power of *eminent domain*);
- depressed market conditions; and,
- any other unforeseen or fortuitous circumstances that are beyond the control of the taxpayer, such as the death of a key employee.

It would be particularly helpful in proving a profit motive if a business that has experienced a series of losses that are attributable to one or more adverse developments or business reverses can show that those years were preceded by a series of years that produced income from its activities.

The amount of occasional profits, if any, that were earned. The explanation accompanying this factor stresses that it is the relative size of any profits realized from an activity as compared to either the size of any losses realized from the activity or the amount of the taxpayer's assets and investment devoted to it that is important. An activity is likely to be considered as not having been entered into for profit if the following are true.

- The activity generates an occasional small profit but often generates large losses.
- The activity generates an occasional small profit and the taxpayer has devoted a large investment or large amount of assets to the activity.

Conversely, the earning of profits will only occasionally still support a taxpayer's contention that he or she has engaged in an activity for a profit if the following are true.

- The profit earned, although only occasional, is substantial.
- The occasional profit earned by the taxpayer is modest, but so are the losses sustained in unprofitable years and the amounts of the assets and investment devoted to the activity are small.
- There is the potential to make a substantial ultimate profit despite the fact that the taxpayer has actually sustained losses or only occasional small profits.

The financial status of the taxpayer. If a taxpayer has no other income source or accumulated wealth with which to cover his or her living expenses, it is an indication that the taxpayer engaged in the activity with the objective in mind of making a profit. If a party has other substantial income or wealth with which to meet his or her living expenses, it is likely that an unprofitable activity will be considered to have been engaged in for purposes other than making a profit. That is even more likely to be the conclusion when the losses would generate significant tax benefits for the taxpayer, if they could be used for tax purposes to offset other income, or if the taxpayer derives personal pleasure or recreational value from the activity.

Elements of personal pleasure or recreation. When a taxpayer engages in an activity that offers absolutely no other benefit than the potential to make a profit, the party's objective for engaging in the activity is clear. However, Regulation Sec. 1.183-2(b)(9) clearly states that it is not necessary that maximizing, or even making a profit, be the exclusive reason that a party engaged in an activity in order for him or her to be considered to have been motivated to engage in the activity for a profit. The fact that a taxpayer engaged in an activity for other purposes, along with a profit motive, will not prevent the activity from being considered to have been engaged in for a profit.

EXAMPLE: Sydney is a CPA and his wife works for the local telephone company. Among his clients is a small company that manufactures and sells components that are used to increase the horsepower output of automobile engines. Many of the people working at the manufacturing company spend their spare time building high performance engines for their own use, and through his association with them, Sydney became interested in building an engine of his own. After completion of his first engine, he saw ways to improve on what he had done, so he sold that engine at a loss of $500 and began building a second engine, which he also sold at a loss so that he could build still another engine. Since Sydney could only work on his engines when he had time free from his accounting practice, it took him about a year to build each engine.

Applying the factors provided in Treasury Regulation Sec. 1.183-2(b), Sydney would not be considered to have engaged in the activity of building engines for a profit. He does not carry on the activity in a business-like manner; has little expertise in engine building; works at the activity on a limited basis; cannot reasonably expect appreciation in the value of assets used in the activity; has no history of success in making a profit building engines; has never made a profit from his current activity of building engines; supports himself from his income as a CPA; and apparently, engages in the activity strictly for pleasure.

However, after three years of building engines and selling them at losses, Sydney built an engine that was used to win a race. That resulted in requests for him to build racing engines for other drivers. Sydney closed his CPA practice, set up a larger shop at his home, and hired an experienced mechanic to help him fill the orders to build engines.

Applying the factors of Regulation Sec. 1.183-2(b) to Sydney's new situation, he would be considered to have engaged in the activity for a profit from the time that he discontinued his CPA practice and set up the larger shop. From that time forward, he had organized the activity in a more business-like way; had developed some expertise in engine building; had hired another party with the needed expertise; had discontinued his other source of livelihood; had become dependent on engine building for his income; and, had started to devote his full-time efforts to building engines. Also, despite the facts that he enjoys building engines or that he might have made more money as a practicing CPA, there is also ample evidence to support the contention that Sydney expects to make a profit from the activity.

The fact that his wife has income from her job should not adversely affect Sydney's position that he entered the new level of engine building for a profit since he and his wife have been dependent on his income, which now must come from engine building.

APPLYING THE HOBBY LOSS RULES TO BUSINESS ENTITIES

The primary purpose of the IRS categorizing a taxpayer's activity as a hobby rather than a venture for profit is to prevent the losses from the activity from being used to offset income from sources such as wages or salary from a job (or the income earned by a spouse when the parties file a joint return). Because of this, the hobby loss rules not only apply to the activities of individuals, but also to those of S corporations, partnerships, estates, and trusts. Hobby losses from each of those entities would otherwise be available to offset wages, salaries, and income from other sources. Although it has not yet been formally addressed by the IRS, the relatively new limited liability company (LLC) presumably will also be subject to the hobby loss rules when an election is made to tax it as a partnership.

On the other hand, C corporations are not subject to the hobby loss rules since losses sustained by them can be used only to offset past or future income earned by the corporation, rather than being passed through to shareholders. Therefore, an LLC that elects to be taxed as a C corporation should not be subjected to the hobby loss rules when it sustains a loss.

The prohibition on using losses generated by a hobby to offset income and reduce a party's tax liability can be a significant detrimental consequence of the hobby loss rules. However, there may also be an advantage to having an activity classified as a hobby. If the activity were to generate a profit in some years, the income from the hobby—although subject to income tax—should not be subject to self-employment tax, since the activity is not considered to be a trade or business.

Factors that Qualify an Activity as a Trade or Business

◆ Activities are assumed to be engaged in for a profit if the taxpayer makes a profit in three or more years of five most recent consecutive years. Taxpayer may combine various activities to meet the test if:

- there is sufficient organizational and economic relationship between the activities;
- a business purpose is served by carrying on the activities together; or,
- the undertakings have similarities in common.

◆ If involved in breeding, training, showing, or racing of horses, the taxpayer must show a profit in two or more of seven most recent consecutive years.

◆ If a taxpayer fails to make a profit in the requisite number of years to be considered to be engaged in an activity for a profit, the party must prove it by showing one of the following.

- The activity was conducted in a business-like manner, complete with books and records, with adoption of techniques consistent with a profit motive.
- The taxpayer has or acquired the necessary business expertise for success or consulted advisors with that expertise and applied it to the activity.
- The taxpayer devoted substantial time and effort to the activity or hired a qualified party to do so.
- Assets obtained for use in the activity are expected to appreciate.
- The taxpayer had success in conducting other businesses.
- The taxpayer had realized profits from the activity in years preceding the five most recent years, but had most recently encountered unusual circumstances (such as fire or theft) that led to losses.
- The taxpayer has made profit only occasionally, but it has been large, or there is potential for a large profit.
- The taxpayer did not have another income source or accumulated wealth.
- The taxpayer's primary incentive for engaging in the activity was profit rather than pleasure or recreation.

Chapter 3
Phantom Income

Self-employed taxpayers are often stunned to discover that they have earned substantial income for a given year, but do not actually have those earnings at their disposal. As a result, they are put in the uncomfortable position of having a tax liability without the necessary cash flow with which to pay it. This *phantom income* that shows up on the taxpayer's profit and loss statement, but not in his or her bank account, can result from several sources. One of the most common sources involves an expenditure that the taxpayer mistakenly believed would be tax deductible in the year in which it was made, but either cannot be deducted at all or can be deducted only in partial increments over a period of years.

One of the most popular misconceptions among those who start a trade or business is that as long as they do not take money out for themselves, they will not have to pay taxes on the profits that they earn. This is simply not true. This misconception is undoubtedly fostered by the fact that many self-employed individuals either previously worked for someone else as an employee or are employed by another person or company while they are involved in their self-employment ventures, and they are still thinking as an employee. From that perspective, they see employers and employees as separate entities, whereas self-employed individuals actually serve as both employer and employee in their trade or business, and there is no separate company in which to leave profits.

To the degree that a self-employed person has merely allowed self-employment income to accumulate in the bank—rather than taking it out as a distribution—in hopes of postponing various taxes on the profits, the taxpayer will suffer no real ill effects upon learning that those earnings are currently taxable income. At tax time, he or she will have to go to that bank account and write a check to cover the tax liability. However, self-employed taxpayers who have chosen to reinvest their profits in their trades and businesses are most likely to suffer a hardship when they discover that these profits are currently taxable, despite the fact they were reinvested. It does not matter if they believed that those profits would not be taxed as long as they were not distributed to themselves or they believed that they must make such a reinvestment to avoid taxation.

Among the more common business profit reinvestments made by taxpayers that have the potential to create cash flow problems are:

◆ increases in inventory;

◆ equipment purchases;

◆ payments to buy out former owners, investors, or partners;

◆ principal payments on debts; and,

◆ cost of acquiring an additional existing trade or business.

THE TAX CONSEQUENCES
OF INCREASES IN INVENTORY

Self-employed individuals who are engaged in the sale of goods will generally find it necessary to carry an inventory of goods that they hold for sale. Obviously, to the degree that the sale price of goods represents the cost of those goods, the seller should not be taxed on that revenue. However, the process for separating the cost of acquiring goods from the gross profit earned from the sale of those goods is accomplished by determining the cost of goods that were actually sold (rather than the cost of goods that were merely acquired for resale but have not actually been sold).

The method for separating mere purchases of inventory from the goods that were actually sold is clearly illustrated on Schedule C of Form 1040, which is a profit and loss statement used by self-employed taxpayers to report net income from self-employment activities. After entering gross income from self-employment on line 1 of Schedule C and adjusting it by deducting returns and allowances, self-employed taxpayers reduce their gross self-employment income by the cost of goods sold on line 4 of Schedule C.

The cost of goods sold is actually calculated on the reverse side of Schedule C. The calculation starts with the taxpayer's beginning inventory, followed by expenditures for newly acquired goods (including the cost of materials and labor associated with production of goods held for sale). The total of the taxpayer's beginning inventory plus expenditures to acquire additional goods is then reduced by the party's ending inventory. This procedure causes increases in inventory to show up as profit on the self-employed taxpayer's return.

EXAMPLE: Nelle has a shop in which she sells ceiling fans. At the beginning of the year, her inventory was $51,000. Business was good and Nelle decided to use her profits to acquire inventory for a second location. As a result, her inventory at the end of the year was $110,000. Her sales were $320,000 and her various deductible expenses—other than her cost of goods—were $110,000. She spent $210,000 on the purchase of fans and other goods for resale. It may appear at first glance that Nelle made no profit, since her deductible expenses, plus what she spent for fans and other goods was equal to her revenue from her shops for the year. However, by following the dictates of Schedule C of Form 1040, Nelle's cost of goods sold will be calculated as follows.

$51,000	Beginning Inventory
+ $210,000	Purchases of Goods for Resale
$261,000	*Total*
- $110,000	Less Ending Inventory
$151,000	**Cost of Goods Sold**

As a result, Nelle's gross sales will be reduced by her deductible expenses of $110,000 and her cost of goods sold of $151,000, and she will realize a net income of $59,000 from her shops for the year. However, Nelle will not have any increase in her cash account due to her profit, since the entire profit will take the form of an increase in inventory. She still will be expected to pay taxes on that income.

TAX CONSEQUENCES OF EQUIPMENT PURCHASES

Just as many taxpayers mistakenly believe that they can avoid paying taxes on their profits to the extent that they reinvest them in inventory, there are also those who believe that they can avoid taxation of their profits by investing them in equipment or other assets used for business purposes. In some instances, they will be right. However, there are also instances in which taxpayers will be unable to avoid taxation of their profits by using them to acquire equipment and other business assets. This makes it all the more important for those in business for themselves to understand the rules pertaining to such deductions in order to avoid being faced with an unexpected tax liability.

To the extent that a taxpayer is permitted to take a deduction for an expenditure in the year in which was made, the party can use profits to make such an expenditure, offset the profits with the deduction, and avoid having to pay taxes on those profits. However, since U.S. tax law requires taxpayers to depreciate assets that have an expected life in excess of one year, the allowable deduction for depreciation for the year in which an asset is acquired can be significantly less than the cost of that asset. Therefore, to the degree that a taxpayer uses profits to acquire equipment or other depreciable assets and is unable to offset the profits with a depreciation deduction, the party will have taxable income. However, the income will be unavailable to pay those taxes since it will have been spent to acquire business assets.

If self-employed taxpayers who acquired depreciable assets had no alternative to depreciation for deducting the cost of those assets, whenever they used their profits to acquire such assets, a portion of those profits would always be taxable. The portion of the expenditure that would be eligible for a depreciation deduction in the year in which the expenditure was made would always be less than the full amount of the expenditure. But I.R.C. Sec. 179 provides some taxpayers with the option of fully expensing the cost of capital assets in the year in which they were acquired, thereby fully deducting the expenditure in the year in which it was made.

For many years, Sec. 179 permitted self-employed taxpayers, as well as various small business entities, to elect to expense up to $25,000 worth of depreciable property placed in service during the tax year. The *Jobs and Growth Tax Relief Reconciliation Act of 2003* (JGTRRA) temporarily raises the limit for the value of depreciable property eligible to be expensed from $25,000 to $100,000 for such property placed in service between 2003 and 2005. After 2005, the limit will drop back to $25,000 unless Congress takes action to extend the increased limit.

Property that is used only 50% or less in a taxpayer's trade or business is ineligible for expensing under Sec. 179. This provision will eliminate the option for many self-employed parties who use some of their assets, such as a motor vehicle, only partly for business. Still another provision of Sec. 179 limits the amount of depreciable property that may be expensed by phasing out the eligible amount dollar-for-dollar to the extent that the party places depreciable property in service in excess of $400,000 in value in a taxable year.

To the extent that a taxpayer can use Sec. 179 to deduct the cost of acquiring capital assets that were paid for from the party's profits, he or she can avoid having to pay taxes on those earnings since they will be fully offset by the deduction. Another advantageous aspect of the provisions of Sec. 179 is that taxpayers are permitted to elect to expense only the amount of their eligible capital expenditures that they choose to expense, rather than having to take an *all or none* approach. This allows them to utilize the write-off to the degree that it offsets income that will be taxed in relatively high brackets and depreciate the balance in future years in anticipation of income that would be taxed in higher brackets. Since taxpayers may use Sec. 179 to take a deduction for the cost of capital assets only to the extent of their profits, they cannot use such deductions to generate a loss to carry back and offset profits in previous years.

EXAMPLE: In 2004, Chang decided to buy a dump truck and become a self-employed operator of the truck, hauling loads as an independent contractor for various construction companies. He spent $78,000 to acquire his truck. After taking all of his allowable deductions and exemptions, only $28,000 of his taxable income for 2004 would be taxed at the 25% rate if he had not been eligible to take any deduction for the year in connection with his acquisition of the truck. The remainder of his taxable income for 2004 would be subject to federal income tax rates of only 15% or less. Therefore, Chang decided to take a Sec. 179 expense deduction and write off only $28,000 of the cost of the truck rather than take a larger deduction and avoid taxes on income that was to be taxed at such low rates. By doing so, Chang will be able to depreciate the remaining $50,000 cost of the truck in future years, when he anticipates higher income.

To the degree that taxpayers acquire depreciable assets, those who qualify to take a Sec. 179 expense deduction can take a much larger initial deduction than they would be allowed to take were they limited to depreciating those assets. Conversely, taxpayers must amortize the cost of intangible assets to the degree to which they acquire those assets (such as customers lists and goodwill). Deductions for amortization generally yield much smaller initial write-offs since most such assets must be written off in equal portions (the equivalent of straight-line depreciation) over a period of fifteen years. (For a more detailed discussion of amortization, see page 71.)

TAX CONSEQUENCES OF USING PROFITS TO BUY OUT OTHER OWNERS

It is not uncommon for self-employed owners of a trade or business who have decided to sell their operations to accept at least part of the payment that they are to receive in the form of future installments. Buyers of existing trades or businesses are often unable to obtain all of the funds that they need to complete their purchases, but feel sure that they can make periodic payments toward owner-financed acquisition costs from their profits from the newly acquired activity. Therefore, using owner financing to permit a buyer to acquire a self-employed taxpayer's trade or business frequently appears to be the ideal way to structure such transactions. However, the tax consequences of such an arrangement may pose unexpected problems for the buyer.

Self-employed purchasers of existing trades or businesses who pay at least some portion of the purchase price from profits often treat the payments that they make to the previous owner as if they were a salary. Also, in order to avoid having to pay FICA taxes, the payments may be treated as a consulting fee or other form of compensation to an independent contractor. The result of such a tax treatment of those payments is that the new owner of the business would take a deduction for the payments as a salary expense, which would offset the taxable income used to make the payments. This is an improper treatment of such payments for tax purposes.

If the IRS were to audit a taxpayer who had taken a salary deduction for payments from profits, when the compensation was actually installment payments for the purchase of a trade or business, the IRS would recharacterize those payments and properly show them as payments from the new owner's profits toward the acquisition cost of the trade or business. The result would be that the new owner would still have to report his or her full income from the newly acquired trade or business, including the portion paid to the previous owner as installment payments on the cost of acquiring the enterprise. Further, the new owner would not be allowed to deduct the installment payments made from those profits as a salary expense.

If a purchaser buys a trade or business rather than its assets, the installment payments made by a taxpayer to cover the unpaid balance of the acquisition cost of the trade or business must merely be added to the new owner's basis in the enterprise and reflect the party's investment in it, as opposed to generating an immediate deduction. If a taxpayer acquires the assets of an existing trade or business rather than the actual business, the buyer will be faced with the same limitations inherent in the purchase of assets that are paid for with profits (as previously discussed).

The result of a taxpayer paying at least part of a newly acquired enterprise's profits to a former owner as an installment payment for the acquisition of the trade or business is that the party will have *phantom income* to the extent of such payments. Since the payments will have been made directly to the previous owner, the new owner will not have the cash in his or her account, but will be subject to taxation as if he or she had received the profits from which the payments were made. As a result, the owner of the newly acquired enterprise will have a tax liability from the profits used to make the installment payments to the former owner, but will not have the part of those profits needed to pay the tax liability on them. Therefore, it is an absolute necessity for taxpayers who acquire a trade or business with an arrangement whereby some or all of the acquisition costs are paid on installments from their profits to allow for the tax liability that they must pay on those payments. It may necessitate negotiating for smaller payments over a longer period of time in order to reduce the amount of phantom income realized each year or negotiating payments as a percentage of profits after allowance is made for taxes.

The IRS audits only a very small percentage of the returns filed each year. Because of this, some taxpayers who have entered into arrangements to buy existing enterprises and pay at least part of the purchase price in installments from future profits may be tempted to knowingly misclassify the payments as a deductible form of compensation to the former owner in hopes of eluding detection. However, this is an ill-advised approach. Detection of an inappropriate deduction for such payments is not likely to come from a random audit, which admittedly, would be rare.

Instead, the IRS would likely be alerted when the seller objects to the buyer sending him or her a Form W-2 or Form 1099-MISC showing the payments as compensation for services, or the seller files a tax return showing the payments as an installment payment received from the sale of an asset and not compensation for services. The seller of a trade or business would have a strong incentive to object to installment payments made as part of the acquisition cost of a trade or business being improperly classified as compensation for services. Compensation for services would be taxed as ordinary income, which is subject to rates as high as 35%, as well as either self-employment taxes or FICA taxes. Payments received for a capital asset, such as ownership interest in a trade or business (that was held for over one year), would qualify as long-term capital gain—with a maximum tax rate of 15%—and would not be subject to either self-employment taxes or FICA taxes.

There are instances in which taxpayers purchase a trade or business and make future payments to former owners, and those payments are deductible compensation expenses. In order for future payments to former owners to be deductible, they must be made for the former owner's continued services rather than as installment payments for acquisition of the business. Consulting contracts or employment arrangements between former owners and purchasers of a trade or business are common, and will be respected as such by the IRS—even though such ongoing relationships may have a bearing on the sale price of the trade or business. In order to avoid a challenge by the IRS that payments by the purchaser of an existing trade or business to the seller are installment payments toward the purchase price rather than compensation for services, the following should be done.

- ◆ The parties should have a written employment or consulting agreement.
- ◆ The former owner should actually perform the agreed on services.
- ◆ The compensation should bear a reasonable relationship to the services performed.
- ◆ The new owner should send the appropriate Form W-2 or Form 1099 to the former owner reflecting the payments made as compensation for services.

Payments by an owner of a trade of business to fellow partners or investors to acquire their interests in an existing trade or business are likely to generate the most serious type of phantom income problem for the acquiring party. A taxpayer who buys out a fellow partner or investor is acquiring an ownership interest in an existing trade or business rather than individual assets. Because of this, the buyer will be permitted to use the acquisition cost as an increase in basis in the trade or business and will not be allowed to expense, depreciate, or even amortize any of the acquisition cost. As a result, to the degree that a tax-payer uses profits to buy out a fellow partner or investor in an existing trade or business, that profit will be fully taxable, without any offsetting write-offs from the expenditure, despite the fact that none of those profits will be available to cover the tax liability.

TAX CONSEQUENCES OF USING PROFITS TO MAKE PRINCIPLE PAYMENTS ON DEBTS

Rather than acquiring the assets of an existing trade or business by paying the entire purchase price to the seller, the buyer often pays the seller for only the equity in the enterprise and agrees to assume indebtedness owed against the newly acquired assets. In such cases, the taxpayer would likely understand that the cash payment made to the seller would be investment in the newly acquired enterprise that cannot be expensed unless it can be shown that the payment was made to acquire assets that are eligible for expensing under I.R.C. Sec. 179. To the degree that the buyer of an existing trade or business buys a going business concern rather than the assets of the concern, the payment will merely become the buyer's basis in his or her investment in the enterprise.

Regardless of whether a buyer acquires an actual existing trade or business, or merely acquires the assets of that trade or business, the buyer is not likely to be concerned about the tax consequences of using income to service the debt on the assets that was assumed as part of the acquisition costs of the assets or the trade or business. After all, payments made to cover the interest expense on indebtedness on business assets will be deductible as a business expense by self-employed taxpayers on Schedule C of Form 1040. This deduction will offset a corresponding amount of otherwise taxable income attributable to the enterprise. However, interest payments are only a part of debt service.

To the degree that payments from profits are made to retire the principal on a debt incurred to acquire an existing trade or business, or its assets, the taxpayer will realize taxable income, since payments toward principal are not a deductible expense. If the buyer of an existing trade or business makes principal payments toward acquisition of tangible assets of an existing trade or business, the taxable income used to retire principal on the indebtedness on those assets will be offset. It will be offset to the degree that those assets may be expensed or depreciated under the provisions of I.R.C. Sec. 179. However, to the degree that the buyer makes principal payments from profits to retire indebtedness on those assets and the payments exceed the depreciation or expense deduction allowed for those assets the buyer will have taxable income that is not available to pay the tax liability on it.

The taxpayer who agrees to acquire intangible assets, such as goodwill, from an existing trade or business and pay for them on installments from future profits is even more likely to realize phantom income from the part of those payments attributable to the retirement of principal. Those assets cannot be either expensed or depreciated, but instead must be amortized, most commonly over a period of fifteen years. Unless the installment payments for such assets are scheduled over an uncharacteristically long period of time, it is likely that the amount of a buyer's installment payments that is attributable to retirement of principal will significantly exceed the amount of amortization to which the party is entitled for the asset. This will result in a correspondingly significant level of phantom income.

Finally, if a taxpayer acquires an existing trade or business rather than merely acquiring its assets, installment payments made from future profits toward that acquisition will be fully taxable to the acquiring party, even if the installment payments are made directly to the seller. The buyer will not be entitled to any expense deduction, depreciation, or amortization to help offset the income used to pay the principal portion of the installments.

Admittedly, installment payments made to cover principal toward the purchase price of an existing trade or business will increase the buyer's basis in the newly acquired trade or business. However, in light of the potential cash flow problems associated with phantom income, most taxpayers would prefer immediate write-offs to offset phantom income rather than a larger basis to reduce capital gains in the event of a future resale of the trade or business.

EXAMPLE: Rob was a teacher in a private school earning only $24,000 a year with little likelihood of significant increases in salary. Ottmar, an acquaintance of his, was a manufacturer's representative for several lines of goods sold in hardware and discount stores. The key to businesses like Ottmar's is developing a relationship with manufacturers so that they will give the representative a contract to exclusively sell their goods in exchange for a brokerage fee on all the company's goods that are sold in the representative's territory. Also, since such contracts are generally terminable by either party upon a mere thirty days notice, it is imperative that representatives establish a good performance history and maintain a good working relationship with the manufacturers they represent.

Ottmar had such a relationship with several companies, and after expenses, had earned a net income of $86,000 as a self-employed manufacturer's representative in the previous year. Ottmar was ready to retire and suggested to Rob that he come and work with him a few months, become acquainted with the customers and the manufacturers, and then buy his business from him for $120,000. Ottmar was willing to allow Rob to pay him $5,500 a month for two years to cover the purchase price plus interest.

Rob went through with the plan and agreed to buy the business. He figured that even after paying Ottmar $66,000 of his anticipated $86,000 annual net income, the remaining $20,000 would be close enough to the $24,000 that he had been making that he could survive for two years and then have the full $86,000 income for himself. Rob had anticipated that the income he paid to Ottmar would be taxable to Ottmar and not taxable to him. However, the accountant that did Rob's tax return after his first year in business explained to Rob that, since the only asset that he got from Ottmar was goodwill, he would be required to fully recognize the entire income that he received from the business.

This turned out to be $87,500, less the portion he paid Ottmar that was interest, which totaled $5,800, and less an amortization deduction of $8,000 ($120,000/15). Therefore, although Rob paid all but $21,500 of his income as a manufacturer's representative to Ottmar, he will have to pay both income tax and self-employment tax on $73,700. The self-employment tax alone will be $10,413. If Rob was a single taxpayer with no additional dependents who took the standard deduction, his income tax liability (for 2004), would push his combined total of self-employment taxes and federal income taxes to more than $21,000. This leaves Rob with virtually no after-tax income for the year.

THE TAX CONSEQUENCES OF USING PROFITS FROM A TRADE OR BUSINESS TO ACQUIRE AN ADDITIONAL TRADE OR BUSINESS

Along with the misconception that as long as an owner leaves profits from a trade or business in that business that those profits will not be taxed, there is also the misconception that self-employed taxpayers can put their profits into ANY business and avoid taxes on those profits. The simple truth is that if a self-employed taxpayer makes a profit from a trade or business, that profit will be taxable. The fact that profits are used to acquire an additional trade or business will not affect the taxability of those earnings from the business that generated them. Even if a taxpayer has his or her trade or business pay profits to which he or she is entitled directly to someone else to acquire that party's trade or business, the taxpayer who was originally entitled to the profit will still be liable for taxes on it (despite having never taken actual possession of the profit). Such payments will be regarded as having been *constructively received* by the party who was originally entitled to them and taxed accordingly. The actual recipient of the profits will be regarded as having received the funds from the buyer as payment for the seller's trade or business, or its assets, as the case may be.

The profits that a taxpayer receives—either actually or imputed from a trade or business—that are used to acquire still another trade or business or its assets will constitute the acquiring party's basis in that business or its assets. Even if the cost of acquiring a trade or business that is paid from the profits of a previously owned trade or business does qualify for some form of tax write-off, any available write-offs will likely offset only a small portion, if any, of the profits used to make the acquisition. This is because the full payment will have likely been made from the previously owned company's profits from a single year, and perhaps even from its profits from the year prior to the purchase. By contrast, the write-offs available to a taxpayer to offset profits used to make installment payments to retire principal indebtedness incurred to acquire the trade or business that is generating the profits will coincide with the profits.

Therefore, taxpayers who use profits from one business to acquire another trade or business (or its assets) will need to be especially careful to allow for their tax liability on those profits, rather than counting on a tax write-off from the acquisition, offsetting the profit. This is especially important when the write-off will not be available until the year following the year in which the profit was realized, or the write-off will offset only a small portion of the profit.

EXAMPLE: John, a self-employed homebuilder, had an especially profitable year in 2004, realizing a net profit of $200,000. In January of 2005, he used $100,000 of his profit from 2004 to acquire the assets of Prestige Cabinet Company. Because virtually the entire purchase price that John paid for the cabinet shop was for its tools and machinery, John intended to expense the $100,000 acquisition cost under I.R.C. Sec. 179 and offset the taxes that he would otherwise pay on the $100,000 used to buy the cabinet company's assets. Since John is on a calendar year for his tax year, he will be required to pay taxes for 2004 on the full $200,000 of profit that he made, even though he used $100,000 to acquire assets of another business. He will not be allowed to take the write-off allowed by Sec. 179 against his profit since the purchase occurred in 2005. Furthermore, since Sec. 179 cannot be used to generate a loss, if John's profits in 2005 are not at least $100,000, his eligibility to take a Sec. 179 expense deduction will be limited.

Most Common Sources of Phantom Income

- ◆ Use of profit to acquire additional inventory
- ◆ Use of profit to purchase more equipment
- ◆ Use of profit to buy out former owners, investors, or partners
- ◆ Use of profits to acquire another trade or business
- ◆ Using future profits to acquire a trade or business on installments
- ◆ Increased accounts receivable if a taxpayer on the accrual method of accounting

SECTION 2:
SAVING MONEY

Chapter 4
Business Deductions for the Self-Employed

One of the most significant tax advantages available to self-employed taxpayers is their right to take deductions for business-related expenses as a step in arriving at their taxable income. Most taxpayers are familiar with the concept of tax *deductions*. It consists of expenditures or other allowances that may be subtracted from earnings before applying tax rates to incomes to determine tax liabilities. However, many taxpayers are unaware that there are different categories of deductions available to various taxpayers, and furthermore, that each of these different categories can have a significantly different effect on a party's eventual tax liability.

The most significant factor in determining the impact of a deduction on a taxpayer's tax liability is whether it is an *above the line* deduction or a *below the line* deduction. The *line* referred to in making the determination is the line on tax returns that contains the figure for *adjusted gross income*. Calculations of a party's tax liability begins with his or her gross income, which is reduced by above the line deductions to yield adjusted gross income. Below the line deductions are then subtracted from the taxpayer's adjusted gross income as a further step toward arriving at his or her *taxable income*. Therefore, above the line deductions are commonly known as *deductions FOR adjusted gross income*, whereas below the line deductions are commonly known as *deductions FROM adjusted gross income*.

Deductions for adjusted gross income consist of business expenses that a taxpayer incurred in earning his or her gross income, as well as a second category comprised of a relative handful of specific expenditures that various sections of the I.R.C. have labeled as deductions for adjusted gross income. Both categories of deductions for adjusted gross will reduce the amount of an eligible taxpayer's income that is eventually subject to income taxation by the amount of the deduction. However, the deductions for adjusted gross income consisting of business expenses *also* reduce the amount of a taxpayer's gross income that is subject to self-employment tax. The specific deductions from adjusted gross income that are created by various sections of the I.R.C. do not affect the amount of a taxpayer's gross income that is subject to self-employment tax.

Not only do deductions from adjusted gross income not reduce the amount of a taxpayer's income that is subject to self-employment tax, but they may not even reduce the amount of a party's income that is subject to income taxation. This is due to the fact that several of the deductions from adjusted gross income, which are known as *itemized deductions* and are reported on Schedule A of Form 1040, are subject to limitations.

For example, a deduction for medical expenses is available to taxpayers, but only to the extent that those expenses exceed 7.5% of a taxpayer's adjusted gross income for the year. Moreover, taxpayers are permitted to take a *standard deduction* of several thousand dollars, depending on the individual taxpayer's filing status, in lieu of itemizing deductions on Schedule A. As a result, unless a party's itemized deductions exceed his or her allowable standard deduction, he or she would be better off to taking the standard deduction. In this case, no benefit is incurred from expenditures that qualify as an itemized deduction. (A detailed discussion of deductions from adjusted gross income can be found in Chapter 8.)

BUSINESS DEDUCTIONS

Those who work for others as employees will virtually never be eligible to take a deduction for adjusted gross income for business expenses that they incur while earning their wages or salaries. Self-employed workers will almost always be allowed to take deductions for adjusted gross income for their business expenses. Whether or not a given expenditure qualifies as a business deduction for adjusted gross income is determined by I.R.C. Sec. 162, which permits such deduction for *ordinary and necessary expenses paid or incurred during the taxable year in carrying on a trade or business.* As is often the case with relatively broad provisions, application of I.R.C. Sec. 162 can prove troublesome and is often the source of conflict between taxpayers and the IRS.

QUALIFYING TO TAKE BUSINESS DEDUCTIONS

Among the specific provisions of I.R.C. Sec. 162 is the requirement that a taxpayer must incur expenses in the course of carrying on a trade or business in order to be allowed to deduct the expenses. Most cases in which there is a question as to whether a person is actually engaged in a trade or business arise when the participant is involved only part-time or sporadically. In order to be considered to be carrying on a trade or business, a self-employed taxpayer must:

- begin an endeavor with the intent of making a profit;
- participate in the venture consistently and significantly;
- demonstrate a commitment to the enterprise; and,
- conduct the operation in a business-like manner.

The fact that the activity actually generates a loss rather than a profit will not be fatal to its being considered a trade or business, as long as it was started with the intent to make a profit. Commitment to an enterprise may be demonstrated by such things as attendance at seminars or trade shows, taking formal courses to gain expertise in operation of the business, or engaging in any other activity aimed at improving the party's ability to operate the enterprise profitably. If a purported business activity is determined not to be a trade or business, it will likely be classified as a hobby. The allowable deduction for expenses of a hobby is limited to the amount necessary to offset gross income from the activity, thereby eliminating the deductibility of any losses generated by the venture. (A detailed discussion of the factors that determine whether an activity is considered to have been engaged in for a profit or must be considered a hobby for tax purposes, as well as the tax consequences of such a determination, is contained in Chapter 2.)

It is common for self-employed taxpayers to have jobs as employees and carry on separate self-employment activities in order to supplement their wages or salaries. The fact that a taxpayer works as an employee for another party will not prevent the worker from being allowed to take deductions associated with a separate trade or business that is conducted on a self-employment basis. However, the worker must maintain separate accountings for expenses associated with his or her employment and those associated with his or her self-employment income. The worker must also limit the deductions taken against self-employment income to those associated with the self-employment activity.

EXAMPLE: Eddie is a manager of a retail electronics store. He also buys and sells photographs, videotapes, and other items associated with UFO's, aliens, and paranormal activity. He markets his goods over the Internet and at paranormal conventions. Eddie was asked by the owner of the electronics store to attend an electronics show at which distributors would be showing the latest products available. Eddie, at his own expense, drove 200 miles to attend the show on a Thursday afternoon and rented a room in a hotel so that he could also attend the Friday morning session of the show, which ended that day at noon. Since there was a paranormal convention scheduled Saturday in a city that was only seventy-five miles further away, Eddie drove there Friday afternoon, rented a room, and attended the show. He sold some of his photos and tapes from a booth that he had rented there.

In determining the amount of the deduction that he is entitled to take against his income from his self-employment activity of selling photos, videos, and other items, Eddie will not be permitted to take a deduction for costs associated with attending the electronics show. However, he will be allowed to take a deduction for the costs of the additional driving necessary to attend the paranormal convention, as well as his eligible food and lodging associated with attending the convention and the cost of renting the booth.

Employees who incur expenses in connection with their jobs and are not reimbursed for those expenditures are entitled to take a deduction for those expenses, but only as a deduction from adjusted gross income. As a result, deductions available to employees for work-related expenses may not reduce their tax liabilities at all. This can be demonstrated by the previous example in which Eddie had deductions for adjusted gross income in connection with his marketing of items connected with paranormal activities, as well as deductions from adjusted gross income in connection with his job as an electronics store manager. Eddie's deductions for adjusted gross income, incurred in connection with his self-employment sales activities, will reduce the amount of his revenue from the activity that is subject to self-employment taxes. The deductions from adjusted gross income that he incurred in connection with his job as manager of an electronics store cannot be used to reduce the amount of his wages from that job subject to FICA taxes, which are an employee's alternative to self-employment taxes.

With a nominal self-employment tax rate of 15.3%, the right to use deductions *for* adjusted gross income to offset income that would otherwise be subject to that tax is advantage enough to give taxpayers a strong preference for deductions for adjusted gross income. However, deductions for adjusted gross income are also more likely to reduce a taxpayer's income tax liability than are deductions from adjusted gross income. This is due to the fact that deductions for adjusted gross income reduce a taxpayer's taxable income dollar-for-dollar, but deductions from adjusted gross income may not. For example, an employee's unreimbursed, job-related expenses must first be reduced by an amount equal to 2% of the party's adjusted gross income. The remainder may be added to the taxpayer's other deductions from adjusted gross income on Schedule A of Form 1040.

Furthermore, only if the total of the itemized deductions on Schedule A exceeds the standard deduction allowed for the taxpayer will he or she benefit from the specific itemized deduction. Moreover, even if a taxpayer's itemized deductions exceed his or her standard deduction, once he or she achieves a relatively high income level, the party must begin to reduce the amount of his or her deductions from adjusted gross income. (The specifics of this reduction are discussed in Chapter 8.)

The significantly different tax impact of deductions *for* adjusted gross income compared to deductions *from* adjusted gross income makes it readily apparent why the IRS scrutinizes the returns of self-employed taxpayers to make sure that they are not including improper deductions. The IRS is also sensitive to the possibility that taxpayers may attempt to include their personal expenses with their business expenses in an effort to increase the size of their deductions for adjusted gross income. Attempts by taxpayers to take personal expenses as a business deduction are often challenged by the IRS on the basis that they simply are not ordinary and necessary business expenses, as is required by I.R.C. Sec. 162 in order to qualify as a business deduction.

The Ordinary and Necessary Requirement

In the event that the IRS challenges the validity of a business expense deduction, the taxpayer will have the burden of proving that those expenses are *ordinary and necessary*. Several allowable business expenses that are deductible by self-employed taxpayers are enumerated in I.R.C. Sec. 162. Included are salary expenses, travel expenses, and rent. These are just a starting point. Any other business-related expenses may be deducted, as long as they are shown to be both ordinary and necessary.

There is no clear-cut test to determine whether or not an expense is *ordinary*. There have been numerous court cases in which the question of whether or not an expense was ordinary was raised. In general, the courts have traditionally considered the issues of whether a business expense should be considered ordinary for a given taxpayer from two distinctly separate points of view. On the one hand, courts consider whether a given expense that a party had deducted was appropriate in light of the type of activity involved. Courts have not required that the expenditures of the type for which a deduction is sought be typical of taxpayers in their field or even that they were historically incurred by the party in question. The key determinant seems to be whether the expenditure was a reasonable one for that taxpayer at the time it was made. As long as there was a reasonable business purpose for the expenditure, it will likely be regarded as reasonable—and therefore, ordinary—even if it does not result in any improvement in the profitability of the business activity.

EXAMPLE: LaShara is a self-employed seamstress who makes curtains and slip covers for furniture. She operates from her home and does not advertise. A friend of hers suggested that if she put a website on the Internet that she could really get a lot of business. LaShara hired someone to design her site and put it on the Web for a fee of $3,500. Since no other seamstress have websites, LaShara thought that hers might give her a competitive advantage. However, after a year, she had not managed to get a single new customer through her website. Despite the fact that her website did not produce the desired result, and even though neither she nor any other seamstress had used such a marketing tool before, LaShara's $3,500 expenditure for website services should be considered ordinary since there was a reasonable business purpose for it.

Another aspect of ordinary that courts analyze in considering whether or not a business expense should be deductible deals with the issue of whether the *amount* of the expenditure was reasonable. Expenditures for business purposes that are clearly ordinary will likely still be considered nondeductible if they are considered extravagant. This approach to determining deductibility of business expenses is supported in I.R.C. Sec. 162. It specifically provides for a deduction for *traveling expenses*, but only as long as the expenditures are not *lavish or extravagant,* and for salaries and wages provided that they are *reasonable*. The determination as to whether a business expenditure is reasonable or lavish must be made on an individual basis, depending on the circumstances of the expenditure and the nature of the taxpayer's business.

EXAMPLE: Shawn decided to start a landscaping business. He billed his customers by the amount of time that he spent on each one of their jobs and had to acquire a watch in order to keep up with his time. Shawn would be entitled to choose a watch of sufficient quality to withstand the conditions that he will subject it to in his line of work and the expenditure should still be considered ordinary. However, if Shawn were to spend $10,000 for a diamond-studded fashion watch, the expenditure could hardly be considered ordinary under the circumstances. He should not be allowed to take a tax deduction based on the cost of that watch.

The concept of *necessary* as it is used in determining whether a business expenditure qualifies as a deductible business expense has also been the topic of analysis in numerous court cases. It is clear that the word *necessary*, as it is used in I.R.C. Sec. 162 to describe deductible business expenses, is not to be construed as essential or indispensable. In practice, the requirement that an expense must be necessary in order to be deductible is not much different than the requirement that it must be ordinary. As long as it can be shown that an expenditure was reasonable, both from the perspective that it would be beneficial to the self-employed taxpayer in conducting his or her business, and that it was not lavish, it should qualify as a necessary expenditure for tax purposes.

SOME SPECIFIC BUSINESS DEDUCTIONS

A basic checklist of deductible business expenses available to self-employed individuals can be found on the very forms provided by the IRS for filing their annual income tax returns. Schedule C of Form 1040, which is the form that sole proprietors must use to report their business income, contains a list of twenty-six specific deductible business expenses. The 27th line of the form, labeled "Other expenses," provides space for the total of the expenses that are unique to the particular taxpayer's business.

Wage and Salary Expenses

The allowable deductions for employee compensation, as provided in I.R.C. Sec. 162, is addressed on Schedule C of Form 1040. It provides separate lines for *commissions* and *fees* and *wages*, and still further breakdowns for the components of employee compensation consisting of *employee benefit programs* and *pension or profit-sharing plans*. Payments of income from business activity by a self-employed person to him- or herself are not to be included in the deductible salary expenses shown on Schedule C. These are not included even if they are paid on a regular, periodic basis (such as weekly) and even if the amounts paid are typical of what a reasonable salary would be for the work done by the self-employed person. Self-employed taxpayers simply do not earn salaries from their self-employment activities. Their earnings from self-employment activities take the form of self-employment income, which is essentially the net profit or loss that they generate from those activities. Schedule C is merely a profit and loss statement that is used for tax purposes to calculate taxpayer's net profits and losses from self-employment activities.

Payments to parties who subcontract to provide services as independent contractors in order to help self-employed taxpayers carry on business activities are fully deductible. Payments to independent contractors who provide business services directly to self-employed taxpayers are also deductible, if the cost of those services qualify as ordinary and necessary business expenses. Payments to independent contractors should not be included as salaries, wages, or commissions, since such a practice may, at the least, cause the IRS to question the taxpayer as to why no FICA taxes were paid on those earnings. Also, erroneously reporting payments to independent contractors as wages (or the equivalent) may jeopardize a taxpayer's argument that certain workers were independent contractors, rather than employees, in the event of an audit.

In some instances, it may be appropriate to report payments to non-employees on the line labeled "Legal and professional services" on Schedule C of Form 1040. In other cases, it may be more appropriate to designate a line as *subcontract labor* (or something similar) in the section provided for "Other expenses" on Schedule C and report the payments there.

Various Deductions Listed as Line Items on Schedule C

A designated line for the deduction of *rent payments*, as provided for in I.R.C. Sec. 162, is also provided on Schedule C, as is a line for deducting *interest expenses*, as is provided in I.R.C. Sec. 163. Schedule C also provides specific lines for the deduction of expenditures for *business-related insurance*, *office expenses*, *repairs and maintenance*, *supplies*, and *utilities*. There is also a specific line on Schedule C for *taxes and licenses*, but I.R.C. Sec. 164, which permits the deduction, excludes any deduction for federal income taxes, thereby limiting the deduction for income taxes to those paid to state or local governments. However, a self-employed taxpayer would still be eligible to take a deduction for any FICA taxes and federal unemployment taxes that he or she paid on behalf of any employees. State sales taxes that were collected from customers and paid to a state government are deductible if they must be included in the taxpayer's gross receipts, but are not deductible if the taxes are not included in the taxpayer's gross receipts.

Advertising

Still another expense provided for on Schedule C is the cost of *advertising*. However, if an advertising expenditure involves acquisition of an asset with a useful life in excess of one year, the expenditure must be capitalized. The expense of advertisements aimed at increasing current sales or enhancing goodwill may be fully deducted in the year in which they were incurred.

EXAMPLE: Chad opened a men's clothing store that he operated as a self-employed sole proprietor. He ran several advertisements on radio, television, and in newspapers to promote his store. He also bought an electronic scoreboard that he installed in a local high school's gym that had his store's name on it and flashed advertisements for the store as it kept score. Chad will be allowed to deduct the cost of his media advertisements, even though some of the benefit of those ads will last into the future. However, Chad must take the deductions for the scoreboard over its expected life in the form of depreciation, a practice known as *capitalizing* the expenditure.

Other Business Expenses

There are innumerable expenses that are not listed on a separate line of Schedule C, but that are legitimately deductible as business expenses. The key to deductibility is whether a given expense is an ordinary and necessary business expense for the taxpayer in question, which is determined by the nature of the business involved.

EXAMPLE: Alagiri became involved as a self-employed individual in the activity of developing instruments for use in micro-surgery. It was absolutely imperative that his lab be free of any contaminants so he contracted to have a special team come to decontaminate and *clean* his lab twice a week. Due to the thoroughness required, the cost of the services was $2,500 a month. In light of the nature of Alagiri's activity, the cleaning and decontamination services should clearly pass the ordinary and necessary test and be fully deductible.

If Alagiri had been an accountant who had insisted on such a cleaning procedure for his office due to an irrational phobia on his part, the expenditures would not qualify as an ordinary and necessary business expense, and would not be deductible. However, if Alagiri had been an accountant and had employed a cleaning service to provide janitorial services that are typical for accountants, he would have been entitled to take a tax deduction for that expense.

BUSINESS DEDUCTIONS THAT ARE SUBJECT TO SPECIAL LIMITATIONS

Although I.R.C. Sec. 162 specifically provides for deductibility of traveling expenses associated with carrying on a trade or business, quite a number of past disputes have arisen between taxpayers and IRS auditors over allowance of specific travel-related deductions. As a result, rather than merely relying on the ordinary and necessary test for determining their deductibility, expenditures for *auto expense* and for *meals and entertainment* have been singled out and more extensive guidelines concerning their deductibility have been set forth. Extensive guidelines have also been promulgated concerning the allowance for *depreciation and depletion* that businesses may take as a deductible business expense, and for the deduction allowed for a self-employed taxpayer's office that is located in his or her home.

Depreciation

Still another line on Schedule C that is set aside for deductions of a specific business expense is the one designated for "Depreciation and section 179 expense deduction." When tangible assets that are used in a business activity have a useful life in excess of one year, U.S. tax law has traditionally required taxpayers who are eligible to take a deduction for the cost of such assets to allocate the deduction over the asset's assigned useful life. The *useful life* assigned to an asset for purposes of calculating depreciation may be a fairly accurate estimate of the asset's actual useful life, or it may be a somewhat arbitrary assignment of its life expectancy.

Through the years, Congress has adjusted the law concerning depreciation, including the methods for assigning *useful lives* to assets. This is often done in an attempt to influence economic activity in the nation by either stimulating investment, by allowing more rapid depreciation, or slowing the economy down by requiring taxpayers to depreciate assets more slowly. Useful lives, known as *recovery periods*, are assigned to assets by I.R.C. Sec. 168(e)(3) and must be used by taxpayers in calculating their depreciation allowance on their business assets.

No depreciation is permitted for the cost of acquiring shares of stock in a corporation or ownership interest in some other formal business activity. Depreciation of eligible assets owned and used by formal business entities must be taken by those entities. If an individual were to choose to acquire an existing business rather than start one, and he or she wanted to be able to depreciate any assets acquired and use his or her purchase price allocable to those assets as the basis for the depreciation, it would be necessary to purchase the assets of the business rather than the actual business entity. Those who purchase a business entity will be required to continue to depreciate the assets of the business within the confines of the business entity and on the same schedule used by the business before they acquired it. This could result in little or no depreciation being available to a new owner of a business if the assets had already been substantially or fully depreciated prior to acquisition of the business.

In the most recent versions of the Internal Revenue Code, the provisions that address depreciation refer to it as *Asset Cost Recovery System* (ACRS). (A *Modified Asset Cost Recovery System* (MACRS) exists for certain situations.) The amount of depreciation deduction that a party may take when an asset is used for business is determined by the depreciable value of the item, the length of time over which the depreciation must be taken, the method of depreciation used, and the time of year in which the asset was placed in service.

Auto Expenses

Car and truck expenses are common deductions for most businesses. This deduction lends itself to abuse by taxpayers and is generally targeted for close scrutiny by the IRS in audits. For many years, a major issue in considering the deductibility of a taxpayer's automobile expense was whether or not the use of an expensive luxury car was an ordinary and necessary business expense. Taxpayers who represented clients or dealt with customers who were high-income earners, or who aspired to be, would argue that it was absolutely necessary that they drive expensive cars in order to create the image necessary to attract and keep such clientele. The IRS would argue that the use of an automobile that cost several times more than the average car was extravagant rather than ordinary and necessary, and therefore, the deduction for the use of such a car should be reduced accordingly.

Eventually, Congress intervened and placed limits on the automobile deduction that taxpayers may take. Thus, the maximum deduction that taxpayers may take for wear and tear, in the form of depreciation, for passenger cars per year is now set forth in annual Revenue Procedures from the IRS. No matter how costly a luxury passenger car may be and no matter how essential a taxpayer may feel that an expensive car is in helping create the business image desired, only the depreciation deduction set forth in the appropriate Revenue Procedure will be allowed.

In addition to depreciation, taxpayers may deduct the cost of fuel, maintenance, insurance, and license fees that they incur in connection with an automobile used for business purposes. However, the deduction for depreciation and expenses associated with an automobile is limited to its use in business matters. Deductions are not allowed to the degree that an automobile is put to personal use.

Also, taxpayers are prohibited from taking a deduction for automobile expenses and depreciation for miles driven to and from their places of employment. Therefore, if a vehicle is used for business purposes as well as personal or commuting use, it is essential that records be kept for each type of use in order to support taking a deduction for the business portion of the expenses and depreciation. Such a record usually takes the form of a logbook in which the beginning and ending mileage on the vehicle's odometer are recorded each time the vehicle is used for business purposes.

It is also necessary that receipts or other records of automobile expenses be kept in support of the deduction for business use of a car or truck. If an automobile is used only partly for business, the deductions for depreciation of the vehicle, and for the expense of operating it, must be prorated based on the percentage of business use. For example, if the taxpayer's logbook showed that a vehicle had been driven a total of 20,000 miles during the tax year, and 15,000 of those miles had been for business, a deduction of only 75% of the allowable depreciation and expenses from gross business income would be permitted. This is because the business miles driven equal 75% of the total miles driven.

More and more businesses and individuals are leasing their vehicles. In such cases there will be no deduction for depreciation, even for the vehicle's business use. Instead, when a leased vehicle is used for business, the taxpayer may deduct the appropriate portion of the lease payments. However, in order to prevent parties from taking deductions for luxury cars, limitations have been placed on the amount of the lease payments that are considered deductible. The limitations on the deductibility of lease payments for automobiles used in business are designed to start at the level of the lease payments on a vehicle with approximately the same fair market value as that of a vehicle on which a taxpayer may take a depreciation deduction without limitation.

As an alternative to taking a deduction for depreciation or lease payments, and then a further deduction for the actual expense of operating an automobile, Sec. 1.61-21(e) of the Regulations allows taxpayers the option of a deduction on the basis of a specified number of cents per mile driven for business purposes. The actual amount of the cents allowed as a deduction for business use of an automobile is set each year and may even vary during the course of a single year. Taxpayers who use the cents-per-mile option for calculating their deduction for automobile use will not be required to keep receipts and other proof of their actual expenses associated with the vehicle's operation. However, they will still need to keep a detailed log of miles driven for business purposes. Using the cents-per-mile option is not available if the provisions of I.R.C. Sec. 179 were used to offset any of its cost during the year of acquisition if:

- the vehicle has been depreciated using any method other than straight-line;
- the vehicle is used for hire (such as when used in a limousine service);
- more than one vehicle is used by the taxpayer for business use at the same time; or,
- the vehicle has been leased by the taxpayer rather than purchased, and the taxpayer has taken a deduction for the lease payments made for the year.

Meals and Entertainment

Additional business expenses that have historically been closely scrutinized by the IRS are the costs of business meals and entertainment. A deduction for meal expenses incurred while away from home on business is permitted by I.R.C. Sec. 162 as long as the meal is not considered lavish or extravagant. However, I.R.C. Sec. 274(n) limits the amount of the deduction to 50% of the amount of the expenditure.

Even though a taxpayer is not away from home, he or she may be still be allowed a business expense deduction for the cost of meals while on business with customers or potential customers. Section 1.274-2 of the Treasury Regulations sets forth the criteria that must be met in order for such expenditures to be deductible as a business expense. It requires that the taxpayer be able to show that the expenditure for such meals *was directly related to the active conduct of the taxpayer's trade or business, or ...that the expenditure was associated with active conduct of the taxpayer's trade of business.* One or both of these criteria will generally be met if bona fide business discussions take place before, during, or after the meal. The same I.R.C. Sec. 274(n) limitations apply to these meals as well.

Another requirement of I.R.C. Sec. 274 is the keeping of detailed supporting records in order to qualify the cost of the meals provided for business associates as a deductible business expense. The most popular way to meet this requirement is to pay for such meals with a credit card and write down the names of those present at the meals and a brief description of the business discussed on the back of your copy of the credit card receipt.

Rules concerning the deductibility of expenditures for entertainment of business clients are also set forth in I.R.C. Sec. 274. The same requirement for deductibility that the expenditure must be *directly related to* or *associated with* the active conduct of the taxpayer's business, applies for expenses incurred for entertainment for clients as it does for meals provided for clients. However, in order to be eligible to take a business deduction for the cost of entertainment provided to clients, the taxpayer must pass a far more stringent application of the test to determine if an expense is either directly related to or associated with the party's business. Treasury Regulations Sec. 1.274(c)(3) states that, in order for an expenditure for entertainment to be considered directly related to a taxpayer's trade or business, each of the following requirements must be met.

- ◆ At the time of the entertainment expenditure, the taxpayer had to have an expectation of acquiring some specific trade or business rather than merely developing goodwill.
- ◆ During the entertainment period, but either before or after the entertainment event (rather than during it), there must have been

an active business meeting or transaction for the purpose of obtaining specific trade or business.

◆ The principal character or aspect of the activity must have been the active conduct of the taxpayer's trade or business.

◆ The cost of the activity must have been allocable to the taxpayer and the person or persons with whom he or she sought to actively conduct trade or business, rather than their companions or friends who were disinterested in business negotiations.

Treasury Regulation Sec. 1.274(c)(3) goes on to say that it is required that activities engaged in that were in furtherance of the taxpayer's business during the entertainment activity had to have occurred in a *clear business setting*. Therefore, attempting to qualify entertainment expenditures as a business deduction by casually discussing business matters during the course of an actual entertainment event simply will not work.

Also, I.R.C. Sec. 274(3) specifically disallows any deduction for payment of dues for membership in clubs that are *organized for business, pleasure, recreation, or other social purposes*. Even when the expenditures for entertainment qualify for a business deduction under the Code and Regulations, I.R.C. Sec. 274(n) limits the deduction to 50% of the amount of the qualified expenditure.

EXAMPLE: Paul is a self-employed civil engineer. In an effort to get a contract as a consultant with a local construction company, he called the owner and asked if they could meet for about an hour, after which Paul would take the owner out to dinner and to a basketball game at a local college. During the meeting, Paul talked about the project that he had done for other companies, his formal training and education, and his hourly rates. Afterwards, Paul drove them to a nearby restaurant. On the way, Paul pointed out a building that he had been involved with when it was being built. At the ballgame, he mentioned that he had formerly been employed by the engineering firm that had done work for the construction company that had built the basketball arena.

Provided that the cost of the meals and entertainment provided by Paul were not extravagant, the expense should qualify for the allowable deduction. A *bona fide* business meeting clearly associated with Paul's business was held in the prospective client's office, which is a *clear business setting*, prior to the meal and entertainment. Had the meeting prior to dinner not taken place, it is doubtful that Paul would qualify to take a business deduction for the meal and entertainment. His comments on the way to dinner do not appear to constitute a *bona fide* business discussion and his comments at the ballgame were not made in a clear business setting.

The depreciable value of *personal property*, such as equipment used in business, is generally the full purchase price paid for it by the taxpayer. However, depreciation can be taken only for *improvements on* realty. Therefore, the cost of acquisition of realty must be reasonably allocated between the actual real estate and the improvements, such as buildings, and the value of the realty must be excluded from the basis upon which the depreciation is calculated. No depreciation is allowed for a taxpayer's inventory or stock in trade.

The method of depreciation and the recovery period assigned to an asset determine the rate of its depreciation. The most basic method of recovery is straight-line, which entails a *pro rata* allocation over the depreciable life of the asset. For example, if a taxpayer placed a piece of equipment in service at the beginning of the year that cost $10,000 with a five-year depreciable life, and depreciated it using the straight-line method, he or she would be able to take one-fifth of its value per year as his or her deduction for depreciation on the item. Other methods of depreciation allow up to double the straight-line rate for the first year in which the asset is placed in service, but this accelerated write-off in the earlier years comes at the cost of reductions in depreciation for those assets in later years.

There have been times when the tax laws have permitted deduction for a full year's depreciation for the first year of an asset's business use, regardless of the time of year in which the asset was placed in service. Under such provisions—which are designed to stimulate investment—a full year's depreciation could be taken on depreciable assets that were not even placed in service until the last day of the taxable year. However, in recent years, U.S. tax laws have penalized parties who have waited until the fourth quarter of the year before investing in business property.

If more than 40% of an entity's investment in new business assets, excluding realty, occurs in the fourth quarter of its taxable year, it must use a mid-quarter convention to compute its cost recovery allowances for all such property placed in service for the taxable year. This means that, for depreciation purposes, such property is treated as having been placed in service at mid-point of the quarter in which it was placed in service. If an entity does not place over 40% of its new business assets, exclusive of realty, in service during the last quarter of its taxable year, it uses half-year convention to calculate its cost recovery allowances on such assets. This results in such assets being regarded, for depreciation purposes, as having been placed in service at mid-point of the year in which they were placed in service.

Forcing a business entity to use the mid-quarter convention will usually result in less first-year depreciation deduction than allowing it to use the mid-year convention would. Therefore, you should view the last day of the third quarter of your taxable year as an investment decision deadline. Consult with your tax advisors in advance of that date so that you can time your investments to avoid any adverse consequences of inadvertently finding yourself forced to use the mid-quarter convention.

The *Section 179 expense deduction* that is linked with depreciation refers to deductions permitted by I.R.C. Sec. 179, which permits some taxpayers to fully deduct the cost of some assets that are actually depreciable property. This practice is known as *expensing*. Under provisions of the *Jobs and Growth Tax Relief Reconciliation Act of 2003* (JGTRRA), up to $100,000 of depreciable property placed in service between 2003 and 2005 may be expensed for the year. After 2005, the amount is reduced to the pre-JGTRRA level of $25,000. By expensing an asset, a taxpayer deducts the full amount paid for it in the year it is placed in service rather than depreciating it. This provision is aimed at self-employed taxpayers and small businesses as evidenced by the fact that if the taxpayer places over $400,000 worth of business assets in service in a taxable year, the amount eligible to be expensed begins to be phased out.

Of particular importance to self-employed taxpayers is the provision that no taxpayer may use a Sec. 179 expense deduction to generate a loss from a trade or business. Also, some property, such as that used 50% or less in the taxpayer's trade or business, is ineligible to be expense under Sec. 179.

Any deduction taken by a taxpayer for depreciation on assets that were first placed in service during the year for which the tax return is filed must be shown on a Form 4562, as must any Section 179 expense deduction. The form must be attached to the party's tax return. Form 4562 is also required if depreciation is taken on *listed property*, regardless of when it was placed in service. Listed property includes:

- automobiles and other assets used for transportation;
- cellular telephones and other communication equipment (unless it is used exclusively in the taxpayer's trade or business or at his or her regular business establishment); and,
- computer or peripheral equipment (unless it is used exclusively at a business establishment and owned or leased by the party operating the establishment).

The right to take depreciation is not without its cost. As annual deductions are taken for depreciation, or Section 179 expense is claimed in lieu of depreciation, the depreciable value of the asset, know as its *basis*, must be reduced by the amount of those deductions. As a result, the basis of depreciable property will eventually be exhausted and no further deductions for depreciation for that property will be available. Furthermore, if a taxpayer sells property that has been depreciated for tax purposes, the gain or loss from the sale of the property will be determined by subtracting the taxpayer's basis in the property, rather than the cost of acquisition, from the net proceeds from its sale.

EXAMPLE: George acquired a bait shop that he operated as a self-employed sole proprietor. His total purchase price for the shop included

$150,000 for the shop building and land that it was on. He allocated $25,000 of the price to the land and $125,000 as his basis in the building for purposes of taking depreciation deductions on it. After several years in business, George sold the business at a net price of $165,000 for the building and land. Since George had taken depreciation of $50,000 on the building when he had owned it, his basis in the shop building must be reduced by the depreciation that he took. As a result, his original basis of $150,000 will be reduced to $100,000. When deducted from the net sale price of the $165,000, it will result in a taxable gain of $65,000 to George, despite the fact that he actually got only $15,000 more for the building than he had paid for it.

Another potentially troublesome aspect of the law concerning depreciation is the fact that I.R.C. Sec. 167, which provides for deductions for depreciation, states such a deduction reflecting exhaustion or wear and tear of an asset used for business purposes shall be *allowed*. Therefore, once an asset is placed in service for business purposes, taxpayers *must* take the depreciation deduction that they are allowed by the I.R.C. to take, until such time as the asset is no longer used for business purposes. As a result, a taxpayer must reduce the basis of depreciable property by the amount of depreciation that was *allowable* for each tax year that it was in business service even if the party's income was so low that no tax benefit was realized from the depreciation. If a taxpayer fails to take the fully allowable depreciation on a business asset in an effort to *save* the depreciation for a later year, Treasury Regulation Sec. 1.167(a)-10(a) requires that the depreciation deduction be adjusted. It must reflect *the allowable method of depreciation used by the taxpayer for such property or under the straight-line method if no allowance has ever been claimed for such property.*

EXAMPLE: Jerry went into business as a self-employed sole proprietor engaged in grinding up tree branches and stumps for tree trimmers. He had to acquire a large grinding machine at a cost of $100,000, which he chose to depreciate on the straight-line method over a period of five years. The depreciation of $20,000, which he took for the first full year that the machine was in service, greatly reduced both his income tax liability and his self-employment tax liability.

However, during his second full year of operation, Jerry decided to perform services exclusively for a single company that went bankrupt, owing him a substantial amount of money that he will never be able to collect. As a result, Jerry's net income for the year was only $20,000 before taking any depreciation deduction for his machine. His exemptions and personal deductions will offset all of his income, causing him to pay no income taxes. Therefore, if he uses his depreciation deduction to offset his income, he will save no income taxes (although he will avoid having to pay self-employment taxes on his $20,000 income).

Jerry has entered into a contract with the city where he lives and expects to make a substantial income grinding limbs and stumps for the city maintenance department, and would prefer not to use up his depreciation in a year in which it will save him little in taxes. But Jerry will have no choice. He must take the allowable $20,000 depreciation and reduce his year two income to zero.

Taxpayers must reduce their basis in business assets by the amount of the depreciation allowable for those assets for each year that they are in service. It would therefore probably be advisable, for those who have sufficient income to take advantage of the deduction, to make use of Section 179 and fully expense newly acquired assets rather than risk facing the possible future situation of having too little income to benefit substantially from depreciation deductions.

Of course, taxpayers who have modest earnings in the year in which they acquire business assets should not take a Section 179 expense deduction for capital assets placed in service that year. They would want to use straight-line depreciation in order to conserve as much of their depreciation deduction as possible for use in future, more profitable, years. If practical, taxpayers who know that their incomes from self-employment activity for the year will be low should postpone acquisition of depreciable business assets until the following taxable year in order to postpone the year in which mandatory depreciation of the assets must start.

Amortization .

Some of the intangible assets that self-employed taxpayers acquire for use in their businesses have life expectancies in excess of a year. In such cases, taxpayers are allowed to take deductions for those assets over the course of their lives in much the same way that they are permitted to take depreciation on tangible assets. However, assets that must be *amortized* cannot be expensed under I.R.C. Sec. 179, since it is applicable only to tangible assets and there is no similar provision in the Code for intangible assets.

There are several I.R.C. sections that provide for amortizing various categories of tangible assets. I.R.C. Sec. 197 covers the largest number of categories among the sections dealing with amortization. It also covers the ones that are most commonly encountered by taxpayers. The intangible assets covered by Section 197 must generally be amortized over a period of fifteen years using the straight-line method. The specific intangible assets addressed in Sec. 197 include the following.

Goodwill

Taxpayers who purchase existing businesses generally pay more for them than merely the total value of the assets owned by the businesses. The premium paid by a purchaser in excess of the value of the tangible assets of a business may be attributable to any of a number of intangible assets that are a part of the business. One of the most common intangible assets that is acquired in the purchase of any business is *goodwill*. Treasury Regulation Sec. 1.197-2(b)(1) defines goodwill as *the value of a trade or business attributable to the expectancy of continued customer patronage*. The Regulation goes on to state that such an expectancy may have been created by the fact that a trade or business has established a recognizable name, a good reputation, or due to *any other factor*.

Going Concern Value

Whenever a trade or business is started, there is usually a period of delay from the time start-up activity is begun, until such time as revenues are actually generated and received. Some business activities even have licensing requirements that necessitate fully establishing a business operation that then must pass inspection by a governmental licensing agency before any business may be done. If a party can purchase a trade or business that is past the start-up phase and can continue to seamlessly operate without any delays, that opportunity should have value to most buyers. It is this ability of a trade or business (or part of a trade or business) to continue functioning or generating income without interruption that Treasury Regulation Sec. 1.197-2(b)(2) defines as *going concern value*.

Although going concern value and goodwill may seem so similar as to be virtually identical, they are not. A trade or business that has met all of the requirements to begin operating would have going concern value, even if no business has actually been done by its organizer at all. In order to develop goodwill a party must have actually done business with customers since it is the expectation of continued customer patronage that gives rise to goodwill.

Workforce in Place

The success of most trades and businesses is highly dependent upon the people employed by that enterprise. Self-employed proprietors who conduct business without having to engage the services of employers, agents, or independent contractors will not be faced with the often difficult task of hiring and training employees or finding reliable agents and independent contractors, and developing a relationship with them. Many proprietors who decide to start a trade or business realize they will be required to have employees, agents, or independent contractors in order to operate. They may be faced with the unappealing and expensive choices of either locating, recruiting, and training the workers that they need or entering into a bidding war to lure them away from jobs at competitor's businesses. Having a *workforce in place*, as can be acquired through the purchase of an existent trade or business, avoids such costs, as well as adding the additional value that comes from the greater efficiency of a fully trained and experienced workforce over an untrained and inexperienced group.

In determining the amortizable cost of a workforce in place, Treasury Regulation Sec. 1.197-2(b)(3) provides that the amount paid or incurred for workforce includes:

- ◆ any portion of the purchase price of an acquired trade or business attributable to the existence of a highly-skilled workforce;
- ◆ an existing employment contract (or contracts); or,
- ◆ a relationship with employees or consultants (including, but not limited to, any key employee contract or relationship).

Alternately, the cost of training workers will largely be expensed in the form of salaries and wages paid to trainees and those who train them.

Information Base

It takes time for those engaged in a trade or business to compile information that may be useful, or even indispensable, in carrying on that activity. To the degree that the purchase price paid for an existing business or trade includes payment for that operation *information base*, I.R.C. Sec. 197(d)(1)(c)(ii) incorporates that expense among those that are amortizable. Treasury Regulation Sec. 1.197-2(b)(4) specifically includes customer lists, information concerning current or prospective customers, and any other customer-related information among those items that comprise the amortizable information base of a newly acquired trade or business. The Regulation also specifically mentions technical manuals, training manuals or programs, data files, accounting or inventory control systems, subscription lists, patient or client files, and lists of newspaper, magazine, radio or television advertisers as examples of amortizable information bases when they are present in a newly acquired trade or business.

Business Know-How

Those considering starting a trade or business are often enticed to consider the purchase of an existing operation in order to acquire that operation's business know-how. I.R.C. Sec. 197(d)(1)(c)(iii) includes *business know-how* among the amortizable intangible assets that buyers of an existent business operation may acquire. Treasury Regulation Sec. 1.197-2(b)(s) specifically names patents, copyrights, formulas, processes, designs, patterns, package designs, computer software, and interests in sound recordings, video tapes, books and similar property, as well as *know-how* itself, as amortizable components of *business know-how*. These are considered when they are part of an existing trade or business that is bought by a taxpayer. However, Treasury Regulation Sec. 1.197-2(c)(4) creates an exception for computer software that is *readily available to the general pubic on similar terms, is subject to a nonexclusive license, and has not been substantially modified*. Software that qualifies for the exception may be expensed rather than amortized.

Customer Based Intangibles

Whereas goodwill is a general expectancy that the customers of a trade or business will continue to patronize that concern, *customer based intangibles* are those specific things that, although intangible, make continued patronage likely. Treasury Regulation Sec. 1.197-2(b)(6) provides that the value of customer based intangibles is derived from the anticipated income that will be earned from supplying goods or services to customers either pursuant to a contract or due to a non-contractual relationship that was developed with customers in the ordinary course of doing business.

The Regulation offers examples of specific contracts, such as investment management contracts, mortgage servicing contracts, or contracts to supply future goods or services to customers. It also provides examples of non-contractual customer based intangibles, such as having necessary insurance in force, or having met qualifications required in order to be allowed to supply goods or services to a particular customer. To the degree that any of the purchase price of an existing trade or business is attributable to customer based intangibles, that expenditure is amortizable, but cannot be expensed.

Supplier Based Intangibles

In some business activities, establishing a source of supply of goods or services to be sold is one of the most difficult, and yet most essential, elements for success. For example, wholesale automobile dealers buy cars that are traded in at new car dealerships and sell them to other used car dealers. Rather than deal with a wide array of wholesale dealers, new car dealerships interact with a few wholesale dealers who they have found to be reliable buyers that promptly pay for the automobiles that they have agreed to buy. Someone wanting to become a wholesale automobile dealer would probably have a difficult time establishing a relationship with a new car dealership in order to buy vehicles that were traded in. However, the purchase of an existing wholesale automobile dealer's operation should include an established relation with a new car dealership.

To the degree that the purchase price of any existing trade or business is attributable to intangible relationships with suppliers that will likely result in the buyer's ability to acquire goods or services from those suppliers in the future, it is subject to amortization, but cannot be expensed. Treasury Regulation Sec. 1.197-2(b)(7) explains that *supplier based intangibles* can include favorable noncontractual relationships with suppliers, favorable relationships with those who provide distribution services (such as display space at a retail outlet), or a favorable credit rating. However, if the right to acquire goods or services from a supplier is not acquired as part of the purchase price of a trade or business, I.R.C. Sec. 197 does not apply to that right and the cost of cultivating the relationship can likely be expensed.

Licenses, Permits, and Other Rights Granted by Governmental Units

Another common motive for acquiring an existing trade or business (rather than starting a new one) is to acquire the existing operation's *license, permit,* or *other government sanction.* There are situations in which the governmental authority in charge of granting business privileges has either chosen to limit the number of participants in a given activity or is forced, often by lack of physical space, to restrict the number of participants. Treasury Regulation Sec. 1.197-2(b)(8) specifically cites liquor licenses, taxi-cab licenses, airport landing and takeoff rights, and television and radio broadcasting licenses as examples of intangible items that are amortizable to the extent that part of the payment for an existing trade or business is made to acquire them.

Covenants Not to Compete and Other Similar Arrangements

In order to retain the goodwill of a business for themselves, buyers of business operations often require sellers to enter into *noncompetition agreements*. To the degree that the purchase price of an existing business represents payment for such agreements, I.R.C. Sec. 197 provides that the payment is amortizable. Payments for noncompetition agreements that a seller had negotiated with former owners or employees would also be amortizable.

Franchises, Trademarks, and Trade Names

Treasury Regulation Sec. 1.197-2(b)(10) defines a franchise as *any agreement that provides one of the parties to the agreement with the right to distribute, sell, or provide goods, services, or, facilities within a specified area.* It defines a trademark as *any word, name, symbol, or device, or any combination thereof, adopted and used to identify goods or services and distinguish them from those provided by others.* Trade names, according to the Regulation, are similar to trademarks, but are used to distinguish a particular business operation from any other business operation, rather than distinguishing particular products from other products. Expenditures to acquire a *franchise*, *trademark*, or *trade name* are amortizable under I.R.C. Sec. 197(d)(1)(F). However, payments for a franchise, trademark, or trade name may be part of a series of substantially equal payments that are made no less frequently than annually and are contingent on productivity, use, or disposition of the franchise, trademark, or trade name. I.R.C. Sec. 1253(d)(1)(B) allows those payments to be treated as a trade or business expense and fully deducted in the year they were made.

In addition to expenditures to acquire any of the specific intangible items enumerated in I.R.C. Sec. 197, Treasury Regulation Sec. 1.197-2(b)(11) provides for amortization of payments made for the right, by contact or otherwise, to merely use such intangible property. Also, Regulation Sec.

1.197(b)(12) provides for amortization of intangible property that is not specifically listed in I.R.C. Sec. 197 but is *similar in all material respects* to the property that is specifically listed therein.

Start-Up Expenditures

Individuals who decide to become self-employed operators of their own trades or businesses often spend substantial sums of money investigating the feasibility and requirements of creating or acquiring an active trade or business. Once the decision is made to start or acquire an active trade or business, organizers usually incur substantial expenses, such as attorney's fees, travel expenses, the cost of accounting services, or the cost of promotional activities, before the operation actually becomes an active trade or business. I.R.C. Sec. 195 defines such expenses as *start-up expenditures* and prohibits taxpayers from expensing them. However, I.R.C. Sec. 195 permits taxpayers the option of amortizing their start-up expenditures over a period of not less than sixty months, beginning in the month in which the party first begins to actually operate an active trade or business to which the expenses apply.

Taxpayers who are already involved in the same or similar business as the one they are investigating for the purpose of possibly acquiring it are allowed to fully deduct the expenses associated with that investigation in the year in which they were incurred or paid. The expenses will be considered to be ordinary, necessary business expenses under I.R.C. Sec. 162. Those who incur expenses starting a new operation that is the same or similar to a trade or business that they are already in will also be allowed, by I.R.C. Sec. 162, to fully deduct those expenses in the year in which they were paid or incurred.

EXAMPLE: Bud is engaged in the business of manufacturing storm windows in Memphis. He has learned that a man in Little Rock with a similar small operation engaged in the manufacturing of storm windows wants to sell his operation and retire. Bud flew to Little Rock, where he stayed several days and hired an accountant, an attorney, and an appraiser of small businesses to work with him in investigating the advisability of acquiring the Little Rock manufacturing operation.

Lou, an executive with a large food brokerage firm will soon be without a job when his company is acquired by another, even larger, food broker. Lou's experience with his employer has caused him to consider using his severance pay to acquire the Little Rock storm window manufacturing company and become self-employed. Lou traveled to Little Rock from Dallas and incurred expenses quite similar to those incurred by Bud. If Lou does not acquire the Little Rock manufacturing operation, he will not be allowed to take a deduction for any of his expenses that he incurred in investigating its purchase.

If Lou does purchase the Little Rock manufacturing operation, he would be permitted under I.R.C. Sec. 195, to amortize the costs that he incurred in investigating the feasibility of the purchase, over a period of not less than sixty months, but he would not be permitted to expense the costs under I.R.C. Sec. 162. By contrast, Bud would be allowed to fully deduct his expenses under I.R.C. Sec. 162 in the year in which he paid or incurred them, even if he decides not to acquire the Little Rock facility.

The reason that taxpayers are not allowed to take an I.R.C. Sec. 162 deduction for investigation or start-up costs for a trade or business that they were not already involved in is that Sec. 162 requires that taxpayers be actively engaged in a given trade or business in order to qualify to take business deductions for it. Those who are not already actively engaged in the same or a similar trade or business simply do not meet the requirement. Therefore, taxpayers who are attempting to qualify expenditures for an I.R.C. Sec. 162 deduction, rather than having to amortize them, should postpone as many expenditures as possible until they have acquired or started up a trade or business and begun to actually operate it. In fact, those who are contemplating multiple locations or divisions within their trade or business may want to consider starting a small part of their operation early. They could then start the balance of their trade or business when they have qualified themselves to fully deduct the expenses of the latter phases of their operation in the year in which those expenses were incurred or paid.

Research and Experimental Expenditures

Most self-employed taxpayers cannot afford the luxury of devoting their limited resources to research and experimentation in an attempt to develop new products. However, the occasional self-employed individual who does incur research or experimental expenditures will be given options by I.R.C. Sec. 174 as to how to take a tax deduction for those expenditures. If a taxpayer does not elect another method for writing off *research and experimental expenses*, they must be capitalized and written off only when the research and experiments are abandoned or become worthless. In the alternative, taxpayers who incur research or experimental expenditures have two choices. They may elect to either expense them and fully deduct their costs in the year in which they were incurred or they may amortize the costs and write them off on a straight-line basis over a period of not less than sixty months.

Generally, taxpayers attempt to maximize their tax deductions each year. Therefore, it would be reasonable to expect most parties to choose to expense the costs of research and experimentation and fully deduct them at the earliest possibility. However, a self-employed person who incurs research and experimentation expenses may well incur such expenditures at the inception of his or her trade or business when income from the activity is low. He or she will have had little or no time to exploit the benefits derived from the development of new products or processes. Therefore, in such cases, it may be beneficial for a self-employed individual to amortize research and experimentation expenses, rather than expense them, and save much of the write-offs for years when his or her income from the marketing of newly developed processes or products has begun to generate significant profits.

There may be some confusion as to what constitutes research and experimentation for purposes of I.R.C. Sec. 174. Treasury Regulation Sec. 1.174-2 states that such expenses *as used in section 174, means expenditures incurred in connection with the taxpayer's trade or business which represent research and development costs in the experimental or laboratory sense.* The Regulation further states that such expenditures include those incurred to either develop or improve a product or to *eliminate uncertainty concerning the development or improvement of a product*. In addition to the costs directly related to research and experimentation, such as the salary expense of researchers or the cost of supplies, the costs of obtaining a patent—including attorney's fees—also qualify as a research and experimentation expense. However, Treasury Regulation Sec. 1.174-2(3) states specifically that the list of expenditures that do not qualify as research and experimental expenditures includes:

- quality control testing of materials or products;
- efficiency surveys;
- management studies;
- consumer surveys;
- advertising;
- literary or historical research projects; and,
- the cost of acquiring another party's patent, model, or method of production.

Depletion

No depreciation is allowed for the cost of real estate. However, taxpayers who are in the business of extracting oil and gas, mineral deposits, or timber from land are permitted, by I.R.C. Sec. 611, to take a deduction for the *depletion* of the resources being removed from the land. Few self-employed individuals are engaged in such activities, but those who are involved in such activities are allowed to take a depletion deduction using a technique known as the *cost depletion method*. This method involves estimating the total recoverable units available, then dividing that total into the adjusted basis of the property from which the resources are extracted, and then multiplying the resulting allowance per unit times the number of units recovered for the tax year.

Those who extract a daily average of no more than 1,000 barrels of oil, or an average of six million cubic feet of natural gas or less per day, are permitted to take a depletion allowance using the *percentage depletion method*. This simply involves deducting a percentage of the taxable income attributable to the resource as the depletion deduction. I.R.C. Sec. 613, which established the percentage depletion method, provides the allowable percentage for depletion for oil and gas, as well as for a number of natural resources, such as sulphur, gold, silver, copper, some clay, and even sand and gravel.

Common Business Deductions

- ◆ Wage and salary expenses (but payments by self-employed parties to themselves are NOT deductible)
- ◆ Advertising
- ◆ Depreciation
- ◆ Auto expense (subject to maximum limits)
- ◆ Meals and entertainment (50% is not deductible)
- ◆ Amortization
- ◆ In-home office expense
- ◆ Rent
- ◆ Utilities
- ◆ Telephone
- ◆ Supplies
- ◆ Professional services (such as accountants, consultants, and attorneys)
- ◆ Insurance
- ◆ Maintenance
- ◆ Pension and retirement benefits for employees (but not those paid for the self-employed owner)
- ◆ Repairs
- ◆ Professional dues and license fees
- ◆ Cost of goods sold
- ◆ Interest on business loans
- ◆ Taxes
- ◆ Payments to independent contractors
- ◆ Miscellaneous expenses—shown on Schedule C as "Other expenses"—consisting of expenses unique to a given business, plus items such as:
  - • Postage
  - • Costs of training workers
  - • Publications
  - • Fees paid in behalf of clients

Chapter 5
In-Home Office Expense Deductions

Since self-employed individuals often conduct their self-employment activity as a supplement to their full-time jobs, it is usually imperative that they hold their expenses to a minimum. One common way in which many self-employed taxpayers minimize their business expenses is by operating their trade or business from their homes, rather than renting commercial space. Those who do rent commercial space for their trade or business will generally be permitted to take a deduction for the full amount for the rent they pay. Those who operate a trade of business from office space within their homes or otherwise devote part of their homes to business use will not write a check specifically for the use of that space. However, taxpayers who devote part of their homes to business use may still qualify for a business deduction for that space, provided they meet certain qualifications set forth in I.R.C. Sec. 280A.

USES THAT MUST BE BOTH EXCLUSIVE AND REGULAR

As long as part of a taxpayer's residence is used exclusively and regularly for business, Sec. 280A(C)(1) permits a deduction if the use is:

◆ as the principal place of business for any trade or business of the taxpayer;

♦ as a place of business that is used by patients, clients, or customers in meeting or dealing with the taxpayer in the normal course of the trade or business; or,

♦ in the case of a separate structure that is not attached to the dwelling unit, in connection with the taxpayer's trade or business.

The requirement that a party must use some portion of his or her residence exclusively for business use in order to qualify for a deduction is a strict one. When exclusive business use is required, there is no tolerance and even minimal nonbusiness use will disqualify the expense for a deduction.

EXAMPLE: Jean, a self-employed typist set up her living room as her office and usually kept the room covered with books and papers. On major holidays and a few other occasions during the year, Jean would clean out the room and use it to entertain her family and guests during parties. Even though these non-business uses of her living room were very limited, they would disqualify her from taking a business deduction in connection with its business use.

It is not necessary to devote a separate room of a residence to business use as long as there is a definite area devoted to regular, exclusive business use. Congregating business related furnishings and equipment into a single area rather than scattering them throughout various parts of the residence would likely be essential in establishing exclusive business use of a definite part of a residence.

Even if a taxpayer conducts more than one business in the part of his or her home set aside for business use, he or she may still take the appropriate deduction, provided that each business use would qualify. Employees who, in addition to their primary employment, also operate a business of their own from their residence must be especially careful in order to preserve their right to take a deduction for the business related use of their residence.

Even if a taxpayer's use of the home in connection with his or her own business would qualify for a deduction, if work is also done for a primary employer in the same area of the home that is set aside for the self-employment activity, the right to take the deduction will be lost. This may not happen if it can be shown that having business-related space in the home was required for the convenience of the employer. Absent a showing that a party was required to have space in his or her residence set aside for regular, exclusive, business use for the convenience of an employer, a taxpayer's use of space in the home to conduct business for his or her employer is regarded the same as personal use of the space.

EXAMPLE: Rob was employed as a stockbroker. He also started two of his own businesses, one as a self-employed landscape designer and the other as a self-employed marketer of collectible dolls over the Internet. Rob operated both of his self-employment activities from the same office space in his home. The office space in Rob's home was used regularly and exclusively for his two businesses. The fact that Rob operated a landscape design service and marketed collectible dolls from the same space will not disqualify him from taking a business deduction for the space. However, if Rob also worked from his home office in connection with his job as a stockbroker, he would be disqualified from taking any deduction for his home office (unless he can show that the home office was maintained for the convenience of his employer).

Section 280A offers no guidance as to what constitutes regular use of a space for business purposes. Therefore, the term *regular* should be given its ordinary meaning, which would require a steady, on-going, and frequent use, as opposed to a sporadic or occasional use, even if the total hours of sporadic use exceeded the total hours of on-going use.

In determining whether a taxpayer is using space in his or her residence as his or her *principal place of business* and thereby qualifies for a deduction of its use, IRS Publication 587 offers significant guidance. It states that a self-employed person will be considered to have established the home office as his or her principal place of business, as required in Sec. 280A(c)(1) in order to qualify for a deduction for the office, if:

◆ he or she is regularly using part of the residence exclusively for an office to perform *administrative or management activities* (such as processing orders or bills in connection with a business) and

◆ he or she has no other fixed location from which a substantial part of the activities are performed.

Even if a taxpayer also conducts business from a vehicle, motel rooms, or other places that are not fixed locations, he or she can still take a deduction for a home office if he or she otherwise qualifies for it.

Occasionally conducting minimal administrative or management activities from a fixed site other than his or her home office will not disqualify a taxpayer from the right to take a deduction for the home office, as long as it still qualifies as his or her principal place of business. Publication 587 helps in determining whether one's home office is his or her principal place of business when business is also conducted from one or more other fixed locations. Publication 587 states that *the relative importance of the activities performed at each location* should be considered first, and if that is not determinative, the next factor to consider is the relative amount of time spent at each location.

Certain actions will not affect a taxpayer's right to take a deduction for a home office if the party otherwise qualifies for it. These actions include contracting with others to perform administrative activities at their premises, performing non-administrative activities at a fixed site other than a home office, and choosing to use a home office rather than space available outside the home.

EXAMPLE: Chris is a computer consultant who has an office in his home, used regularly and exclusively to calculate and write payroll checks, pay bills, and handle other administrative duties connected with his business. He has no other fixed site from which he operates, but he usually meets customers at their homes or businesses and often works up estimates on the spot, either in the customer's home or in his van. Chris will qualify for a deduction for his home office since he has no other fixed location that he uses for conducting his trade or business.

EXAMPLE: Mauricio is a self-employed affiliate real estate broker. State law requires that he be sponsored by a licensed broker who must provide him with office space. Mauricio uses the space he is provided to meet with clients, check for available homes for sale, and collect data in order to prepare a market analysis for each client whose house he seeks to list for sale. He also has a home office that he uses regularly and exclusively to keep records of past clients and to prepare brochures to mail out to previous clients and prospective new clients. He spends about an equal amount of time at each office.

Unless Mauricio can show that what he does from his home office is significantly more important than what he does at his broker's office, he will not be allowed to take a home office deduction. If what he does at his broker's office is more important than what he does at his home office, he will definitely not qualify for a home office deduction. If Mauricio had decided to do all of his work either from his home office or at client's homes, he would be permitted a deduction for his home office despite the fact that office space had been available for him at the broker's place of business.

Even if a self-employed person has his or her principal place of business at a fixed site away from home, Sec. 280A still allows a deduction for that part of his or her home that a taxpayer regularly uses exclusively to meet or deal with patients, clients, or customers. However, Publication 587 states that *occasional meetings* and *telephone calls* in the taxpayer's home office are not enough to qualify it for a deduction for use of residence as a meeting place.

EXAMPLE: Balzar, a self-employed architect, works Monday through Friday from 8:00 a.m. to 6:00 p.m. He also has an office in his home, which he uses exclusively for the purpose of meeting with clients by appointment on Saturdays. This enables him to get business from clients whose work schedules do not permit them to come to his office during regular business hours without requiring him to open his office on Saturdays. Balzar will be entitled to take a deduction for his home office since he meets clients there as a regular part of his business and not merely occasionally.

The third general deduction provision in Sec. 280A applies to business use of structures located on the premises of a taxpayer's residence but that are not attached to the dwelling. Publication 587 explains that such free-standing structures as a *studio, garage,* or *barn* would qualify for the deduction. The language of publication 587 also indicates that the entire structure, rather than a mere part of it, must be used exclusively and regularly for the taxpayer's trade or business. However, Sec. 280A does not require that a separate structure located on the site of a taxpayer's residence be the primary place that a party conducts a trade or business. It also does not require the party to meet patients, clients, or customers there, in order to take a deduction for it, as long as it is used exclusively and regularly in his or her trade or business.

EXAMPLE: Nick operates an auto repair shop from a commercial location that he rents. He uses a workshop behind his personal residence exclusively and regularly for the purpose of rebuilding motors and transmissions that he then installs at his repair shop. Since he uses the workshop at his him home exclusively and regularly in his business, he will be permitted to take a business deduction for its use.

USES THAT MUST BE REGULAR, BUT NOT EXCLUSIVE

A taxpayer who regularly uses some part of his or her residence to provide day care for children, persons who are at least 65 years-of-age, or individuals who are incapable of caring for themselves due to mental or physical incapacity, is allowed by Sec. 280A to take a deduction for the part of the residence used for that business. It is not necessary that the part of the residence used for a day care be exclusively used for that purpose as long as the space is available for regular use in providing day care services and is used for that purpose more than merely occasionally, according to Publication 587. However, Sec. 280A provides that a deduction for use of a part of one's residence as a day care will be denied if the party providing the care has not obtained the necessary authority under state law, such as a license, to legally provide such services, or can show an exemption from such requirements.

There is another deduction provided for in Sec. 280A that requires regular use of part of a residence for business purposes, but does not require exclusive use. This is the one for allocation of space within one's residence for the purpose of storing inventory or product samples in connection with the party's trade or business of selling products at either the retail or wholesale level. Although the area used for storage does not have to be exclusively used for that purpose in order for the taxpayer to be eligible for the deduction, Sec. 280A does require that the party's residence be *the sole fixed location of such trade or business* in order to qualify for the deduction.

EXAMPLE: Pat, a manufacturer's representative, sells carpet cushion. The sole fixed location of his business activity is his home. In addition to allocated office space in his home, Pat has set aside the largest bedroom in his house to store samples of carpet cushion and some inventory to supply customers who unexpectedly run out of carpet cushion. Pat also stores his sales brochures and display materials in the room, as well as an old motorcycle. To the degree to which Pat uses the room for storage of samples and inventory of his carpet cushion, he can take a deduction for that use. He is not entitled to a deduction for the part of the room used to store brochures and display materials, nor is he entitled to take a deduction for the part of the room used for storing the motorcycle. However, the fact that the brochures, display materials, and motorcycle are stored in the same room as the carpet cushion used as samples and inventory will not disqualify him from taking a deduction for the part of the room used to store the samples and inventory.

Allocating Percentage of Use for Calculating the Deduction

In calculating the deduction for qualifying business use of one's residence, the first step is to determine the appropriate percentage of the residence that qualifies for the deduction. Deductions for use of part of a residence as a primary place of business, a place to meet clients, patients, or customers, or for storage of samples of inventory are generally based on the percentage of square footage in the entire structure that is devoted to the qualifying business use.

EXAMPLE: Rusty used most of a bedroom in his house to store samples of various products that he sold in connection with his business as a self-employed manufacturers' representative. Since his residence is his sole fixed business location, he qualifies for a deduction for the space devoted to storage of samples. Rusty will be allowed to take the deduction only for the part of the room actually used for storage.

Rusty's house contains a total of 2,500 square feet. The bedroom that he used for storage is 15 feet wide and 18 feet long. By multiplying the length of the bedroom by its width, Rusty determined that the room contains 270 square feet. He used 20 square feet of the room to store old clothes, leaving 250 square feet devoted to business use. By dividing the square footage used for business by the total square footage in the house (250/2500) Rusty determined that he devoted 10% of the total square footage of his home to business use.

Calculating the appropriate percentage of expenses to deduct for a qualifying business use of part of a residence is more difficult when the part used is a free-standing structure than when it is actually part of the main residence. If the detached structure and the main residence are of similar quality and, therefore, of similar value to each other, it would still be appropriate to use a *percentage-of-square-footage* approach in order to calculate the business use deduction. However, when there is a significant difference in the nature of the square footage of the separate structure and that of the main dwelling, calculating the deduction on the basis of the percentage of overall square footage used for business is not appropriate.

Space in a barn or garage is simply not as valuable per square foot as space in the typical house. Space in a specifically designed and outfitted recording studio or research laboratory may be far more valuable than the space used for living quarters in a house. In such cases, a deduction could be calculated by using the *fair rental value* of the separate structure or by still using the relative amount of square footage used for business, but with an adjustment to reflect the relative value of the space in the separate structure compared to space in the main residence.

EXAMPLE: Melissa lives in a house containing 2,000 square feet. She is now a self-employed computer repair specialist. There is a separate shop building on the premises that contains 500 square feet and she uses it exclusively and regularly as her only fixed business location for repairing computers. The shop building has special lighting, wiring, and climate control equipment to facilitate computer repair. The cost to construct such a shop would be twice the cost to construct the house.

Melissa chooses to calculate her business deduction for the value of the shop on the basis of square footage. She must adjust the square footage of the shop to allow for its relative value compared to the value of the square footage of the house. Therefore, since square footage of the shop is worth twice the total square footage of the house, she should take twice the total square footage of the shop and add that result to the total square footage of the house. The result would be that Melissa would add twice the shop's 1,500 square feet (3,000) to the 2,000 square feet in her house for a total of 5,000 square feet. She would then divide the 3,000 square feet allocated to the shop by the 5,000 square feet allocated to the total of both structures and the result would be a 60% allocation for the value of the shop.

In the alternative, if Melissa could show that the fair rental value of the shop would be $3,200 a month, and the shop and the house together are either currently renting for $5,000 a month—or would have a fair rental value of that amount if the property is not actually being rented—she could calculate the allocation for the shop for a business deduction. This would be done by dividing the $3,200 fair rental value of the shop by the $5,000 total fair rental value for a 64% allocation.

Allocating the percentage of use of a residence devoted to a qualifying *day care* operation is the most complicated calculation among the deductible business uses of part of a residence. The calculation starts with a determination of the percentage of the residence that is available for regular use as a day care. Once that determination is made, if the area within the taxpayer's residence is used exclusively to provide day care, the percentage of square footage used for day care is calculated in the same manner as it is in calculating the percentage of use for a principal business. A deduction is available for the part of a residence used for day care, even when the use is not exclusive. If that is the case, after determining the percentage of the residence used to provide day care, the taxpayer must then further adjust that percentage to reflect the amount of time that the space is devoted to personal use for the year.

EXAMPLE: Vernon is a self-employed, licensed, day care operator. He uses 1,000 square feet of the 2,000 square feet in his home to provide day care to elderly patrons from 7:00 a.m. to 6:00 p.m., six days a week. At all times that he is not providing day care services, his entire house is used by his family for residential purposes. Vernon uses 50% of his home for a day care, but only does so eleven hours a day for six days a week, a total of sixty-six hours weekly (or 3,432 hours annually). Since there are 8,736 hours in a year, his net percentage of use of his residence as a day care would be calculated as follows:

50% (percentage of house used for day care) x 3,432 (hours of day care operation) ÷ 8,760 (total hours in a year) = 19.59%

EXPENSES ELIGIBLE FOR HOME OFFICE DEDUCTION

Once the percentage of business use of a residence is ascertained, the next step is to apply that percentage to the eligible general expenses associated with the residence. Included among those expenses are insurance, property taxes, repairs, utilities, mortgage interest, and the cost of maintaining a security system. If the taxpayer is renting a residence, the business use percentage should be applied to the rental payments to determine the deductible portion of them. If the party who is qualified to take a deduction for business use of a part of his or her residence owns the residence, regardless of whether or not it is mortgaged, he or she is entitled to take a deduction for depreciation on the part of the residence used for business. The depreciation is calculated by taking the lesser of the residence's adjusted basis or its fair market value, deducting the value of the land that it is on, and dividing the remainder by thirty-nine. Then, apply the percentage of the residence that is devoted to a qualified business use.

Adjusted basis of the residence is usually its acquisition cost plus the cost of any permanent improvements (such as additions or replacement of electrical systems), less the past deductions for either depreciation or losses in value due to destruction (such as by fire or storm not covered by insurance). These losses are known as casualty losses. *Fair market value* is the price for which the property would sell in an *arms-length transaction* between a knowledgeable buyer and seller. The value of the land is deducted from the total value because land is not eligible for depreciation. The depreciable value of the property is divided by thirty-nine because the current law requires that nonresidential real property be depreciated in even increments, known as the straight-line method, over a period of thirty-nine years. Since the deduction is for business use of the property, the nonresidential rules for depreciation apply.

DRAWBACKS TO TAKING A DEDUCTION FOR BUSINESS USE OF A RESIDENCE

Although taking a deduction for depreciation for the part one's home used for business will likely result in a reduced tax liability, there is a down side to taking the deduction. Under I.R.C. Sec. 121, if a taxpayer has owned a residence for at least two years and occupied it as his or her primary residence for at least two of the last five years, he or she may exclude up to $500,000 of such gain from taxation. These are not mere postponements of taxation, but are permanent exclusions. However, Sec. 121 does not permit exclusion of gain that was brought about due to any depreciation that was allowed on the property after May 6, 1997.

EXAMPLE: Liz's adjusted basis in her home is $150,000, of which $30,000 is attributable to the value of the lot. The fair market value of the house is $200,000, of which $50,000 is attributable to the lot. Liz uses 20% of her residence regularly and exclusively as her only fixed place of business as a self-employed artist. The depreciation that Liz is entitled to take on her business use of her residence is calculated as follows:

> $150,000 (adjusted basis) − $30,000 (part of basis attributable to the land) = $120,000 (depreciable basis) x .20 (percentage of business usage) = $24,000 ÷ 39 (number of years over which property must be depreciated) = $615.38 (allowable depreciation)

If, after owning the house for five years (during which time she had used 20% of it for business each year and deducted a total of $3,076.90 in depreciation), Liz were to sell it for a net of $200,000, she would have a gain of $53,076.90 ($200,000 net sales price, less $145,923.10 adjusted basis). This is because adjusted basis in her house must be reduced by any depreciation allowed. However, only $50,000 would qualify for exclusion under Sec. 121 and the $3,076.90 gain attributable to depreciation would be ineligible for such exclusion.

SPECIAL RULES CONCERNING DEDUCTION FOR BUSINESS USE OF A RESIDENCE

Although prorating costs based on square footage to determine the deduction for business use of a residence concludes calculation of the deduction in most instances, there are cases that call for further refinements. Normally, such expenses as the cost of utilities or security systems are allocated on the basis of square footage devoted to business, just as are rent or depreciation. However, if the business deduction is attributed to a barn, garage, or other free-standing structure with such a different value per square foot than the main residence that the square footage of the separate structure had been adjusted to reflect the disparity in value, using square footage to allocate such expenses as utilities and the cost of a security system would likely be inappropriate. Also, to the degree that a taxpayer places equipment in use exclusively for business purposes, the entire cost should be treated as business related.

EXAMPLE: Amir owns and occupies a house that contains 2,000 square feet and has a detached garage containing 1,000 square feet. He decided to quit his job as a salesman at a local automobile dealership and start his own pottery business from his garage. He had the electrical wiring upgraded in the garage in order to be able to operate an oven for baking the pottery and installed an oven and various shelves and racks. Once he started to operate the business from his garage, his utility bill doubled. The value of the space of Amir's garage is worth only about 40% as much as the space in his house. For purposes of allocating depreciation, taxes, and other general expenses to the garage, Amir would have to figure the square footage of the garage at only 40% of its actual size since it is valued at only 40% as much as the square footage in his house. The allocation would be calculated as:

400 (square footage allowed for garage) ÷ 2,400 (square footage allowed for garage + 2,000 actual footage of house) = .1666 (16.66%)

Since Amir can show from his prior bills that his utility bill doubled upon opening his pottery business in his garage, he should be entitled to deduct half of his utility bill for business usage rather than merely 16.66%. Also, the oven, shelves, and racks that Amir had installed are entirely business equipment and he will be entitled to take a depreciation deduction for them without regard to the percentage of square footage of his residential property that is devoted to business.

Amir will not be entitled to deduct the cost of upgrading the electrical wiring in his garage since this is a permanent improvement to the property and will merely increase his basis in it. However, if Amir had merely been renting the property, he would be entitled to take a write-off for the cost of the wiring.

Day care operators who devote part of their residence to their business may also be entitled to certain refinements of their business deductions associated with their residence. If the part of a day care operator's home that is used to provide day care services is not exclusively used for that purpose, not only does that party have to allocate a percentage of his or her residence to day care in figuring the business deduction, but the deduction must also be further reduced to allow for the time the part of the residence is used for non-business purposes. The net result is then applied to what are referred to as *indirect expenses*, which are those that apply to the entire house, such as utilities or general upkeep. However, if expenses incurred in connection with the area devoted to day care are *direct expenses*, then the only adjustment necessary to calculate the business deduction allowed for that expense is to determine the percentage of time that the space is used for business and apply that percentage to the expense. Direct expenses are those that are specific to the space used for that operation, such as the cost of painting the area devoted to day care.

EXAMPLE: Reg operates a day care in his residence. He uses 50% of the home for that purpose and is open 40% of each day, every day of the week. Last month, Reg spent $1,000 having the part of his house used for day care painted. His utility bill was $300. Since the cost of painting was a direct expense and the area that was painted is used for day care 40% of the time, he is allowed to take a business deduction of 40% of the painting cost. The utility bill is an indirect expense and will limit Reg's deduction to 40% (part of each day open for day care) of 50% (part of the residence devoted to day care), which is 20% of the bill.

LIMITATIONS ON THE HOME OFFICE DEDUCTION

Despite the fact that a taxpayer may meet even the most stringent requirements of Sec. 280A and qualify for a deduction for business use of his or her residence, I.R.C. Sec. 280A(c)(5) prohibits the deduction to the extent that it results in a loss from the business involving the residence. This holds true if there would have been no question about the deductibility of such expenses had the business been operated from a location other than the residence. However, the deductions may not be totally lost since taxpayers who cannot take deductions for business use of their residence because the deductions will generate a loss can carry the deductions forward and used them in subsequent years, provided that they do not create a loss in those years.

Section 280A also prohibits any deduction for an employer for expenses incurred in connection with an employee renting any part of his or her residence to his or her employer for business use. Apparently, the potential for abuse in such cases outweighs the justification for allowing such deductions.

Taxpayers also face limitations as to the timing for taking deductions for expenses associated with allowable home office write-offs. For example, when expenses, such as insurance premiums, are paid on an annual basis, taxpayers cannot use the entire premium in calculating the deductible portion allocated to their business. The degree to which a payment covers expenses attributable to the following tax year, it should be appropriately reduced to calculate the deductible expense for the current year. Also, taxpayers who itemize deductions, such as home mortgage interest and real estate taxes must remember to reduce those deductions by the amount allocated and taken as a deduction for the business use of their residences.

Chapter 6

Deductions for the Cost of Goods Sold

Many self-employed taxpayers are in the business of providing some sort of service in exchange for the payments they receive. Such parties will have no deduction for the cost of goods sold and will limit their deductions to the expenses that they incurred in connection with the performance of the services that they provided, as well as allowances for depreciation and amortization of assets used in providing those services. Even self-employed service providers who also furnish an incidental amount of goods along with the services that they provide usually deduct the cost of those goods as a form of *supplies* rather than reporting them as a component of their cost of goods sold. For example, an independent contractor who installs satellite dishes for customers who have purchased the dishes from a retail store would likely furnish some cable and some fittings in the process of the installation but would likely deduct the cost of the cable and fittings as supplies on Part II of Schedule C of Form 1040.

For self-employed taxpayers who sell goods it is imperative that they carefully account for the cost of the goods that they sell. Otherwise, to the degree that a person in the business of selling goods fails to deduct the cost of those goods from his or her gross receipts, the taxpayer will pay taxes on funds that were actually a mere recovery of expenditures for inventory, rather than profit.

The *cost of goods sold* deduction for self-employed taxpayers is provided for on line 4 of Part I of Schedule C of Form 1040. However, the amount of the deduction for the cost of goods sold that is permitted on Schedule C is actually calculated on page 2 of the form in Part III. After some preliminary questions concerning the method used by the taxpayer to determine inventory values, the calculation of the cost of goods sold begins with the value of the taxpayer's inventory at the beginning of the year.

There is a reason that the calculation begins with the taxpayer's beginning inventory. Since no deduction is allowed for expenditures to acquire inventory, sellers of goods must be allowed a deduction for the amount of their sales that were made from their previously acquired inventories or they will not otherwise be allowed any deduction for those expenditures. Therefore, including the cost of previously acquired, but unsold, inventory in the calculation of the cost of a seller's goods sold will allow the taxpayer to write off the cost of the carried over inventory when it is sold.

The next step in the calculation of the cost of goods sold is to add in the value of the taxpayer's purchases of goods acquired for resale to the extent that those purchases were made during the tax year for which the cost of goods sold is being calculated. Once a taxpayer adds the cost of goods purchased to his or her beginning inventory, this will provide the total of all of the party's expenditures for goods that were available for resale for the tax year. Any amount withdrawn for personal use must be reduced from the total, since the cost of those goods was not a business expense. The deduction for the cost of goods withdrawn for personal use is made by reducing purchases of goods by that amount before entering the net expenditure for the purchase of such goods on line 36 of Schedule C. The deduction of the value of the taxpayer's inventory at the end of the year, which is made necessary by the fact that a deduction for purchases of goods for resale is not allowed until the goods are actually sold, is taken on line 41 of Schedule C.

Self-employed business operators who actually manufacture the goods that they sell—including those who merely fabricate components for goods that they purchase for resale or modify such goods prior to sale—must include the costs of their manufacturing activities in their calculations for their costs of the goods that they have sold. This is accomplished by including the cost of labor employed in the manufacturing process, as well as the costs of raw materials and supplies used in the manufacture, fabrication, or modification of goods offered for sale. The deduction for labor costs incurred in the production of goods for sale is provided for on line 37 of Schedule C and deductions for raw materials and supplies is provided for on line 38. There is even a provision for *other costs* of production on line 39.

Payments to self-employed individuals from the trades or businesses that they operate must, for tax purposes, take the form of profits. Therefore, self-employed taxpayers are not allowed to reduce profits by taking a salary deduction for payments that they make to themselves. It is common for self-employed individuals to write themselves checks from their profit on a weekly or other periodic basis. However, the fact that they distribute their profits to themselves in a manner that resembles a salary will not transform the nondeductible profit distributions into deductible salary expenses.

The expenditures for materials and supplies used in the manufacture, fabrication, or modification of goods offered for sale must not be confused with the deductible *supplies* expense provided for on line 22 of Schedule C. Expenditures for materials and supplies that are incorporated into goods that a taxpayer produces should be included in the cost of goods sold. Expenditures for things such as office supplies, sales aids, and expendable items used in providing service should be deducted as a supplies expense. Likewise, inclusion of expenditures for labor as a cost of goods sold should be limited to payments to workers engaged in the actual manufacture, fabrication, or modification of goods offered for sale. Payments to workers who operate the taxpayer's business by providing services, selling products, or dealing with suppliers or customers, but who are not involved in the production of products that are offered for sale, should be deducted as an expense in Part II of Schedule C. They should not be included in the calculation of the cost of goods sold.

As is the case when taxpayers strictly sell goods that were bought rather than produced by them, those who are involved in the production of goods for resale must also deduct the value of their ending inventories from the sum of their beginning inventories, plus their expenditures for goods acquired for resale, less the value of goods withdrawn for personal use. The only difference in the calculations is that those who produce goods for resale will have costs of labor, materials, supplies, and perhaps some additional costs that are associated with the production process to add to their beginning inventories and purchase of goods for resale before subtracting their ending inventories in order to arrive at their cost of goods sold.

Requiring taxpayers to subtract their ending inventories in calculating their cost of goods sold prevents them from manipulating their tax liability by simply loading up on inventory in an attempt to reduce their profits. However, although increases in inventories will result in increased taxable income to a taxpayer, since the party's cost of goods sold will be reduced by the increase, the additional inventory will be available for future sales. When it is sold and not replaced, the inventory will be deductible as part of the net cost of goods sold.

Chapter 7
Non-Business Deductions Available to Self-Employed Taxpayers

Unlike business deductions that are made available to self-employed taxpayers by I.R.C. Sec. 162, non-business deductions are permitted only if they are specifically provided for by Congress in the Internal Revenue Code (I.R.C. Sec. 162 permits the deduction of any expenditure as a business expense as long as it was *ordinary and necessary*.) The non-business deductions that Congress has authorized for self-employed taxpayers are broken into deductions *for* adjusted gross income and deductions *from* adjusted gross income. Business-related deductions are deductions that self-employed taxpayers are permitted to subtract from gross income in order to arrive at their net self-employment income, referred to on Schedule C as *net profit or (loss)*, which is a component—if not the sole source—of their income.

Both the business-related deductions available to self-employed taxpayers and the deductions *for* adjusted gross income permitted for them are deducted from their income in arriving at adjusted gross income. However, deductions *for* adjusted gross income differ from their business deduction counterparts in that the non-business deductions *for* adjusted gross income do not reduce the amount of the taxpayer's income that is subject to self-employment taxes, as do the business deductions available to self-employed taxpayers. Therefore, if a self-employed taxpayer were to have a choice of taking a deduction as a business deduction or as a non-business deduction, it would generally be preferable to take the write-off as a business deduction.

However, some of the deductions that self-employed taxpayers are permitted to take simply will not qualify as a business deduction under the requirements of I.R.C. Sec. 162.

NON-BUSINESS ADJUSTMENTS FOR ADJUSTED GROSS INCOME

Unlike business expense deductions, which are netted against a self-employed taxpayer's gross receipts on Schedule C of Form 1040 rather than being shown on the form itself, the non-business deductions for adjusted gross income are listed on the front of Form 1040. Taxpayers begin the actual calculation of their taxable income by listing all the various sources of income, such as wages and salaries, interest, dividends, business income, capital gains, farm income, rental income, various sources of retirement income, alimony, and unemployment compensation. There is even a line for *other income*, on which taxpayers are to list odd items that do not fit specific categories, such as jury duty pay.

As with business income, the various income components that are calculated on separate schedules, such as Schedule F for farm income, are reported as a net figure with all allowable expenses associated with the earning of that income having been deducted on the schedule used to calculate that income. The taxpayer's income components, which are listed on lines 7 through 21 of Form 1040, are netted together and the figure is entered on line 22 as *total income*. The total of the taxpayer's deductions for adjusted gross income, listed on lines 23 through 32a of Form 1040 are totaled on line 33 and subtracted from the party's total income. Since the deductions are known as *adjustments* in tax parlance, the remaining income after subtraction of the deductions for adjusted gross income is known as adjusted gross income.

Of the ten deductions for adjusted gross income provided for on Form 1040, there are some that the fact that the taxpayer is self-employed will not at all increase the likelihood that the party will qualify for them. Among them are the deduction allowed for alimony paid, the deduction for the payment of interest on student loans, the deduction for penalties imposed for the early withdrawal of savings, and the deduction allowed for qualified educator expenses.

MOVING EXPENSES

Among the deductions for adjusted gross income that are available to both self-employed taxpayers and those who are employees is the deduction for *moving expenses* that is provided for on line 27 of Form 1040. The cost of moving from one residence to another will not give rise to a tax deduction for most taxpayers. Only those who meet the requirements of I.R.C. Sec. 217, which established the moving expense deduction, will be allowed to take the deduction. The objective of the moving expense deduction is to give tax relief to those who have been out of the job market altogether or working only part-time for a substantial period and must relocate to secure full-time employment. It also offers relief to those who must move because they changed employment or were transferred by an employer.

Regardless of whether a taxpayer moves in order to take a job with an employer or to engage in a trade or business as a self-employed worker, Sec. 217 permits the moving expense deduction when certain qualifications are met. Although among those who qualify to take the moving expense deduction the majority are employees, undoubtedly a larger percentage of qualifying self-employed taxpayers actually take the deduction. A large number of employees who would otherwise qualify for the deduction are reimbursed for those expenses by their employers, which renders the employees ineligible for the deduction. Self-employed workers have no employers to reimburse them. The two primary requirements that taxpayers must meet in order to qualify for the moving expense deduction are that the party must move a certain minimum distance or more and the party must be employed at the new location for at least a minimum length of time after the move.

The Distance Test

The distance test that taxpayers must meet in order to qualify for the moving expense deduction is a *fifty-mile test*. However, application of the test is often not as simple as it may sound. Taxpayers who relocate to engage in a trade or business as a self-employed person, who have either never had any previous type of employment or who are reentering the workforce on a full-time basis after a substantial period of only part-time employment or unemployment, must merely take employment that is at least fifty miles from their former residence. The rules are different if a self-employed taxpayer gives up a full-time job and moves to pursue a trade or business as a self-employed person or leaves one self-employment activity to pursue another. In that situation, I.R.C. Sec. 217(c)(1)(A) requires that the taxpayer's new principal place of employment be at least fifty miles further from his or her former residence than his or her former principal place of employment was from his or her former residence.

EXAMPLE: Bill, who lived twelve miles from his primary place of employment, quit his job to become a self-employed computer consultant in a nearby town. His new primary place of employment is fifty-five miles from his residence. If Bill moves to be closer to the site of his new business activity, he will not be entitled to take a moving expense deduction. His new place of employment, being fifty-five miles from his home, is only forty-three miles further than the twelve mile distance of his residence from his former place of employment. In order to qualify for the moving expense deduction, should he choose to move, Bill's new place of employment would have to be at least sixty-two miles away from his residence. If not, he would not have begun a self-employment, activity that was at least fifty miles further from his home than his old place of employment, and he would fail the distance test.

The distance test is the same for both employees and self-employed workers. In measuring the distances of a taxpayer's old and new locations of employment from his or her residence, Treasury Regulation Sec. 1.217-2(c)(2)(iii) requires the party to use the *shortest of the more commonly traveled routes*.

Self-employed taxpayers often work as employees on one job and work in a self-employed capacity on a part-time basis, often in hopes of eventually developing the self-employment activity sufficiently to be able to give up working as someone else's employee. It is particularly important that such workers understand how their place of employment will be determined for purposes of meeting the requirements necessary to take the moving expense deduction. In applying the distance test to determine qualification for the moving expense deduction, a party's place of employment will be his or her main job location, determined by the amount of time spent there, as compared to other locations where he or she may also be required to spend time while at work. The primary job location for those who have more than one job is determined by the total time spent at each job and the comparative earnings from each job.

EXAMPLE: Mary worked as a sales manager making $50,000 per year. On weekends she worked at a gym as a fitness trainer for $200 a day. Mary lived only two miles from her job as a sales manager, but lived twenty-eight miles from the gym. While at a fitness seminar, she met Juliet, who had recently started a business as an independent self-employed fitness consultant and trainer for people wanting individualized attention. Juliet had recently been diagnosed with arthritis and approached Mary about buying her business. Mary knew that Juliet did not have enough clients to provide her with sufficient income to meet her needs, but bought Juliet's business with plans to keep her job as a sales manager and work her new business on weekends and evenings until she could build the business. Since it was easier to commute a long distance to her main job, rather than to various customers' homes for short sessions, Mary moved fifty-five miles to the city where Juliet and her clients lived.

Mary will not qualify to take a moving expense deduction since she did not make the move as a result of a change of her primary job. Had Mary quit her sales manager job and made the move, she would have met the distance test to qualify for the moving expense deduction. Her new place of primary employment would be fifty-three miles further from her residence than her former residence was from her former place of employment. The distance of her former residence from the gym, where she had worked on weekends, would be irrelevant, since her weekend job was not her primary employment.

The Time Test

Subject to a few exceptions, those who retire from working and move are not entitled to a moving expense deduction. Such a move does not meet the fundamental requirement that the move be work-related. Generally, a taxpayer must establish the fact that a move was work-related by actually working at a qualifying job at the new place of residence. Furthermore, the employment at the new place of residence must be for more than just a short-term, token period that was merely a ploy by the taxpayer to qualify for the moving expense deduction. Although both employees and self-employed taxpayers must meet a time test in order to qualify for the moving expense deduction, they are not subjected to the same test.

Employees will be considered to have met the time test to qualify for the moving expense deduction if they work sufficient hours to be considered full-time for the type of work involved and for at least thirty-nine hours of the first twelve months after relocating. Employees are not allowed to count periods of self-employment to meet the time test, but as long as work done as a full-time employee is performed in the same general commuting area, it will count toward fulfillment of the time test (even if the weeks of work are not continuous and are not done for the same employer).

In order for self-employed taxpayers to qualify to take the moving expense deduction, they must pass a two-pronged time test. They must work in qualifying employment for at least thirty-nine weeks of the first twelve months after moving *and* for a total of at least seventy-eight weeks of the first twenty-four months after moving. As with the time test for employees, in order for work to qualify in meeting the time test, it must be done in the general commuting area to which the party relocated and must be considered full-time. However, unlike employees, self-employed taxpayers may count both the work performed as employees as well as work done while self-employed to meet each part of their two-pronged time test.

EXAMPLE: Ralph left his job as a mechanic in a large city on January 1ˢᵗ and moved 100 miles to a small town to take a job running a small engine repair shop. After six months, the owner closed the shop and Ralph rented space at a local gasoline station and began doing auto repair on his own as a self-employed worker. Ralph worked full-time without any periods of interruption for the full year. Since Ralph failed to work as an employee for at least thirty-nine weeks of the first twelve months following his relocation, he must meet the test for duration of work for a self-employed person in order to qualify for the moving expense deduction. Since Ralph actually worked a full fifty-two weeks in the first twelve months following relocation, if he works only twenty-six weeks in the second twelve-month period, he will have met the test for length of employment to qualify for the moving expense deduction.

Treasury Regulation Sec. 1.217-2(c)(4) sets forth a few factors to consider in determining whether a given employment situation satisfies the requirement for duration of employment and thereby qualifies moving expenses for a deduction. Among those factors is that a worker who takes seasonal employment is still considered to have worked during the *off season,* as long as the off season is less than six months, and in cases involving a self-employed seasonal worker, the party worked full-time both before and after the off season. Also, when a married couple with relocation expenses files a joint return, either party's time spent employed full-time can be used to meet the time requirement, but the weeks of full-time employment of each of the two parties cannot be added together to meet the requirement. The Regulation also provides that taxpayers may count weeks missed from work for vacation, or due to illness, strikes, layoffs, natural disasters, and other sources beyond their control, as if they were worked full-time for purposes of meeting the test for duration of full-time employment.

EXAMPLE: Sidney moved to become a self-employed ride operator at an amusement park. He will qualify for a moving expense deduction if he works the required amount of time following the move. He started the job June 1ˢᵗ and worked daily until the park closed on November 1ˢᵗ for the winter. It reopened on April 1ˢᵗ, and Sidney resumed his duties for the full season. For purposes of meeting the test for duration of employment following relocation, Sidney will be considered to have worked full-time during the period in which the park was closed, since he worked both before and after it closed and it was closed less than six months. He will qualify for the deduction.

Moving Expenses Qualifying for Deduction

Not every expense incurred by a taxpayer in connection with relocating is deductible even when the party qualifies for the moving expense deduction. A general definition of *moving expenses* is provided by I.R.C. Sec. 217(b). It limits the deduction to the *reasonable* cost *of moving household goods and personal effects from the former residence to the new residence, and of traveling (including lodging) from the former residence to the new place of residence*. It specifically excludes the expense of meals from inclusion as a part of the costs of the *traveling* component of moving expenses.

Treasury Regulation Sec. 1.217-2 offers specific guidance on the deductibility of moving expenses. It states that the costs of packaging and crating household goods and personal effects, as well as the costs of storing and insuring them while they are in transit are all part of allowable moving expenses. However, the Regulation provides that the following do not qualify as moving expenses for the purpose of determining the allowable deduction:

- storage costs following transit;
- costs of acquiring a new residence;
- costs and losses from disposing of a former residence;
- penalties from breaking a lease or prematurely paying off a mortgage;
- the costs of refitting furnishings to a new residence; and,
- losses from disposing of club memberships or forfeiting prepaid tuition.

Several limitations are placed on the deductibility of travel expenses as a moving expense. The travel expense of the qualifying taxpayer and all members of the party's household are eligible for the deduction, but it is limited to the cost of only one trip, although it is not necessary that all of the parties travel at the same time. Once a party moves out of the old residence, a deduction is permitted for the cost of only one day's lodging in the vicinity of the old residence. Since a deduction may be taken only for the reasonable cost of lodging for the taxpayer and members of the party's household during the course of the move, this rules out deductions connected with side trips along the way or stays in extravagantly expensive hotels. Once a taxpayer arrives at the site of the new residence, no further deductions are allowed for travel expenses, even if temporary accommodations had to be secured while waiting for a new residence to become available, or while awaiting the arrival of furnishings.

No additional moving expense deductions are allowed for travel expenses incurred by a taxpayer to return to the place of the old residence in order to promote or complete the sale of the former residence. If parties who are eligible to take a deduction for moving expenses travel in their own motor vehicle, they may take a deduction for either the actual expenses associated with their use, such as the cost of fuel and tolls, provided they keep records of the expenses, or they may take a deduction based on the number of miles driven.

TUITION AND FEES DEDUCTION

There are a wide array of provisions available to taxpayers that provide tax relief on payments that they make or which are made on their behalf in order to cover the costs of tuition and certain other costs of education. Employees are afforded a major tax advantage by I.R.C. Sec. 127 that allows employers to provide up to $5,250 per year in education assistance to each of their employees and exclude the payments from the recipient's gross income on the party's Form W-2. However, self-employed workers are not considered to be their own employers for purposes of Sec. 127 and are, therefore, ineligible for this exclusion.

It is common for self-employed taxpayers (or those who are contemplating becoming self-employed) to enroll in job-related educational programs. This may be because they want to enhance their skills needed to conduct their trade or business or because they must meet certain minimum requirements in order to become licensed to engage in their chosen profession. Self-employed taxpayers will gain the greatest benefit from deductions for education expenses to the degree that they are allowed to take them as a business deduction on Schedule C of Form 1040 as provided for in I.R.C. Sec. 162. However, Treasury Regulation Sec. 1.162-5 sets forth some very stringent requirements that self-employed taxpayers must meet in order to qualify their education expenses for a business deduction. The primary requirement that self-employed taxpayers must meet in order to qualify their educational expenses as a business deduction is that they must have obtained the education either:

- ◆ to maintain or improve skills required for employment or
- ◆ to meet requirements imposed by law or by the party that engaged them in order to maintain employment and not suffer a reduction in level of employment or compensation.

The Regulation specifically disallows a business deduction for expenses for education that the taxpayer must have in order:

- ◆ to meet minimum educational requirements needed to qualify for the job in question or
- ◆ to qualify the party for a new trade or business.

This disqualification applies even if the education also is necessary in order for the party to acquire the skills necessary to meet the requirements to maintain existing employment.

EXAMPLE: Doris works at a discount chain store checking out customers. In an effort to increase her income, she enrolled in evening classes at a local college with the intention of majoring in accounting and becoming a CPA. Doris will not qualify to take a business expense deduction for these educational expenses since their purpose is to qualify her for a new trade or business. However, if Doris were already a CPA and enrolled in courses in order to meet her state's continuing professional education requirements, the cost of those courses would qualify as a business expense that, if she is self-employed, would be deductible on her Schedule C.

A self-employed person whose education expenses do not qualify for a business deduction may still be entitled to a *tuition and fees* deduction on line 26 of Form 1040. Although such a deduction will not reduce the amount of a taxpayer's income that is subject to self-employment tax, as would a business deduction for an education expense, it offers one significant advantage over the business expense deduction for education expenditures. A tuition and fees deduction of up to $4,000 is available in 2004 and 2005 (subject to extension by Congress) for expenditures for qualified education expenses incurred on behalf of a taxpayer, the party's spouse (when filing a joint return), or any dependent. Therefore, one who pays education expenses for a spouse or dependents may still be entitled to a deduction, whereas it is very rare that education expenses paid for such parties can be shown to be a business expense.

Married taxpayers who file joint returns and whose adjusted gross income does not exceed $130,000 for the year are allowed the maximum deduction per year for qualified education expenses. Taxpayers filing under a status other than married and filing jointly are allowed the full deduction as long as their modified adjusted gross income did not exceed $65,000, except for those who are married and choose to file separately, in which case they are ineligible for the deduction. There is a $2,000 maximum deduction for qualified personal education expenses. It is phased out for married taxpayers filing joint returns whose modified adjusted gross income exceeds $130,000 but is not more than $160,000, and for taxpayers of other filing statuses whose modified adjusted gross incomes exceed $65,000 but are not over $80,000. Those who are married and file separately are ineligible for the deduction.

In order for an education expense to qualify for the deduction it must have been for tuition and related fees paid directly to a qualified educational institution as a condition of enrollment. Therefore, tuition expenses and student activity fees will generally qualify for the deduction, whereas payments for room and board or the cost of books and supplies will not. Qualified educational institutions include any post-secondary educational institution that the U.S. Department of Education considers eligible to participate in student aid programs that it administers.

To the degree that expenditures for education qualify as a business deduction, there will be no limitations, such as the taxpayer's filing status, income level, or nature of the expenditure that will restrict the party's eligibility to take the deduction. This is still another reason why it is almost always preferable to be able to claim a business deduction for education expenses, rather than a tuition and fees deduction on Form 1040. However, it must be remembered that they are not eligible for any type of deduction to the degree that education expenses are paid from tax-free sources, such as scholarships, grants, or employer-provided programs, or are used to qualify for an education tax credit (discussed in Chapter 10).

DEDUCTION FOR ONE-HALF OF SELF-EMPLOYMENT TAX

The deduction for one-half of self-employment taxes paid, which appears on line 28 of Form 1040, is available only to taxpayers with self-employment income. The purpose of the deduction is to achieve a degree of equity between self-employed taxpayers—who must pay self-employment taxes at a nominal rate of 15.3%—and employees—whose share of FICA taxes are only 7.65%—since their employers are paying a matching share of FICA taxes. The deduction does not alter the fact that the nominal rate of self-employment taxes is twice that of an employee's share of FICA taxes. However, it does prevent taxation of that part of self-employment taxes that is the equivalent of the employer's share of FICA taxes which, despite being paid on behalf of employees, is not considered to be taxable income to them.

The deduction for one-half of self-employment taxes is actually calculated on Schedule SE of Form 1040, which is used by self-employed taxpayers to calculate their self-employment tax liabilities. Once a party calculates his or her self-employment tax on Schedule SE, there is a line beneath the amount of the tax for the taxpayer to enter one-half of that liability, which is then transferred to Form 1040.

SELF-EMPLOYED HEALTH INSURANCE DEDUCTION

One of the biggest disadvantages to being self-employed is the lack of employer-provided health-care coverage. Employers commonly enroll in health insurance plans that offer group rates that are generally far lower than individual policies. The employers also usually pay a substantial amount, if not all, of the premiums for the coverage. Furthermore, despite the fact that the insurance premiums paid by employers for their employees are clearly a form of compensation to those employees, the amount of the premium payment is not regarded as taxable income to the employees. Therefore, in order to give self-employed taxpayers similar tax treatment regarding health insurance premiums, Congress enacted I.R.C. Sec. 162(1). It allows self-employed taxpayers to deduct their health insurance premiums as an adjustment for adjusted gross income.

Prior to this provision the only deduction for health insurance premiums allowed for self-employed taxpayers was as part of their itemized medical expense deductions on Schedule A of Form 1040. An itemized medical deduction on Schedule A is allowed only to the extent that it exceeds 7.5% of a taxpayer's adjusted gross income. Therefore, hardly any self-employed taxpayers had enough medical expenses to take an itemized deduction, even though they generally paid out considerably more in health insurance premiums than did taxpayers who worked as employees.

Self-employed individuals are not eligible to take the deduction for self-employed health insurance premiums that they pay if they are eligible for coverage in a subsidized health plan offered by an employer or a spouse's employer. A subsidized plan is one in which an employer pays some or all of an employee's premium for the insurance coverage. Since this qualification is determined on a monthly basis, a self-employed party who is eligible for subsidized group coverage for only part of the year will still be entitled to take the deduction for the months when no subsidized coverage was available.

EXAMPLE: Phillip worked as a self-employed marketing consultant. His wife, Carole, worked for an airline January through April, and was provided with subsidized health care for her and Phillip. After Carole left her job, Phillip acquired health insurance on the two of them and paid the full premium himself. Even though Phillip had subsidized coverage for the first four months of the year, he will still be allowed a self-employed health insurance deduction for the last eight months of the year since he had no subsidized health insurance available to him for those months.

The self-employed health insurance deduction that is available to self-employed taxpayers is further limited by the amount of self-employment income that each of them earns. No matter how much a self-employed taxpayer may pay in qualified health insurance premiums, the deduction on Form 1040 cannot exceed the party's profits from self-employment.

EXAMPLE: Mary retired from her job as a sales clerk. She was not old enough to qualify for Medicare and her former employer provided no subsidized health-care insurance for the company's retirees. In order to be able to pay her $650 monthly health insurance premiums, Mary started providing day care services as a self-employed operator. She netted a profit of $6,000 for the full year from her day care activity. Although she paid out $7,800 in health-care insurance premiums for the year, she will be allowed a self-employed health insurance deduction of only $6,000 on Form 1040, since that is all that she earned in profit for the year.

As with all of the deductions for adjusted gross income allowed on lines 23 through 32a of Form 1040, the deduction for health insurance premiums for self-employed individuals cannot be used to reduce the amount of the tax-payer's self-employment income that is subject to self-employment taxes. Therefore Mary's (from the previous example) entire earnings from her self-employment activity in providing day care will be offset by her deduction for health insurance premiums and totally escape imposition of federal income taxes, but the full $6,000 will be subject to self-employment taxes.

DEDUCTIONS FOR PAYMENTS TO RETIREMENT ACCOUNTS

Another major detriment to being self-employed, rather than working for others as their employee, is that the self-employed individual will not have an employer-provided retirement plan, which is often provided for employees. The conventional wisdom in today's retirement planning is that workers should develop a plan in which Social Security payments are combined with employer-provided pensions and personal savings in order to provide adequate retirement income. Since self-employed workers have no employer to provide them with a retirement plan, it is imperative that they develop a sufficiently large personal retirement plan to compensate for the lack of an employer-provided plan and avoid the prospects of having to live at or near the poverty level in their retirement years. In an effort to encourage self-employed workers to develop retirement plans of their own, Congress allows them to take a deduction for adjusted gross income for certain payments that they make into certain plans.

Payments into Individual Retirement Arrangements

For many years Congress has allowed taxpayers who meet certain qualifications to take a deduction for payments made into a qualified Individual Retirement Arrangement (IRA). The maximum amount of the deduction that is available is as follows.

2004—$3,000, plus an extra $500 for those who are fifty years of age or older;

2005—$4,000, plus an extra $500 for those who are fifty years of age or older;

2006 and 2007—$4,000, plus an extra $1,000 for those who are fifty years of age or older; and,

2008—is scheduled to increase to $5,000, with an extra $1,000 for those who are fifty years of age or older.

A deduction for a payment into an IRA is not restricted to only self-employed taxpayers. Since those who are covered by a retirement plan that is provided by an employer may be partially or even totally ineligible for the IRA deduction, workers who depend solely on self-employment activities for their incomes will not only be more likely to need to establish an IRA, but will also be more likely to qualify for the deduction. Those who qualify for the IRA deduction are to take it on line 24 of Form 1040.

Payments into Self-Employed SEP, SIMPLE, and Qualified Plans

Due to the relatively modest limits on the available IRA deduction, some self-employed taxpayers opt for a retirement plan with larger limits. Although these plans are commonly used by corporations to provide retirement benefits for employees, self-employed taxpayers are also eligible for them.

The *Simplified Employee Pension (SEP)*, which was created by I.R.C. Sec. 408, allows employers to establish either an individual retirement account or individual retirement annuity for each of their employees. It also allows contributions to the account the lesser of 25% of an amount equal to an employee's compensation for the year or $40,000. Since self-employed taxpayers are considered to be their own employers, they qualify to establish a SEP-IRA and take a deduction for eligible contributions.

Another type of plan that qualifies for a deduction for adjusted gross income for contributions made to it is the *Savings' Incentive Match Plan for Employees* (SIMPLE IRA). It allows employers with 100 or fewer employees whose earnings for the previous calendar year were at least $5,000 to establish a retirement account for each employee and either match each employee's contribution up to 3% of the worker's earnings or make a contribution equal to 2% of each worker's earnings without regard to the amount of workers' contributions. As with the SEP, since self-employed workers are considered to be their own employers, they are allowed to establish SIMPLE IRAs of their own and take deductions for qualified contributions.

There are several other types of retirement plans available to employers, such as profit sharing plans and 401(k) plans that self-employed taxpayers may also participate in and qualify for a deduction for adjusted gross income with, since they are considered to be their own employer for purposes of qualifying for the deduction. Such plans are generally more complex than the SEP IRA or the SIMPLE-IRA but may be worth the extra effort since they may offer greater flexibility and larger contribution limits.

It is generally advisable for self-employed parties who wish to take advantage of the SEP IRA, SIMPLE IRA, or any of the other qualified plans to seek professional guidance in establishing and administering the plan in order to be sure that contributions qualify for the deduction. Banks, brokerage houses, and other organizations that market investment choices that qualify for such plans will often gratuitously provide clients with the services that they need to ensure the compliance necessary to qualify for the deduction. Also, there are professional plan administrators who, for a fee, will manage retirement plans so that they qualify for the deduction.

None of the retirement plans for which self-employed taxpayers may take a deduction for contributions made in their own behalves will affect the amount of the parties' self-employment income that is subject to self-employment taxes. There may be some confusion caused by the fact that line 19 on Schedule C of Form 1040 provides for an expense deduction for *pension and profit sharing plans* and any expenses deducted from a self-employed proprietor's gross income will result in a smaller net profit that is subject to self-employment taxes. However, line 19 of Schedule C should be used to deduct *only* payments made to pension and profit sharing plans by self-employed proprietors on behalf of their employees *other than themselves*. Payments made by self-employed taxpayers into retirement plans on their own behalves should be separated from such payments made on behalf of others and shown on line 30 of Form 1040.

Special Characteristics of Deductions for Payments to Retirement Accounts

Regardless of whether a self-employed taxpayer chooses the traditional IRA, SEP IRA, SIMPLE IRA, or some other qualified plan, they all have some specific—and sometimes complex—requirements and limitations that must be met in order to qualify them for a tax deduction. Among the more burdensome requirements common to most plans (other than the traditional IRA), is that if a party has employees, the eligible employees must be included in the retirement plan, as well as the self-employed party who is regarded as his or her own employer. As a result, a retirement plan may prove very costly to a self-employed individual who must make some form of contribution to the retirement plans of every participating employee.

Of course, the self-employed taxpayer who has no employees will reap the entire benefits of any retirement plan that he or she adopts and such plans are usually very easy to administer. These are among the reasons why a self-employed person may find it preferable to engage the services of independent contractors to help them conduct business, rather than hiring employees.

Although the Code sections that authorize them and the forms upon which they are taken refer to the write-offs allowed for payments into qualified retirement plans as *deductions*, they are unlike almost any other available deductions. In reality, they are merely deferments of taxation. It is true that taxpayers may avoid paying taxes on ordinary income used to make qualified contributions into one of the various qualified retirement plans, and will also avoid paying taxes on the income generated by those plans as it is earned. However, when the participant (or the party's heirs) draws money out of the retirement plan, it will be taxed at that time. In theory, participants in retirement plans will profit by sheltering income from taxation at relatively high rates and drawing income out of the plan when their incomes have dropped and they are in relatively low tax brackets. However, this may or may not prove to be the case, depending on what Congress does regarding tax rates. Current law requires participants in most retirement plans to start withdrawing funds from their plans, in amounts based on their life expectancies, once they reach 70½ years of age. They will be taxed on the amount that they are required to withdraw, even if they made no such actual withdrawal.

Non-Business Deductions for Adjusted Gross Income

◆ Educator expenses—up to $250 spent for educational materials by a K through grade 12 teacher, counselor, principal or aide

◆ Student loan interest payments—not available to those who file "married filing separately" or who can be claimed as a dependent by someone else or to those with income in excess of specified limits based on filing status

◆ Tuition and fees paid in behalf of one's self, spouse or dependent to a qualified institution but not available to those filing "married filing separately," those who can be claimed as a dependent by someone else, and nonresident aliens—not available if education credit is taken for the tuition and fees or if income exceeds certain limits based on filing status

◆ Moving expense incurred in connection with job or business or to start a new job

◆ One-half of self-employment tax as shown on Schedule SE

◆ Self-employment health insurance expense—deduction available to otherwise uninsured self-employed taxpayers and owners of over 2% interest in S corporations

◆ Contributions by a qualified party to traditional IRA

◆ Eligible contributions to self-employed SEP, SIMPLE, and Qualified Plans

◆ Penalties imposed on early withdrawal of savings from a time deposit

◆ Alimony paid

Chapter 8
Deductions from Adjusted Gross Income

Once a taxpayer has subtracted his or her deductions for adjusted gross income in order to arrive at adjusted gross income, the only remaining allowable deductions are the deductions *from* adjusted gross income. These deductions are, for the most part, unaffected by whether a taxpayer's income was earned from self-employment activity, work as an employee, or some other source. The allowable deductions from adjusted gross income take the form of either a standard deduction or the total of certain itemized deductions.

ITEMIZED DEDUCTIONS

Taxpayers generally find *itemized deductions* to be the least beneficial type of deduction when they are compared to business deductions and deductions for adjusted gross income. This is because itemized deductions are subject to a number of limitations and also because most taxpayers are allowed to take a relatively sizeable *standard deduction* in lieu of itemizing deductions. This causes itemized deductions to be of absolutely no value to them until they exceed the amount of their standard deduction. Even taxpayers whose itemized deductions exceed their allowable standard deductions will realize tax savings only to the extent of the excess itemized deductions. Therefore, taxpayers who are motivated to incur expenditures because they are *tax deductible* may simply be bringing the amount of their itemized deductions closer to their standard deductions—or just barely over their standard deductions—and will realize little or no tax benefit from the expenditures.

Congress has traditionally allowed most taxpayers to take a federal tax deduction for several categories of expenditures. There is no real pattern or basis to explain why some expenditures may be deducted while others may not, or why some of the deductions are subject to limitations and others are not. Generally, taxpayers must meet rather specific requirements in order to qualify for an itemized deduction and there will be little or no room for argument if those requirements are not met.

Medical and Dental Expenses

I.R.C. Sec. 213 permits taxpayers to take a deduction for *medical and dental expenses* paid for both prevention and treatment or cure of disease, including the cost of prescription drugs, prescribed long-term care for the chronically ill, the cost of transportation to receive medical care, and even premiums paid for health insurance. Even so, very few taxpayers actually realize any benefit from the deduction. Among the provisions that limit the value of the medical and dental expense deduction to taxpayers is that any qualified expenses that are not actually paid by the taxpayer are ineligible for deduction. Therefore, those who have significant amounts of medical and dental expenses, but which are paid by their health insurance companies, will not be allowed to take a deduction for those expenses. Even though health insurance premiums are deductible to the extent that they are paid by an employer, no deduction by the employee will be permitted (although the employer will be allowed a deduction).

In calculating the medical and dental expense deduction, a taxpayer is required to reduce any out-of-pocket qualified expenditures by an amount equal to 7.5% of his or her adjusted gross income. This step in the calculations generally leaves only those taxpayers who had extraordinarily high uninsured medical and dental expenses and health insurance premiums with anything to deduct.

Self-employed individuals who do not have the option of enrolling in a subsidized health insurance plan provided by an employer or a spouse's employer have an opportunity to do some tax planning to maximize the deductibility of their medical and dental expenses. Such self-employed tax-payers are permitted to fully deduct their health insurance premiums as a deduction *for* adjusted gross income, which is not subject to reduction and can be taken *in addition to the standard deduction* (rather than in lieu of it.) Eligible self-employed taxpayers should attempt to maximize their health insurance premium deduction and minimize their out-of-pocket medical and dental expenses. This can be accomplished by choosing health insurance coverage that has higher premiums but relatively small deductibles and copayments.

EXAMPLE: Floyd is a self-employed barber. His wife keeps his books, but neither she nor Floyd have any other jobs. It is time for Floyd to renew his health insurance and his insurance agent has a variety of plans to offer. The least costly plan is a major medical policy that does not pay any benefits until a $2,000 deductible per insured has been paid out-of-pocket. It then pays 80% per person for the next $15,000 in medical costs and 100% for all costs thereafter. The premium for this plan for Floyd's family is $350 per month. Alternatively, Floyd can take a health insurance plan that covers all but a $10 copayment for trips to see a doctor, all but $5 for each prescription, and all but the first $100 of the bill for each hospital stay. The cost of this plan is $750 per month. Last year, insured under a major medical plan, Floyd had $4,900 in uninsured med-ical expenses, all but $500 of which would have been paid by the more comprehensive plan of coverage. He is reluctant to spend the extra $4,800 in premiums to save only $4,400 in medical costs. Floyd's adjusted gross income for the previous year was $72,000.

If Floyd's medical costs and income are about the same for the next year as they were for the previous year, he would be better off to take the more comprehensive coverage even though the addi-tional premiums would exceed the savings from the better policy by $400. This is due to the fact that under the major medical policy, Floyd would get to take the $350 monthly premium as a deduction for adjusted gross income, for an annual total of $4,200, but would get no itemized deduction for his out-of-pocket medical expenses, since they would not exceed 7.5% of his adjusted gross income. On the other hand, he would be entitled to fully take the entire $750 premium for the more comprehensive policy as a deduction for adjusted gross income, for a total of $9,000. If Floyd were in the 25% marginal tax bracket, the $1,200 tax savings from the additional $4,800 deduction would far exceed the $400 by which the added premiums exceeded the added benefits from the comprehensive health insurance policy.

NOTE: *Eligible self-employed taxpayers are permitted to take health insurance premiums as a deduction for adjusted gross income or as an itemized deduction but are not allowed to take both deductions for the same health insurance premium payment.*

Taxes Paid

Among the various taxes that individuals pay, some, such as state, local, and foreign income taxes, and state, local, and foreign property taxes, qualify as itemized deductions under I.R.C. Sec. 164. Still other taxes that individuals commonly pay do not qualify as itemized deductions. Among them are federal income taxes, FICA taxes, estate and gift taxes, and any payments to governmental entities for which goods, services, or personal privileges are received.

Section 164 gives self-employed taxpayers the opportunity to take a business deduction for taxes that were paid as part of the cost of conducting a trade or business, or that were incurred in producing rents, royalties, or other income. Therefore, it is not only possible for self-employed taxpayers to take a business deduction for some of their tax payments that individuals who are not self-employed would not be permitted to deduct, but they are also able to upgrade some of their itemized deductions, attributable to taxes that they have paid, to business deductions. Of course, by maximizing their business deductions, self-employed taxpayers minimize their federal tax liabilities, since these deductions reduce the amount of their incomes that are subject to self-employment taxes, and benefit even those taxpayers who do not have sufficient itemized deductions to exceed the standard deduction.

As previously discussed in the section on deductions for adjusted gross income, self-employed taxpayers are permitted, by specific statutory provision, to deduct one-half of the self-employment taxes that they pay as a deduction for adjusted gross income, apart from any itemized deductions that they may have. This guarantees them a reduced income tax liability, but the deduction cannot be used to offset income subject to self-employment taxes. Qualifying tax payments for a business deduction that will reduce a self-employed taxpayer's income, which is subject to both federal income taxes and self-employment taxes, is a matter of showing that the payment of the taxes was an ordinary and necessary business expense.

EXAMPLE: John wants to erect a sign on his property denouncing George Bush because of his policies that led to the war in Iraq. Sigmund, owner of a neighboring piece of property, wants to erect a sign advertising his business as a self-employed taxidermist. In their township, each will be required to pay a tax of $500 in order to be permitted to erect the sign. John will not be allowed to take a tax deduction for the $500 payment to the township since he is obtaining a personal privilege for the payment and there is no business purpose for it. Sigmund will be entitled to take a business deduction for his $500 payment since the costs associated with a sign for his taxidermy trade would clearly be considered to be ordinary and necessary business expenses.

Itemized Interest Expenses

At one time, U.S. tax law permitted taxpayers to deduct any interest expenses that they incurred as an itemized deduction. However, current law limits the itemized deduction available to individuals for interest expenses to home mortgage interest and investment interest. Even those taxpayers who have incurred interest expenses that qualify for the itemized deduction must meet certain requirements or the right to take the deduction will be lost.

The Home Mortgage Interest Deduction

For purposes of establishing that interest paid constitutes *home mortgage interest* that is deductible under Sec. 163, it must be shown that the loan on which the interest was paid had been obtained to buy a main home or second home, or the loan must have been a second mortgage, line of credit, or home equity loan on a main or second home. Additionally, the taxpayer must be legally liable on a valid, bona fide debt that is secured by a legitimate mortgage on a qualified home and the mortgage must be evidenced by a binding promissory note and collateralized with the property being mortgaged. The specific methods of collateralizing loans on real property differ somewhat from state to state. However, they all share the common denominator of a written grant, such as a deed of trust, that is signed by the owners of the property authorizing a designated party to foreclose on the loan if the debtor fails to make timely payments.

In addition to payments that are specifically labeled as interest, those who itemize deductions are also allowed to deduct discount points, origination fees, late payment fees, and prepayment penalties, since all of these charges are generally considered to be part of the cost of using borrowed money. Generally, the deduction for discount points and origination fees cannot be taken in the year in which they were paid, but must be spread over the life of the loan. This is true unless:

  ♦ the proceeds of the loan were used to buy or build the party's main home and paying points or origination fees of the amount paid is an established business practice in the area where the loan was made;

  ♦ the points or fees are computed as a percentage of the amount of the mortgage, such charges are clearly shown on the settlement statement; or,

  ♦ the funds for the points or origination fees were not borrowed as part of the mortgage.

Fees for services connected with obtaining a home mortgage, such as appraisal fees, mortgage insurance premiums, and the cost to record a deed or mortgage are not deductible as interest.

All the interest on any mortgages originated on or before October 13, 1987 is deductible on Schedule A as home mortgage interest, since that was the last date virtually all interest payments qualified as itemized deductions. Such obligations are referred to as *grandfathered debt.* Mortgages that are originated after October 13, 1987, in order to buy, build or improve a main home or second home is referred to as *home acquisition debt.* Interest on such debts is fully deductible on Schedule A as long as the total of the home acquisition debt and the grandfathered debt on all of the mortgages on the individual's main home and second home combined does not exceed $1 million ($500,000 if the party's filing status is married, filing separately). Otherwise, the interest deduction will have to be reduced to reflect the interest charged on the maximum allowable indebtedness.

Mortgages originated after October 13, 1987—for purposes other than to purchase, build, or improve a main home or second home—are known as *home equity debt.* Interest on home equity debt is deductible on Schedule A. The total home equity debt on an individual's main home and second home combined cannot exceed $100,000 ($50,000 for married couples choosing to file as married, filing separately). The total of grandfathered debt, home acquisition debt, and home equity debt cannot exceed the fair market value of the property that is mortgaged. If the total indebtedness exceeds the fair market value of the property mortgaged, the interest deduction must be reduced to the level that would be paid if the total indebtedness equaled the fair market value of the property mortgaged.

EXAMPLE: Sigourney owns a home worth $400,000 which she obtained with a mortgage that has a $375,000 balance. She just bought a home at a nearby lake for $150,000. She paid her closing costs, which included a $3,000 loan origination fee, in full and obtained a mortgage for $150,000 against the lake property to pay for it.

Sigourney will be allowed to fully deduct the interest on both of her mortgages on Schedule A since they are both home acquisition debt, neither of which exceeds the value of the property on which each mortgage is placed, and the combined total of the two mortgages does not exceed $1 million. The $3,000 loan origination fee is deductible as interest expense on Schedule A, but it must be spread out over the life of the loan for purposes of calculating the interest deduction. If Sigourney had not already owned a home and the lake home had been purchased as her main home, she would likely have been allowed to claim an interest deduction for the full origination fee for the year in which it was paid.

Investment Interest

Section 163(d)(5) of the I.R.C. allows taxpayers to deduct interest that they pay on indebtedness incurred to acquire investments, which I.R.C. Sec. 469(e)(1) defines as items that generate income from interest, dividends, annuities, or royalties not derived in the course of a trade or business. No interest deduction is permitted on investments that generate tax-exempt income, passive activities (those in which a taxpayer did not materially participate), or interest incurred on straddles (taking a simultaneous long and short position in the same security). Also, no deduction for investment interest will be allowed to the extent that the investment interest exceeds the taxpayer's *net investment income.*

Net investment income is the total of interest, dividends, annuities, royalties, or other such income less investment expenses other than interest, such as fees paid to a financial planner or the cost of publications for investors. Commissions charged by brokers to execute a transaction are not regarded as an investment expense, but merely increase the cost of acquisition on purchases and reduce the net proceeds upon sale. Investment expenses are deductible on Schedule A as "Other expenses" to the extent that the total of such deductions exceeds 2% of the taxpayer's adjusted gross income for the year.

To the extent that no deduction is allowed for these expenses due to failure of the total miscellaneous itemized deductions to exceed 2% of a party's adjusted gross income, he or she will not be required to reduce his or her investment income by the amount of those expenses. However, in calculating a party's miscellaneous itemized deduction, all such expenses (other than investment expenses) are applied against the 2% of adjusted gross income limitation first. To the extent that the limitation is exceeded by noninterest investment expenses for which a miscellaneous itemized deduction is then allowed, those expenses must be deducted from the party's gross investment income to determine the net investment income.

To the extent that a taxpayer has insufficient net investment income to enable the party to fully deduct the investment interest, the unused interest deduction may be carried over to the next tax year. Normally, net investment income does not include net gains from the sale of investment property, but taxpayers may elect to include it in order to raise their investment incomes and permit them to fully deduct their investment interest expenses. However, if such an election is made, the gain that was realized must then be taxed as ordinary income, whereas it may have otherwise qualified to be taxed as long-term capital gain, which is subject to a maximum tax rate of only 15%. Therefore, the taxpayer making an election to treat long-term capital gain as investment income would be using the investment interest deduction to offset capital gain that would have been taxed at only 15%. This is instead of carrying the deduction forward and using it to offset ordinary income that could be subject to as much as a 35% rate of taxation, depending on the tax-payer's income and filing status.

EXAMPLE: George, whose adjusted gross income for the year was $60,000, earned interest income of $3,000 from bonds that he had bought partially on credit. The interest on his loan to acquire the bonds was $2,800 for the year and his only investment expense was a subscription to an investment information service that cost $500 per year. George had other miscellaneous itemized deductions subject to the 2% of adjusted gross income limit that totaled $1,200.

George's investment interest deduction is calculated by first subtracting 2% of his adjusted gross income (.02 x $60,000), which is $1,200, from his miscellaneous itemized deductions subject to the 2% of adjusted gross income limit ($1,200 of noninvestment related deductions plus $500 of noninterest investment-related deductions). The total is $1,700, leaving a total deductible amount of $500. Since noninvestment-related miscellaneous itemized deductions must be offset by the 2% adjusted gross income deduction first in calculating the net deduction, the full $1,200 of George's deductions in this category is fully offset.

Therefore, the full $500 of miscellaneous itemized deductions remaining after the 2% of adjusted gross income limitation is applied must be deducted from his investment income ($3,000 – $500) to arrive at his net investment income of $2,500. Section 163 prohibits a taxpayer from taking an investment interest deduction in excess of his investment income. Because of this, George will be allowed to take a deduction of only $2,500, leaving the $300 difference between his investment interest expense and net investment income ($2,800 – $2,500) to be carried forward to the next tax year for deduction.

If an individual has investment interest expense in excess of interest income, has deductible investment expenses other than interest, or has investment interest expenses that were carried over from a prior year, the taxpayer must use Form 4952 to calculate the investment interest expense deduction. It can then be transferred over to Schedule A. Otherwise, individuals may deduct their investment interest expense directly on Schedule A without having to file Form 4952.

Interest Expense Related to Rents and Royalties

To the extent that taxpayers incur indebtedness in order to obtain property that generates either rent or royalty income, they will be allowed to take a deduction for the interest expense associated with that part of the debt for which they are liable. Such deductions are allowed on Schedule E of Form 1040. This is generally preferable to an itemized deduction, since it benefits even those taxpayers whose itemized deductions fail to exceed their standard deduction.

Rental of real or personal property is generally considered to be a *passive activity* from which losses can be used to offset a maximum of only $25,000 of ordinary income, such as wages or interest income. Interest deductions are indirectly limited on rental property to the degree that they contribute to nonpassive activity losses in excess of $25,000. There is no direct limitation on the amount of interest expense deduction that can be taken for indebtedness on property held for the production of rent or royalty income. Also, the right to offset even $25,000 of ordinary income with losses from related activities is phased out for taxpayers with relatively high incomes.

Business Interest

As with other expenditures, to the degree that a self-employed individual can show that a *bona fide* loan was obtained for use in the party's trade or business, the interest on the loan should qualify for deduction as an ordinary and necessary business expense as provided for in I.R.C. Sec. 162. Regardless of whether a taxpayer pledges personal property or business property as collateral for a loan, as long as the proceeds were used in the debtor's trade or business, the interest on the loan would be a deductible business expense. If the proceeds are used for a non-business purpose, the interest would not be a deductible business expense.

Taxpayers benefit from business expenses, even if their itemized deductions do not exceed their standard deductions. Self-employed taxpayers can reduce their federal income tax liabilities by structuring their debts so that as much of their interest expense as possible qualifies as interest on business indebtedness and is deductible as a business expense. Still another incentive for self-employed taxpayers to favor business indebtedness over personal indebtedness is that it reduces their profit that is subject to self-employment taxes. Interest on personal indebtedness, if it is deductible at all, will not reduce the amount of a party's income that is subject to self-employment taxes.

EXAMPLE: Casey, an instructor at a small college, inherited $200,000 upon the death of his father. He owes $93,000 on a mortgage on his home, owes a combined $41,000 on two cars, owes a total of $21,000 on various credit cards, and owes $10,000 on an account at a furniture store. However, rather than use the money to pay off his debts, Casey is seriously considering using the money to open a bait shop at a nearby lake, since that is something that he has always wanted to do. He has free time during the peak summer season to work in such a shop.

If Casey were to decide to open the bait shop, he would be wise to use $165,000 of his inheritance to pay off his personal debts and then borrow the funds that he needed to open his bait shop. By doing so, all of his interest on his new loan would be deductible as a business expense. Only the interest on his home mortgage is deductible among his personal debts, and it will not offset income that is subject to self-employment taxes, as will the business deduction, and it may not even result in a reduced income tax liability if his itemized deductions do not exceed his standard deduction.

However, such a plan would not be workable if Casey could not get a business loan or if the interest rate on the business loan were significantly higher than the rates of interest on the various loans that were paid off. Casey could even pledge the very assets that he paid off as collateral for his new business loan and still be entitled to a business deduction for the interest that he pays on the loan, since the loan proceeds will be used for a business purpose. It would seem likely that he could get as good an interest rate as he had, if not better, unless interest rates had risen in general.

Many self-employed individuals pledge their home as collateral for a new business loan in an effort to raise money for their ventures at a favorable interest rate. Treasury Regulation Sec. 1.163-10T(o)(5) provides that a debtor who secures a loan in the form of a home mortgage that qualifies for the home mortgage interest deduction, but uses the loan proceeds in his or her trade or business, may choose to take the interest payments on the loan as a business interest deduction, rather than a home mortgage interest deduction. This can be done provided that the taxpayer makes an election to treat the debt that is actually secured by a qualified residence as not being secured by a qualified residence. The Regulation does not specify the method for making such an election, however, reporting the home mortgage interest expense as a business interest expense when the proceeds of the loan are used in the debtor's trade or business should be sufficient. But, attaching a statement to the debtor's tax return declaring that such an election had been made may even be advisable.

Although making such an election will permit the debtor to realize the advantage of taking a business deduction in place of the home mortgage interest deduction, the election is not made without a cost. Section 1.163-10T(o)(5) further provides that once an election is made to treat a loan that is secured by a qualified residence as if it were not secured by a qualified residence, the election will be effective not only for the year in which it was initially made, but also for all future taxable years. This will remain in effect unless the Commissioner of the IRS consents to revocation of the election. Therefore, if a taxpayer elects to treat a loan that is secured by a qualified residence as if it were not secured by a qualified residence, and then discontinues the business in which the loan proceeds were used but still owing money on the loan, the party will not be allowed to take a home mortgage interest deduction for the interest expense on the loan. Despite the fact that a business interest expense deduction for the interest that he or she pays on the loan can no longer be taken, only the Commissioner of the IRS can consent to revocation of the prior election.

EXAMPLE: If Casey, from the previous example, were to pay off his home with money from his inheritance and then take out a new loan against his home to get funds to start his bait shop, he would be eligible to elect to deduct the interest payments on that loan as a business expense on his Schedule C of Form 1040. However, if, after two years, he were to close the bait shop, he would no longer be entitled to deduct his mortgage interest as a business expense, since he would no longer have a business. He would be ineligible to take an itemized deduction for home mortgage interest on Schedule A of Form 1040, since he had previously made an election to treat his mortgage interest as if it were not interest on a qualifying residence, unless he can get the permission of the Commissioner of the IRS to revoke the election.

An alternative that Casey may have would be to use funds from liquidation of the business to pay off the mortgage on his home. If he needed funds to pay off other obligations left over from the business, taking another mortgage on his home to obtain those funds, but qualifying to take an itemized home mortgage interest deduction for the interest paid on the latest mortgage. He would not have made an election to treat the interest on that loan as business interest, even though the proceeds of the loan were used for a business purpose.

Charitable Contributions

Under the provisions of I.R.C. Sec. 170, cash contributions and the fair market value of contributions of property made to qualified organizations up to an amount equal to 50% of the individual *donor's* adjusted gross income for the year are generally deductible by the donor as charitable gifts on Schedule A. There are some special criteria if the donation is not to a charitable organization (50% limit organization as defined by the IRS) or is of property on which there is a long-term capital gain, but for most common donations the following rules apply.

No deduction may be taken for a contribution to the extent that the donor received benefits in exchange. However, if the donor receives benefits with a smaller fair market value than the amount of the contribution, a deduction may still be taken for the difference.

No deduction is allowed for gifts made to individuals or to nonqualified organizations. Donors are prohibited from taking a deduction for donations when they stipulate that the benefit of their gift is to go to a specific nonqualified recipient. This is done to prevent donors from being able to give gifts to qualified organizations so that they can take a tax deduction for them, and then having that organization give the gift to the unqualified party that the donor wishes to benefit. However, donors can make gifts to qualified organizations and specify that they are to be used for some particular purpose, such as providing relief to victims of a certain hurricane, and still be permitted to take a deduction for their contributions.

No deduction is available for the contribution of one's time or service, even when the contribution is made to a qualified organization. However, out-of-pocket expenses, such as the cost of transportation or the cost of buying and cleaning uniforms, associated with contributed services, are deductible. The cost of child care necessary to permit a person to perform volunteer work is not a deductible expense as a charitable contribution.

Taxpayers must maintain adequate records to substantiate their charitable contributions. As the amount of the contribution goes up, the record keeping requirement becomes more stringent. Cash contributions, which include donations by check, credit card, and payroll deduction, as well as currency of less than $250, can be substantiated by a cancelled check, an account statement from the recipient, or the taxpayer's own written records. An account statement from the recipient must show the amount and date of the contribution. If substantiated by the taxpayer's own written records, the record must be made at the time of the contribution and show the name of the recipient, and the amount and date of the contribution. As long as no single contribution to a charity exceeds $250, it will qualify as a gift of less than $250 even if other contributions to the same charity would put the combined total of those contributions well over $250.

Deductions for cash contributions, other than by payroll deduction, in excess of $250 each must be supported by a written acknowledgment from the qualified organization receiving them stating the amount of the contributions and the value of goods or services, if any, that were received as a result of the contributions. This acknowledgment must be received by the taxpayer on or before the earlier of the date the taxpayer files a return for the year in which the contribution was made or the due date for such return, including extensions. If a donor makes multiple cash contributions in excess of $250 to the same donee and does not make them by payroll deduction, the deduction of the contributions may be supported by a single acknowledgment showing the party's total contributions or by a separate acknowledgment for each contribution.

Deductions taken for contributions by payroll deduction do not require an acknowledgment from the recipient. However, if $250 or more is deducted from a single paycheck of an employee, proof of the amount withheld (in the form of a pay stub or W-2) must be kept, and documentation must be provided by the recipient stating that the organization did not provide goods or services in return for the contribution made by the payroll deduction.

Noncash contributions require the most stringent documentation to support a charitable contribution deduction. There are four different categories of noncash contributions that have separate requirements for supporting a deduction. The categories are determined by the fair market value of each contribution.

1. Noncash contributions of less than $250 require a receipt from the recipient showing its name and location, the date of the gift, and a reasonably detailed description of the property that is donated. Additionally, for each donated item, the donor must maintain his or her own records that contain:

   ◆ the name and address of the donee;

   ◆ the date of the gift;

   ◆ a reasonably detailed description of the property;

   ◆ the value of the contribution and how it was determined; and,

   ◆ any terms or conditions attached to the gift.

2. A taxpayer who takes a charitable gift deduction for noncash donations of items valued at $250 to $500 must obtain and keep a written acknowledgment of the contribution from the recipient. The acknowledgment must show the name and address of the donee, the date of the gift, a reasonably detailed description of the property, and whether goods or services were given to the donor

as a result of the contribution and, if so, the estimated fair market value of them. The taxpayer must also maintain his or her own records with the same information as the records for noncash gifts valued at less than $250.

3. Deductions for donations of noncash property valued at more than $500, but not over $5,000, must be supported by the same information as for gifts valued between $250 and $500, with the taxpayer keeping additional information as to how and when the donor got the property, and the donor's cost or other basis in the donated property.

4. Those who take deductions for noncash property valued in excess of $5,000 must meet all of the requirements for supporting a deduction for noncash contributions valued at over $500 but not over $5,000, plus they must obtain a *qualified written appraisal* of the donated property. For purposes of determining whether the value of noncash donations exceeds $5,000, taxpayers must combine all similar items donated to all donees during the taxable year. (The appraisal requirement does not apply to donations of publicly traded securities.)

Most taxpayers are permitted to take their charitable contributions on Schedule A of Form 1040. However, taxpayers who take deductions for total noncash contributions of over $500 must also file Form 8283, which calls for extensive information concerning donated property, acknowledgment by the donee, and requires attachment of appraisals when they are necessary.

Unlike other expenditures, such as interest payments, donations by self-employed taxpayers cannot be converted to a business expense by making the donations in the names of the self-employed donors' trades and businesses, rather than making them as personal donations. In fact, even partnerships, limited liability companies, and S corporations are not allowed to take deductions for charitable contributions made by them. They must report the *pro rata* share of the contributions of each owner so that each party can take that amount as part of his or her personal itemized deductions for charitable contributions. Individuals who make payments to charitable entities and get something of value in return are ineligible to take a contribution deduction for those payments (since they are actually purchases rather than gifts). However, if those purchases can be shown to be an ordinary and necessary business expense, they should be deductible. Therefore, a self-employed individual who desires to offer financial support to a charitable organization may be able to provide that support and still take a business deduction by making payments to the charity in exchange for a good or service that benefits the party's trade or business.

EXAMPLE: Phil is an optometrist. He wanted to help the local high school raise money to publish the school annual, so he bought a full-page advertisement for his optometry practice in the annual for $1,000. Phil should be able to deduct his $1,000 payment to the school as an advertising expense.

Band members have an opportunity to participate in a Thanksgiving Day parade in New York City but they must raise money for the trip. Band members approached Phil for a $1,200 donation. The donation would qualify for an itemized charitable deduction, but, in recent years, Phil's standard deduction has exceeded his itemized deductions by a wide margin and this additional itemized deduction would not provide Phil with any tax savings. But Phil is aware that the school publishes a calendar each year that is displayed on all of the bulletin boards throughout the school and is distributed to teachers, parents, and administrators. Phil decided to decline the request that he make a contribution but offered to give the school $1,200 to help finance the band trip if the school would put an advertisement for his optometry practice on the bottom border of its next calendar. If Phil's proposal is accepted, the band will get money that it needs and Phil should be entitled to deduct the payment as an advertising expense as long as the fair market value of the ad is $1,200.

Any charitable contributions that cannot be taken because they exceed the limit for such deductions may be carried over and deducted in a later year for up to five years, but no further.

Casualty and Theft Losses

Individuals are not allowed to take a tax deduction for ordinary wear and tear that diminishes the value of their personal property. However, when a taxpayer's personal property is damaged or destroyed by an identifiable event that is sudden, unexpected, and unusual, such as fire, storm, vandalism, or auto accident, I.R.C. Sec. 165 allows a limited itemized deduction for the loss. Such a deduction is also allowed for losses due to theft, such as burglary, robbery, shoplifting, and even blackmail, extortion, or kidnapping for ransom. No deduction is allowed for property that is merely misplaced.

The amount of a party's casualty or theft loss is determined by subtracting the amount of the decrease in the fair market value of items subject to a casualty or theft loss from the taxpayer's adjusted basis in the items and then further reducing the loss by any insurance or other reimbursement received or expected. The fair market value of unrecovered stolen property and property totally destroyed by casualty will be zero after the loss, and, therefore, the decline in the value of such property due to the loss will be equal to its fair market value. In determining the fair market value of property involved in a casualty or theft loss, no allowance can be included for the fact that:

- replacement cost may exceed the property's fair market value;
- the property may hold sentimental value for the taxpayer; or,
- the taxpayer incurred costs incidental to the loss, such as the need to temporarily obtain a rental car or the necessity to get medical treatment for injuries associated with the loss.

Calculating the Personal Deduction for Casualty and Theft Losses

Once a determination has been made as to the amount of a taxpayer's casualty or theft loss, two separate limits must then be applied in order to determine the amount of the loss that the party will be allowed to take as a personal deduction. First, the total loss from each casualty or theft event must be reduced by $100. Then, the total losses from all casualties and thefts, less the $100 deduction per event, are added together for the taxable year and an amount equal to 10% of the taxpayer's adjusted gross income for the year must be subtracted from that total. The remaining balance is the amount that the taxpayer is eligible to deduct as a casualty or theft loss on his or her personal tax return. If a taxpayer collects insurance or other reimbursements in excess of the adjusted basis for property that is damaged, destroyed, or stolen, the excess must be reported as income.

Casualty and theft losses, as well as any gains on reimbursements from casualties and thefts, are reported on Form 4684, which then calls for the allowable deduction to be reported on Schedule A of Form 1040 and requires that any gains be reported on Schedule D of Form 1040. If a taxpayer's casualty or theft loss exceeds the party's income, it will be regarded as a net operating loss, despite the fact that the loss did not arise from a business operation, and the loss can be carried back and generate a refund for a prior year's taxes or carried forward and used to offset income in subsequent years.

EXAMPLE: Jim bought a 1957 Chevrolet that he had been restoring. He paid $5,000 for the car and spent $1,500 on parts and supplies, plus countless hours of his time. The free-standing garage in his back yard caught on fire due to an electrical problem and burned to the ground, destroying Jim's car as well. The garage, which had cost Jim $8,000, had a fair market value of $10,000. It was insured and he received $8,000 for the loss after his deductible was withheld by his insurance company. Since Jim had not quite finished restoring his car and was not driving it, he had not insured it. The fair market value of the car at the time of the fire was $24,000. Jim's adjusted gross income for the year in which he suffered these losses was $42,000.

The fire that destroyed Jim's garage and car is a classic example of a casualty loss (unless Jim had deliberately set the fire). In calculating the amount of his casualty loss deduction, Jim must first determine the lesser of his adjusted basis in the garage and the car or the decrease in their fair market value due to the fire. Jim's adjusted basis in the car was $6,500, which was comprised of the $5,000 that he spent acquiring it plus the $1,500 in parts and supplies restoring it. He cannot include any value for his time in restoring the car in its adjusted basis.

Since the car had no value after the fire, its decline in fair market value was the full $24,000. Jim's loss for purposes of determining his casualty loss deduction for the car will be limited to his adjusted basis in the car of $6,500 since it is less than the $24,000 decline in fair market value of the car due to the fire. Jim's adjusted basis on the garage is his cost of $8,000, which is the value that he must use in determining his casualty loss deduction, since the decline in the value of the garage from $10,000 to zero is greater than his adjusted basis in it.

He must then combine the $6,500 loss on the car with the $8,000 loss on the garage for a total of $14,500 and subtract the $8,000 insurance proceeds, leaving a remainder of $6,500. Jim must then subtract $100 from that total. Even though two distinct properties were destroyed in a single event, only one $100 exclusion must be applied to the combined uninsured loss. The remaining balance of $6,400 must then be reduced by an amount equal to 10% of Jim's $42,000 adjusted gross income ($42,000 x .10 = $4,200). The remaining $2,200 is the amount of Jim's casualty loss that he will be allowed to deduct on his Schedule A.

The Casualty Loss Deduction for Business-Related Property

To the degree that self-employed taxpayers can show that casualty losses that they suffer involved property that they used in their trade or business, rather than items that were personal property, they will be entitled to a much more favorable deduction for the loss. This is because deductions for casualty or theft losses on business property and income-producing property are not subject to the $100 per event exclusion, the 10% of adjusted gross income exclusion, or even the 2% of adjusted gross income exclusion for miscellaneous deductions. The amount of the loss on such property is still limited to the lesser of its fair market value or the owner's adjusted basis, but that amount is then fully deductible. Equipment owned by a self-employed individual to conduct his or her trade or business, or an office building that is rented out, would be examples of business property. Stocks, bonds, gold, notes, and works of art are all examples of income-producing property.

Self-employed taxpayers report their casualty and theft losses that involve business property in Section B of Form 4684, rather than in Section A, which is reserved for reporting casualty and theft losses of personal property. If a taxpayer's net gain or loss shown in Section B of Form 4684 is attributable to business property, that figure must be entered in the "Net gain or loss from Form 4684" section of Form 4797, which incorporates the figure with other items reported on the form. That total is then reported on line 14 on the front of Form 1040. If there would be no other entries on Form 4797, the figure may be entered directly on the "Other gains (or losses)" line of Form 1040 with the notation "Form 4684" next to that line. By being allowed to take their casualty and theft losses on the front of Form 1040 in the section dedicated to the calculation of total income, self-employed taxpayers not only avoid having to reduce such losses pertaining to business property by the adjustments that apply to personal property. They are also assured of getting the full tax benefit from the losses regardless of whether their itemized deductions exceed their standard deductions.

The casualty or theft loss shown in Section B of Form 4684 that is attributable to income-producing property is to be entered in the "Other Miscellaneous Deductions" section of Schedule A of Form 1040 for individuals. This is not subject to reduction by an amount equal to 2% of the taxpayer's adjusted gross income, as are most miscellaneous deductions. This reporting requirement allows owners of income-producing property who have suffered a casualty or theft loss to avoid having to reduce the amount of such losses by the adjustments that must be applied to casualty or theft losses of personal property. However, unless the total of such a party's itemized deductions, including the casualty and theft losses, exceeds his or her standard deduction, no tax benefit will be realized from the deduction for the loss.

Postponing Recognition of Taxable Gain from Casualty Losses

Since taxpayers generally insure their property for its fair market value, it is common for self-employed taxpayers who have suffered a casualty or theft loss on business property that they have been depreciating to realize a gain on the property from their insurance settlements. Their depreciation allowance will have reduced the basis in those assets to a level that is often well below the fair market value of those assets. However, the gain is strictly an accounting measure in most cases since the replacement cost of assets that were totally destroyed is often greater than the insurance proceeds on the lost assets. The miseries of the taxpayer who has suffered a total loss and whose insurance proceeds will not cover the cost of replacement of the destroyed or stolen assets are further compounded by the fact that capital gains tax will be due on the insurance proceeds to the extent that they exceed the party's post-depreciation basis in the property.

In an effort to alleviate part of the problem faced by taxpayers who find themselves in such a situation, provisions in the tax law allow taxpayers to postpone recognition of such gains if they reinvest an amount equal to the full amount of the insurance proceeds that they receive for their property that sustained a casualty or theft loss in similar property. However, their basis in the new property must be reduced by the amount of the deferred gain. It is not necessary that taxpayers invest the actual insurance proceeds in replacement property in order to qualify for postponement of recognition of gains from casualty or theft losses, as long as they invest an amount equal to the insurance proceeds or other compensation that they receive in settlement of their loss in replacement property.

EXAMPLE: Joe, a self-employed investment counselor, had a computer system that he had acquired for $10,000 for use in his business and he insured it for its purchase price. After taking depreciation in the amount of $8,000 on his computer equipment, it was destroyed by a lightning strike and the insurance company paid him $10,000 for the computer. The new computer system that Joe had to buy in order to run the latest software cost him $12,000. Since the computer manufacturer was offering an interest-free loan on their products, Joe bought the computer on credit and used the $10,000 insurance check to go on a vacation.

Even though he obtained credit to make the purchase rather than using the actual insurance payment, since Joe invested at least as much as he received in insurance proceeds in replacement property, he will be permitted to postpone recognition of his gain in the amount of $8,000 ($10,000 insurance proceeds less $2,000 basis after depreciation). However, his basis in the new computer will be a combination of his basis in the computer that was destroyed ($2,000), plus the amount by which the cost of the replacement asset exceeds the insurance settlement ($12,000 − $10,000 = $2,000), for a total of $4,000.

Miscellaneous Deductions

The final two categories of itemized deductions on Schedule A of Form 1040 are less specific than the other categories of itemized deductions. The category shown on Schedule A as "Job Expenses and Most Other Miscellaneous Deductions" provides for the deduction of unreimbursed business expenses incurred by employees in the performance of their jobs. Included among those deductible expenses are travel expenses, job-related educational expenses, and the cost of their samples and supplies. Self-employed individuals should never take a deduction for expenses that are related to their self-employment activities as a job expense on Schedule A. Self-employed taxpayers are allowed to take their job-related expenses as business deductions on Schedule C, which will be more beneficial than an itemized deduction since business deductions reduce the amount of a party's income that is subject to self-employment taxes. Furthermore, all of the deductions taken under the "Job Expenses and Most Other Miscellaneous Deductions" category must be reduced by an amount equal to 2% of the adjusted gross income of the taxpayer taking the deduction, which will significantly reduce, if not altogether eliminate, such deductions. Therefore, a self-employed party should not only be sure to take the deduction for job-related expenses as a business deduction. He or she should also consider the possibility that other miscellaneous deductions that are subject to the 2% of adjusted gross income reduction, such as tax preparation fees and the cost of a safety deposit box, might also qualify as business expense deductions, and take them as such, rather than taking them on Schedule A.

The final category of itemized deductions on Schedule A is "Other Miscellaneous Deductions." The miscellaneous deductions in this category differ from those in the category that includes job expenses in that their total is not reduced by an amount equal to 2% of the taxpayer's adjusted gross income. There are very few items that qualify for this type of deduction. They are specifically listed in the Schedule A instructions. Among the more common ones are:

◆ casualty and theft losses from income-producing property (as previously discussed);

◆ gambling losses up to the amount of the taxpayer's reported gambling winnings;

◆ expenses incurred by a disabled person that are related to work and necessitated by the party's disability; and,

◆ federal estate tax paid on inheritances consisting of wages that the deceased had earned but not received and that were included in the heirs' earnings for income tax purposes (known as *income in respect of a decedent*).

The fact that taxpayers are not required to reduce their other miscellaneous deductions by an amount equal to 2% of their adjusted gross income may make those deductions more desirable than the miscellaneous deductions that are subject to the reduction. However, since these deductions do not reduce the amount of a party's income that is subject to self-employment taxes, nor will the deductions even reduce the amount of a party's income that is subject to federal income tax unless the taxpayer's total itemized deductions exceed his or her standard deduction, business deductions are clearly preferable over these miscellaneous deductions. Some deductions, such as gambling losses and federal estate taxes paid on income with respect to a decedent, will not qualify for any type of a deduction other than a miscellaneous deduction on Schedule A. At the same time, others, such as work-related expenses incurred by a disabled self-employed taxpayer, should qualify as a business deduction and should be taken as such on Schedule C.

The General Limitations on Itemized Deductions

After reducing qualified medical and dental expenses by 7.5% of their adjusted gross incomes, reducing casualty losses by 10% of their adjusted gross incomes, and reducing job-related and most other miscellaneous deductions by 2% of their adjusted gross incomes, only those taxpayers whose total itemized deductions exceed their allowable standard deductions will benefit from itemizing deductions. Even those taxpayers will benefit only to the extent that their itemized deductions exceed their allowable standard deductions. But having itemized deductions that exceed the applicable standard deduction will not guarantee that a taxpayer will benefit from itemizing deductions. This is due to the provisions of I.R.C. Sec. 68 that requires taxpayers with relatively high incomes to reduce their itemized deductions. The amount of the itemized deductions that is lost increases with increases in income. There is a worksheet in the instructions to Schedule A for calculating the reductions in itemized deductions that are required of those with high incomes.

Schedule A Itemized Deductions

- ◆ Medical and dental expenses not covered by insurance plus medical insurance premiums, to the extent they exceed 7.5% of the taxpayer's adjusted gross income

- ◆ Taxes paid to state and local governments other than sales tax, gasoline tax, or license fees

- ◆ Real estate taxes based on assessed value

- ◆ Taxes on personal property based on assessed value

- ◆ Home mortgage interest paid on a first or second mortgage or home equity credit line on a primary or second home but subject to maximum mortgage limits

- ◆ Investment interest to the extent that it does not exceed investment income

- ◆ Gifts to qualified charities in monetary or nonmonetary form, but not in the form of donation of one's own services. Donations are subject to limits as a percentage of the donor's income and must be supported by the maintenance of certain records

- ◆ Casualty and theft losses to the extent that each loss exceeds $100 and the total of the taxpayer's qualified losses exceed 10% of the party's adjusted gross income for the year

- ◆ Job expenses and most other miscellaneous deductions—consisting primarily of unreimbursed expenses incurred by employees or in connection with their jobs but also including cost of tax preparation, union dues, uniforms, job-related education expenses, investment expenses and the cost of a safe deposit box—the total is deductible only to the extent that it exceeds an amount equal to 2% of the taxpayer's adjusted gross income

- ◆ Other miscellaneous deductions include gambling losses to the extent of winnings, casualty and theft losses of income-producing property, federal estate tax on income with respect to a decedent and expenses incurred by disabled parties to enable them to work (There is no reduction based on the taxpayer's adjusted gross income.)

Chapter 9
Exemptions

In calculating taxable income, a taxpayer is allowed to reduce adjusted gross income by not only the larger of the standard deduction or allowable itemized deductions, but also by any available allowance for exemptions as well. The amount of the exemption deduction, which is stated on the line that is designated on Form 1040 for the total exemption deduction to be taken, is adjusted annually, as provided for in I.R.C. Sec. 151(d)(4). The exemptions that are available are *personal exemptions* and *exemptions for dependents*. Whether or not a party is self-employed will not affect the taxpayer's entitlement to a deduction for exemptions or its amount.

PERSONAL EXEMPTIONS

Each taxpayer is allowed to take a personal exemption for him- or herself, unless he or she can be claimed as a dependent by some other taxpayer. Married taxpayers who file joint returns are allowed to take a personal exemption for each spouse. Even if a married taxpayer files a separate return, the party can still take a personal exemption for his or her spouse, as long as the spouse had no gross income and could not be claimed as a dependent by some other taxpayer, regardless of whether that party actually claimed the spouse. The fact that a party's spouse is a nonresident alien will not affect the right to take a personal exemption for the spouse, as long as the taxpayer is otherwise qualified to do so. If a spouse dies, the surviving spouse may still claim a personal exemption for the deceased spouse for the year of the spouse's death, provided that the surviving spouse did not remarry during that year. No personal exemption may be taken for a spouse if the couple is divorced or legally separated as of the last day of the year, even if the party seeking the exemption had fully supported the former spouse for the entire year in question.

EXEMPTIONS FOR DEPENDENTS

In addition to the personal exemption available to taxpayers and their spouses, exemptions may also be taken for dependents. However, they must meet the five dependency tests to qualify the taxpayer to take an exemption for them.

The Relationship Test

In order for a taxpayer to be entitled to take an exemption for someone as his or her dependent, that party must have either lived with him or her as a member of the party's household for the entire tax year or must be related to the taxpayer to the degree specified in I.R.C. Sec. 152. Those who are considered to be relatives of a taxpayer under the provisions of Sec. 152 are:

- children;
- stepchildren;
- grandchildren;
- great-grandchildren;
- brothers and sisters;
- half brothers and half sisters;
- stepbrothers and stepsisters;
- parents;
- stepparents;
- grandparents;
- great-grandparents;
- aunts and uncles;
- nieces and nephews;

- parents and siblings of a spouse; and,
- sons-in-law and daughters-in-law.

Any of the relationships created by marriage are not terminated by divorce or by the death of the taxpayer's blood relative.

The Citizenship or Residency Test

A person for whom a taxpayer wishes to take an exemption as a dependent must be a citizen or resident of the U.S. or a resident of Canada or Mexico. As long as the party meets this requirement for some part of the calendar year in which the taxpayer's tax year begins, the requirement of the test is considered met for the year.

The Joint Return Test

Generally, if a taxpayer is otherwise entitled to take an exemption for a dependent, but the dependent is married and files a joint return, the taxpayer will not be allowed to take the exemption. The lone exception to this provision is the situation in which a party's married dependent files a joint return with his or her spouse in order to claim a refund of taxes withheld from earnings, but the couple that filed the joint return had such low earnings that no taxes would have been due for either of them if they had filed separate returns.

EXAMPLE: Bernard, while on a job in Hong Kong, contracted SARS in late May and was placed in quarantine. His wife, Cassandra, a student at a local college, moved out of the couple's apartment and moved in with her parents while Bernard recovered. Bernard's recovery took several months, during which time Cassandra's parents fully supported her. Bernard and Cassandra filed a joint return reporting the $34,000 income that he earned before he got sick. Even though Cassandra's parents provided her with most of her support for the year, they will not be able to take an exemption for her since she filed a joint return with her husband who earned sufficient income to have a tax liability.

EXAMPLE: George and Laura, a married couple, were students during the year. They lived with George's parents who supported them, since the only income that George and Laura had was about $2,000 each from summer jobs. A small amount of income tax was held out of each of their salaries, so they filed a joint return to claim a refund for the amounts withheld. If all of the other tests are met, George's parents will be permitted to claim both George and Laura as dependents, despite the fact that they filed a joint return of their own. Both George and Laura had such low incomes that neither of them would have had a tax liability had they filed separate returns.

The Gross Income Test

In order to be entitled to take an exemption for a dependent, the dependent person cannot have gross income in excess of the amount of the exemption deduction. However, a parent is allowed to claim an exemption for his or her dependent child, regardless of how much the child earns, as long as that child is either under the age of 19 at the end of the year or under the age of 24 at year's end and a full-time student for at least five calendar months during the calendar year. Even though parents may be allowed to take an exemption for dependent children with incomes of their own, the result will be that the children will not be allowed to take an exemption for themselves on their own returns.

EXAMPLE: Rekah is a full-time student who lives with her parents and works at a department store. She earns about $12,000 annually. She is 20 years-of-age. The fact that Rekah earns $12,000 will not prevent her parents from claiming her as a dependent, but if they do, Rekah will have to file her own tax return without claiming herself as a dependent.

The Support Test

To qualify to take an exemption deduction for a dependent, a taxpayer who is otherwise qualified to take the exemption must usually provide more than half of the support for that person. However, there are two exceptions to this rule.

Multiple Support Agreements

If two or more otherwise qualified people together provide over 50% of a party's support, but no individual person provides the party with over half of his or her total support, any otherwise qualified person who provides over 10% of the party's support may claim the exemption for the dependent. Every other qualified party who provided over 10% of the dependent's support must sign a Form 2120, *Multiple Support Declaration*, stating that they will not claim the exemption for the dependent. An executed Form 2120 from each otherwise qualified party who is not taking an exemption for someone that they provided over 10% of their support to must be included with the tax return of the taxpayer who does claim an exemption for the dependent. Taxpayers should keep a copy of each Form 2120 for their own records as well.

EXAMPLE: Yoko's four sons, Paul, John, Ringo, and George, fully support her. Paul provides 45% of her support, John and George each provide her with 20% of her support, and Ringo provides 15% of her support. They decided to let Ringo claim Yoko as his dependent and take an exemption deduction for her. As long as Paul, John, and George each sign a Form 2120 each year consenting to Ringo claiming Yoko, he will be entitled to take an exemption deduction for her if he meets the other requirements for doing so since he provided over 10% of Yoko's support.

EXAMPLE: Mattie worked for two attorneys for many years. They decided to retire and close their practice. Mattie was not yet old enough to draw retirement benefits, so the attorneys agreed to provide Mattie with 70% of her support for the next three years and her son provided her with the remaining 30%.

Since the attorneys do not qualify to take an exemption for Mattie due to failing the relationship test, neither of them will be eligible to take an exemption for Mattie, even if her son and the attorney that did not take the exemption had executed a Form 2120. Mattie's son will not be eligible to take an exemption for his mother, even if the attorneys were to execute a Form 2120, since over half of her support is provided by individuals who do not qualify to take an exemption for supporting her. No one will be allowed to claim an exemption for supporting Mattie.

Children of Divorced or Separated Parents

Normally, if a child's parents are divorced, legally separated under a written separation agreement, or have lived apart for the last six months of the calendar year, the parent who had custody of the child for the larger part of the year will be considered to have provided over half of the child's support. That parent will be entitled to claim the child as a dependent for tax purposes. This rule will apply if the noncustodial parent can show that he or she actually provided over half of the child's support for the year.

If there is a divorce decree or a decree of separate maintenance that states which party will be entitled to claim an exemption for the couple's dependent children, that decree will govern. In the absence of such a decree, if there is a written separation agreement designating which parent will receive the exemption for each child, it will govern. A parent who has the right to claim a child as a dependent and take an exemption deduction, either by court decree or agreement or based on custody, may relinquish that right to the other parent for any number of years by executing Form 8332. The form must be attached to the tax return of the party who obtains the right to take the exemption.

THE PHASE-OUT OF EXEMPTIONS

Taxpayers whose adjusted gross income exceeds an amount—which Sec. 151(d)(3)(B) refers to as the *threshold amount*—must reduce their exemptions deductions by 2% for every segment of $2,500 that their income exceeds the threshold amount, up to a maximum of one hundred percent. The threshold amounts are adjusted for inflation each year and are reflected in a worksheet, provided in the Form 1040 instructions, for calculating the exemption deduction phase-out. The exemption deduction phase-out has been partially repealed for years 2006 through 2009. For years 2006 and 2007 the phase-out will be reduced by one-third and for years 2008 and 2009 there will be a two-thirds reduction in the phase-out. In 2010 the partial repeal will cease and the phase-out will be fully reinstated to the pre-2006 level unless Congress extends the repeal either entirely or partially.

Chapter 10
Federal Income Taxes and Common Tax Credits

The method for calculating federal income tax liabilities is not appreciably different whether the taxpayers earned their incomes from self-employment activities or as some form of investment or retirement fund. In fact, it is common for taxpayers to have income from a variety of sources during the course of a taxable year. The only real distinction between the federal income tax calculations of self-employment taxpayers is that at least some, if not all, of a self-employment individual's earnings will be calculated on a Schedule C and then entered on Form 1040. On the other hand, those who work primarily as employees of others will report the majority of their earnings as salaries and wages that were transferred to Form 1040 from W-2 forms that were provided by their employers.

REGULAR FEDERAL INCOME TAXES

Once the various sources of income and loss are transferred from the appropriate forms and schedules onto Form 1040 and all of the allowable deductions and exemptions are subtracted, the remaining balance—referred to as *taxable income*—is then subjected to the applicable rate of taxation. This will determine the taxpayer's federal income tax liability. The U.S. federal income tax is considered to be a *progressive tax* because the rates of taxation increase as taxpayer's taxable incomes increase. This progressiveness is accomplished in the U.S. by establishing income segments, known as *tax brackets*, and applying higher tax rates to higher segments of a taxpayer's income. As a taxpayer's income rises and enters higher tax brackets, the higher rates will apply only to the income in the higher bracket. Therefore, contrary to popular belief, an increase in income cannot cause a taxpayer to incur an increase in tax liability that exceeds his or her increase in income.

Tax brackets vary on the basis of filing status. The bracket that is subject to the lowest tax rate, which is 10%, is the first $7,000 of taxable income for taxpayers filing single for 2004, the first $14,000 for married taxpayers filing joint returns, and $10,000 for those filing as head of household.

In an effort to stimulate the economy, the *Jobs and Growth Tax Relief Reconciliation Act of 2003* temporarily increased the 10% bracket in 2003 and 2004 by $1,000 for single taxpayers and $2,000 for those who are married and filing jointly. The brackets will shrink back to $6,000 and $12,000, respectively, for 2005 through 2007, and then will be restored to their 2003-2004 levels in 2008. There are provisions for some adjustments in the bracket size to reflect inflation. There are also brackets of 15%, 25%, 28%, 33%, and 35%.

The instructions to Form 1040 contain a tax table that shows the tax liability for each filing status at various levels of annual ordinary income up to $100,000. Those who make in excess of $100,000 in ordinary income for the year must use the Tax Rate Schedules provided in the Form 1040 instructions to calculate their tax liability. Taxpayers who have some income in the form of long-term capital gains or dividends must calculate their tax liability on Schedule D of Form 1040 in order to prevent those gains from being taxed in excess of the maximum 15% tax rate that applies to most long-term capital gains and dividends.

ALTERNATIVE MINIMUM TAX

Some taxpayers with relatively substantial incomes have greatly reduced federal income tax liabilities, or even no federal income tax liability at all, due to collecting income from sources that are given special tax treatment and using tax deductions and credits. Congress established the *alternative minimum tax* (AMT) to prevent these taxpayers from avoiding the payment of at least some minimum amount of federal income tax.

The AMT, which is calculated on Form 6251, accomplishes its purpose by requiring taxpayers to determine their alternative minimum taxable incomes, subtracting the AMT exemption, and then applying the AMT rate to the remainder. If a taxpayer's AMT on Form 6251 exceeds his or her regular federal income tax liability, he or she must report the excess as AMT on Form 1040.

Calculating Alternative Minimum Taxable Income

The calculation of *alternative minimum taxable income* (AMTI) is accomplished on Part I of Form 6251 and begins with the taxpayer's adjusted gross income. If a taxpayer itemized deductions, the party is allowed to subtract any allowance for itemized deductions, as shown on Schedule A, from adjusted gross income, but must add back part, or all, of some of the deductions. Among the deductions that must be added back are:

- any deductions taken for property taxes or any other state and local taxes;
- all miscellaneous deductions, including those for employee business expenses;
- any deduction taken for interest on a home mortgage that was not taken out to buy, build, or improve a primary residence or second home; and,
- part of the deduction taken for medical and dental expenses.

A party who takes the standard deduction in calculating regular federal income taxes does not get to take a standard deduction in calculating AMT. Therefore, there is no need to make any adjustment for deductions in that case, and the process of making adjustments to determine AMTI begins with adjusted gross income.

The next adjustment to be made in determining AMTI is to subtract the amount of tax refunds and credits associated with state and local taxes that were included in the taxpayer's income on Form 1040. Since no write-off is allowed for payment of state and local taxes in computing AMTI, it is appropriate in calculating AMTI, to offset refunds and credits from such taxes to the degree that they were included in the taxpayer's adjusted gross income.

Form 6251 then requires adjustments to add back all or part of certain exclusions, known as *tax preference items*, that were permitted in calculating the taxpayer's regular federal income tax liability. The deduction allowed for items such as investment interest expense, depletion, depreciation on certain assets, and research and experimental costs in calculating regular income taxes is larger than the deduction allowed for those items in determining AMTI. In situations involving those types of items, the adjustment involves merely adding back the difference in the two allowances. Other items, such as the exclusion of interest from tax-exempt private activity bonds, exclusion of part of the gain from the sale of small business stock, and intangible drilling cost preferences, have no allowance for any exclusion in calculating AMTI. They must be fully added back in making the calculation. Any deduction for net operating losses taken on Form 1040 must be fully added back, but a somewhat limited net operating loss is allowed as a separate item in calculating AMTI.

Calculating and Applying the Alternative Minimum Tax Exemption

Once a taxpayer has determined his or her AMTI, it is then reduced by the AMT exemption, which is determined by the party's filing status and AMTI. The *Jobs and Growth Tax Relief Reconciliation Act of 2003* (JGTRRA) raised the AMT exemption to $58,000 for married taxpayers filing joint returns and surviving spouses, $40,250 for unmarried taxpayers, and $29,000 for married taxpayers who file separate returns. However, these increases apply only for 2003 and 2004. After those two years, JGTRRA provides that the AMT exemption will revert to its pre-2003 levels of $45,000 for married taxpayers filing joint returns and surviving spouses, $33,750 for unmarried taxpayers, and $22,500 for married taxpayers who file separate returns. The provision that established the AMT, I.R.C. Sec. 55, does not provide for adjustments in the amount of the AMT exemptions to allow for inflation. Nevertheless, whether the applicable AMT exemption is the increased amount provided for in JGTRRA or the lower amount scheduled for reinstatement after 2004, it is actually a tentative exemption that is subject to reduction, or even elimination, based on the taxpayer's AMTI.

As long as their AMTIs do not exceed $150,000, the full AMT exemption is available to married couples who file jointly and to qualifying widows and widowers. An unmarried taxpayer may take the full exemption if the party's AMTI does not exceed $112,500 and married parties who file separately can have no more than $75,000 in AMTI and still qualify for the full exemption. There is no provision to change the limits automatically to reflect inflation, and Congress has not seen fit to alter them since the inception of the current AMT in 1994. If a party's AMTI exceeds the maximum level permitted for deduction of the full AMT exemption, the exemption must be reduced by an amount equal to 25% of the amount by which the AMTI exceeds the maximum level permitted for full deduction. Therefore, a married couple with $382,000 or more of AMTI in 2004 would lose their AMT exemption entirely, as would an unmarried taxpayer with AMTI of $273,500 or more, or a married taxpayer filing separately with AMTI of at least $192,000.

EXAMPLE: Yolanda and her husband, Ziggy, had adjusted gross income in 2004 of $190,000. They also had tax-exempt interest of $30,000 from bonds issued by their city to raise funds to lend to a company to build an amusement park. They took the standard deduction on their joint return. Assuming that they had no income from tax preference items except the interest on the tax-exempt bonds that were issued to fund the private activity of amusement park construction, the couple's AMTI would be $220,000. It would consist of their adjusted gross income of $190,000, plus their $30,000 of interest from the bonds. Since the couple's AMTI exceeds the $140,000 maximum permitted for taking the full exemption by $70,000, their exemption must be reduced by 25% of the $70,000, a reduction of $17,500, leaving them with a deductible exemption of $40,500 of their initial $58,000.

Determining the Alternative Minimum Tax

Once the AMTI is reduced by a party's allowable AMT exemption, the remainder is taxed at the rate of 26% on the first $175,000 ($87,500 for married taxpayers filing separately) and 28% on all over that amount. This calculation yields a result that is further adjusted by deducting foreign tax credits to the degree permitted, which produces a balance referred to as the party's *tentative minimum tax*. The final step in calculating AMT is to deduct the taxpayer's federal tax liability, less foreign tax credits and taxes paid on lump sum distributions from qualified plans from Form 4972, from the tentative minimum tax. The balance, if any, is the party's AMT. If a taxpayer had long-term capital gains, Part III of Form 6251 takes the capital gains rates into consideration in calculating AMT.

Steps in Determining
a Self-Employed Taxpayer's Federal Tax Liability

◆ Report all gross receipts from self-employment on Schedule C of Form 1040.

◆ Deduct the cost of goods sold and ordinary and necessary business expenses incurred in earning self-employment income on Schedule C.

◆ Add the net self-employment income to all other taxable income sources on the front of Form 1040.

◆ Total and subtract all deductions for adjusted gross income listed on lines 23 through 32A of Form 1040 to arrive at adjusted gross income.

◆ Subtract the total allowable itemized deductions or the standard deduction from adjusted gross income.

◆ Multiply the number of exemptions allowed times the exemption allowance and, after making any adjustments due to a high level of income earned by the taxpayer, subtract the total from the balance of adjusted gross income after reducing it by either the itemized deductions or standard deduction, leaving Taxable Income.

◆ Calculate the tax on the taxable income using either tax tables or tax schedules. Use Schedule D to calculate taxes if the taxpayer had long-term capital gains or qualified dividends.

◆ Add alternative minimum tax, if any is due.

◆ Subtract available credits.

◆ Add other taxes—in particular, self-employment taxes.

◆ Subtract payments already credited to leave balance due or refund due.

TAX CREDITS

Just as business deductions are favored over nonbusiness deductions, tax credits are favored over an equal amount of deduction of any kind. What makes tax credits so desirable is that, rather than reducing the amount of a taxpayer's income that is subject to taxation, as deductions do, exemptions actually offset a party's tax liability dollar-for-dollar.

EXAMPLE: Donald, a self-employed magician, and his wife, Daisey, were considering buying a new home. Since their itemized deductions already exceeded their standard deduction they would realize an additional deduction for the extra $2,000 in interest that they would pay each year on the loan that they would need for the new home. Also, Daisey was thinking of going to a local community college to take some computer courses. The $1,000 in tuition that Daisey will be required to pay will entitle her to a $1,000 education tax credit. If Donald and Daisey are in the 25% marginal tax bracket, the $2,000 interest deduction will enable them to avoid having to pay the 25% tax rate on that $2,000 and will save them $500 in taxes. However, the $1,000 education tax credit will reduce their tax liability by the full $1,000, which will cover the full cost of her tuition. Although the couple's added interest deduction of $2,000 was twice the size of their tax credit, it resulted in only half as much in tax savings.

Historically, there have been a number of business tax credits for such things as investment in equipment and other business assets that also benefitted self-employed taxpayers. Today's tax credits that are business-oriented, many of which are components of what is referred to as the *General Business Credit*, are so specialized in nature that not even many corporations qualify for them. Few, if any, self-employed individuals will benefit from them. Only a relative handful of people are likely to benefit from business credits as a result of their self-employment activities. They include self-employed individuals who are involved in qualified rehabilitation of either certified historic structures or structures placed in service before 1936—thereby qualifying for the *Rehabilitation Credit*—or those who are involved in providing housing to low-income tenants—therefore, entitled to the *Low Income Housing Credit*.

PERSONAL CREDITS

Whether or not a taxpayer's income is derived primarily from self-employment or from work as an employee will have no direct bearing on the party's eligibility to take any of the personal tax credits. However, some of the personal tax credits may be of particular interest to self-employed individuals who, by structuring their deductions, may be able to ensure that they qualify for those credits. The following personal tax credits are among those that are most likely to be of interest to self-employed taxpayers.

Nonrefundable Personal Credits

Some of the available personal tax credits can be used only to the extent that the taxpayer who is entitled to the credit has tax liability that can be offset with the credit. These are referred to as nonrefundable tax credits. Some credits may be carried forward to future years to the extent that they exceed a party's tax liability, but other credits are simply lost to the extent that they exceed a party's tax liability. Probably the most significant of these credits to self-employed taxpayers are *The Household and Dependent Care Credit* and *Hope and Lifetime Learning Credits*, the details of which follow.

The Household and Dependent Care Credit

A taxpayer who has a dependent child under the age of 13, or a spouse or other dependent of any age that is physically or mentally incapable of taking care of him- or herself, may be eligible to take a credit of up to 35% of work-related expenditures for household services or care for the qualifying party as provided for in I.R.C. Sec. 21. Such expenditures are considered to be work-related if they are incurred to permit the taxpayer to hold gainful employment. Treasury Regulation Sec. 1.44A-1(c)(1)(I) provides that such expenditures are also considered to be work-related if they are incurred to permit the taxpayer to search for gainful employment.

The maximum amount of qualifying expenditures to which the credit may be applied is $3,000 per qualifying person and the maximum number of qualifying individuals for whom the credit may be taken is two. A taxpayer whose adjusted gross income is $15,000 or less may take the full 35% credit, which could yield a maximum credit of $1,050. The credit is reduced by one percentage point for each $2,000 increment, or part thereof, that a party's adjusted gross income exceeds $15,000.

The Credit for *Household and Dependent Care Services* cannot exceed the taxpayer's earned income. In the case of married taxpayers—who must file a joint return in order to be eligible to take the credit—it cannot exceed the lesser of the taxpayer's earned income or his or her spouse's earned income, unless the spouse is a qualifying individual due to incapacity or is a full-time student. No credit is allowed for payments to the taxpayer's child who is under the age of 19 at the close of the taxable year or for payments to a dependent of the taxpayer or taxpayer's spouse, even though such parties may have provided services that would otherwise qualify for the credit. The *Household and Dependent Care Credit* cannot be used to reduce a party's tax liability below his or her tentative minimum tax, and any unused portion of the credit cannot be carried over to other years.

Many of the self-employed in the U.S. today are housewives who start a trade or business to supplement family income—but who have children and household responsibilities that must be taken care of in their absence. Because of this, the *Household and Dependent Care Credit* should prove to be important to a growing number of self-employed taxpayers. However, in order to qualify for the credit, careful tax planning may be required, since the credit cannot exceed the lesser of the income of the taxpayer or the party's spouse.

EXAMPLE: Ivy's company downsized and he lost his job. The only job that he could find pays him only $25,000, which is substantially less than he formerly earned. In an effort to help cover the lost income, his wife, Patsy, decided to become a self-employed booth operator at a local flea market. In order to have money to operate her business, Patsy and Ivy obtained a home equity loan. Patsy acquired most of the things that she sold by going to yard sales and auctions, which required her to be away from home on occasions when Ivy was not available to be with their eight-year-old daughter. As a result, Patsy sometimes had to hire someone to stay with her child and perform household services in her absence.

During the year, she spent $2,800 on such services. The interest on Patsy's home equity loan was $3,000 which she can deduct as either a business expense, since the proceeds were used for business purposes, or as an itemized deduction, since the loan was a qualified home equity line of credit. Patsy and Ivy always have itemized deductions in excess of their allowable standard deduction, so they will realize a deduction if they elect to take the interest as a personal itemized deduction. Patsy's net income for her first year of operation, without deducting the interest cost as a business expense, was only $2,900. If Patsy takes the interest expense as a personal itemized deduction, she will be entitled to take the Household and Dependent Care Credit since she would have income that exceeds the credit. But, if Patsy were to take the interest expense on her home equity loan as a business expense, she would have no income from her business and would be ineligible to take the credit.

If Patsy chooses to take the interest expense as an itemized deduction so that she can take the credit, her credit would be 28% of her $2,800 expense for household services and dependent care, a total credit of $784.00. Since the couple's combined income was $27,900 and they are required to reduce the 35% credit by one percentage point for each $2,000 increment, or part of such increment, that their combined income exceeds $15,000, they must reduce their credit by 7 percentage points from 35% to 28%. The credit would generate tax savings that would be more than twice as much as the self-employment tax that Patsy would incur by taking the interest deduction as a personal rather than a business deduction.

Hope and Lifetime Learning Credits

The *Hope Scholarship Credit* and the *Lifetime Learning Credit*, which are generally referred to together as *Education Tax Credits*, were established by I.R.C. Sec. 25A. Both credits apply to qualified tuition and related expenses, such as lab fees or activity fees, that are paid to an eligible educational institution for enrollment of the taxpayer, spouse of the taxpayer, or a person for whom the party is allowed to claim a deduction as a dependent. The costs of books, supplies, and other materials are not eligible for either credit unless payment for them must be made directly to the eligible educational institution. Payments for room and board or other personal living expenses are not eligible for the credit, even if they are made directly to the school in which the eligible party is enrolled. Eligible educational institutions are those whose students are eligible for federal student aid. No unused portion of either credit may be carried to another year.

The base amount of the *Hope Credit* was set in 2003 at 100% of the first $1,000 of qualified expenses and 50% of the next $1,000 of such expenses, for a total of $1,500. The amounts to which the credit rates will be applied are subject to adjustments for inflation after 2003. The *Hope Credit* is available only to eligible parties for the first two years of a post-secondary degree program or certificate program. The party must be enrolled at least as a half-time student and can continue to take the credit until completion of two years of the work, regardless of how many years it actually takes to complete the first two years of the curriculum. If a taxpayer is allowed a deduction for education expenses, no *Hope Credit* is allowed in connection with those expenses. An advantage of the *Hope Credit* is that it is available to a taxpayer for as many eligible parties as he or she is entitled to claim as a dependent.

The *Lifetime Learning Credit* is limited to 20% of the first $10,000 of qualified expenditures incurred on behalf of the taxpayer and dependents per year. The *Lifetime Learning Credit* is available for eligible expenditures for even a single course and is available without limitation as to the number of years.

However, if a *Hope Credit* is taken for a student, no Lifetime Learning Credit will be allowed for that student. For 2004 and beyond, the credit cannot be used to reduce tax liability below the party's tentative minimum tax.

The education tax credits are of particular importance to self-employed people because they often find it necessary to take courses in order to become qualified or certified for their self-employment activities. Unfortunately, they will not be eligible to take a business deduction for the cost of the courses, since Treasury Regulation Sec. 1.162-5 forbids such a deduction if the education prepares the taxpayer to meet minimum educational requirements in order to qualify for a job or it qualifies the party for a new trade or profession. Also, there is no provision for self-employed people that is a counterpart to the law that allows employers to pay up to $5,250 per year in tuition on behalf of each employee, and deduct it as a business expense, without the payment being considered as taxable income to the employee.

EXAMPLE: Earl went to work as a clerk in the parts department of an automobile dealership. He showed aptitude for detail and was given a job as a bookkeeper and trained to do the work. When the dealership was bought by a large corporation, Earl was dismissed and he began providing payroll services to small businesses as a self-employed independent contractor. Not content with his $30,000 annual income, he decided to become a CPA and work for a large accounting firm, so he enrolled at a local college and began a degree program in accounting.

Earl's tuition cost for the year was $1,000. Earl will not be entitled to take a business deduction for his tuition expense since the courses that he is taking will qualify him for a new profession. However, he will qualify for the Hope Credit, which will give him a tax credit for the full $1,000 that he spent for tuition for the year. Alternatively, Earl could have taken the tuition and fees deduction on the front of Form 1040 as a deduction for adjusted gross income, but his tax savings would have been far less since the deduction would have merely reduced the amount of his income subject to taxation whereas the credit offsets actual tax liability.

Both the *Hope Credit* and *Lifetime Learning Credit* are phased out at certain levels of modified adjusted gross income. In 2004, the phase-out of both credits began for a single taxpayer with a modified adjusted gross income in excess of $42,000 with a 100% phase-out at a modified adjusted gross income of $52,000. The 2004 phase-out for married taxpayers filing a joint return began at modified adjusted gross income in excess of $85,000 with complete phase-out at $105,000. These income levels for the phase-out are altered annually to reflect inflation. For those whose modified adjusted gross income falls within the phase out range of income, their credit phase out is prorated.

EXAMPLE: Bob was single and had a modified adjusted gross income of $46,000 in 2004. He incurred qualified education expenses of $4,000, which were eligible for the *Lifetime Learning Credit*. If Bob were eligible for the full credit, it would be 20% of $4,000 for a total credit of $800. However, he must reduce the credit by a percentage calculated by dividing the amount by which his modified adjusted gross income ($46,000) exceeds the maximum amount of modified adjusted gross income he can have without having to phase out any of the credit ($42,000), by the total amount involved in the phase out. Since the phase out range runs from $42,000 to $52,000, the total amount involved is $10,000, which, when divided into Bob's excess modified adjusted gross income ($4,000 in this case) yields a result of 40%. Therefore, 40% of Bob's credit will be phased out, leaving him with a $480 credit.

Other Nonrefundable Personal Tax Credits

There are a number of other nonrefundable personal tax credits available to taxpayers, but they are for relatively specialized situations and are not likely to be of any particularly greater benefit to self-employed taxpayers than those who are not self-employed. Among the more noteworthy of those tax credits include the following.

Credit for the Elderly and Permanently and Totally Disabled. The *Credit for the Elderly and Permanently and Totally Disabled* provides a $750 tax credit when a single taxpayer qualifies for the credit or a married couple files jointly and only one qualifies, and provides a tax credit of $1,125 for a married couple who file jointly and both qualify for the credit. In order to qualify for the credit, a taxpayer must either be 65 years-of-age or older before the end of the taxable year or retired on permanent or partial disability. The credit is for elderly and disabled people with relatively low levels of income since the credit is phased out starting at adjusted gross income of over $7,500 for single people, and is fully phased out at an adjusted gross income of $17,500. The credit is phased out for married couples filing jointly beginning at adjusted gross income in excess of $10,000 and is fully phased out at $25,000 of adjusted gross income.

Credit for Adoption Expenses. The *Credit for Adoption Expenses* allows a credit of up to $10,000 for qualified adoption expenses incurred in connection with the adoption of a child under 18 years-of-age, or a person of any age who is physically or mentally incapable of caring for him- or herself.

Credit for Interest on Certain Home Mortgages. The *Credit for Interest on Certain Home Mortgages* allows taxpayers who have obtained certificates issued by their states under special programs that are usually aimed at low income earners and/or first-time home buyers to take a credit for some specified percentage of the interest that they pay on their home mortgages.

Qualified Electric Vehicle Credit. The *Qualified Electric Vehicle Credit* provides for a credit of 10% of the purchase price, up to a maximum of $3,000 in 2004, for new vehicles with at least four wheels that are operated primarily on public streets and are powered primarily by an electric motor. Hybrid vehicles with both internal combustion engines and electric motors do not qualify for this credit. The credit is set to phase-out and will be reduced to $2,000 for qualifying purchases in 2005 and $1,000 for such purchases in 2006, after which the credit is no longer available, unless Congress sees fit to extend it.

Foreign Tax Credit. The *Foreign Tax Credit* allows taxpayers to take a credit for the lesser of tax on income or profits paid to a foreign government, or such tax due to the U.S. government on the same income or profits.

The Refundable Credits

Since refundable tax credits will result in a tax refund to the extent that they exceed a party's tax liability, they are the more highly prized of credits. Several of the refundable credits are actually nothing more than payments that were previously made by taxpayers in anticipation of an eventual tax liability or tax payments from funds that were withheld from earnings by employers and paid to the U.S. Treasury on behalf of their employees. However, there are some refundable personal tax credits that are of particular importance to self-employed taxpayers, and among them are the following.

Credit for Elective Deferral and IRA Contributions

One of the biggest disadvantages to being self-employed is that the worker has no employer-provided pension or other retirement fund. The burden of funding an individual plan to provide retirement income beyond Social Security will rest entirely with the individual when the party has chosen to become self-employed. Most self-employed people are aware of their need to establish some sort of retirement plan, but many—especially those with relatively low incomes—feel that they simply cannot spare the income needed to establish a retirement program. Therefore, they decide to postpone retirement savings until their incomes increase. However, self-employed individuals' optimistic expectations of dramatic increases in income more often than not go unrealized. Even those who do eventually find themselves financially able to start a retirement program will have missed making contributions to retirement funds in the earliest years that would have generated the largest rates of increase from compounding.

In an effort to entice those who earn relatively modest incomes, whether they are self-employed or work as another party's employee, Congress has provided an incentive in the form of a credit for such workers who make payments into certain retirement plans. The credit is available for elective deferrals and IRA contributions generally referred to as the *Credit for Retirement Savings Contributions*, by virtue of I.R.C. Sec. 25B. A credit of up to 50% of the first $2,000 of a qualified party's qualified retirement savings contribution is allowed. A qualified party is someone who is at least 18 years-of-age, who is not claimed as a dependent on someone else's tax return, and who was not a full-time student during five or more months during the calendar year for which the credit is sought. A contribution to a qualified retirement plan or IRA of any type provided for in the I.R.C., a simplified employee pension, a 401(k) plan, or to a plan or annuity of a tax-exempt organization, school, or government entity will be considered to be a qualified retirement savings contribution.

Since the credit for retirement contributions was designed to encourage relatively moderate income earners to make contributions to some type of retirement program beyond Social Security, the percentage of the credit is reduced from 50% to 20% for married taxpayers filing joint returns who have adjusted gross income in excess of $30,000, but not over $32,500. It is reduced to 10% if their adjusted gross income exceeds $32,500 but is not over $50,000, past which they are no longer eligible for the credit. Taxpayers who file as heads of households must reduce their credit to 20% when their adjusted gross income exceeds $22,500 but is not over $24,375 but is not in excess of the $37,500 level at which the credit is lost. For everyone else, the reductions in the percentage of the credit and loss of the credit occur at income levels that are exactly one-half of the levels for married couples filling jointly. Self-employed taxpayers with relatively small income levels may be able to avoid reductions in the credit by electing to take accelerated assets under I.R.C. Sec. 179, in order to cause their incomes to fall below the level that requires reduction of the credit.

The credit for retirement contributions does not affect a taxpayer's right to exclude such contributions from adjusted gross income. In fact, those deductions must be taken first, along with credits for household and dependent care, the elderly and disabled, education, qualified home mortgage interest, the

Child Credit, and the *Foreign Tax Credit*. These must be taken before the *Credit for Retirement Contributions* can be used to offset regular tax liability, as well as AMT. Prior to 2004, the credit was nonrefundable, however, it is refundable in 2004 and thereafter until 2006 when it is set to expire.

Credit for Estimated Tax Payments and Overpayments from Prior Years

Since self-employed individuals do not have an employer to withhold taxes from their earnings, they are expected to make quarterly estimated tax payments of a sufficient amount to equal at least 90% of their tax liability for the year. The estimated payments, which are sent in with Form 1040ES, are due April 15th, June 15th, September 15th, and January 15th. If the due date falls on a weekend or holiday, payment is due on the next business day. If the payment is sent by U.S. mail, it is considered to have been made on the date that the payment is postmarked. If a taxpayer has a refund due on his or her tax return, he or she may stipulate in the *refund* section of Form 1040 that all or part of the refund is to be applied to his or her next year's estimated tax liability.

Taxpayers who file a request for an automatic extension of the deadline for filing their income tax returns are expected to estimate and fully pay any remaining tax liability for the year. Payments that accompany such extension requests are another source of estimated tax payments.

Taxpayers are allowed to take a credit for their estimated tax payments made in each of these ways. The credit is taken by entering the amount of the payment on the appropriate line in the *payments* section of Form 1040. Since estimated tax payments and refunds from prior years that are applied to estimated payments are actual payments that are made by taxpayers, they are fully refundable in the event that a party over-estimates his or her tax liability.

Earned Income Credit

It may seem peculiar to list what is essentially a welfare payment, designed to reward low income earners who remain in the workforce, among the credits that are of particular interest to self-employed workers. However, it is not uncommon for people who decide to become self-employed to initially suffer through one or more years of relatively poor earnings. Since self-employment income is considered to be a component of earned income, self-employed workers may qualify for the *earned income credit*, which can result in such parties getting a tax refund that exceeds the taxes that they paid in for the year. The earned income credit could easily be overlooked by self-employed taxpayers who were formerly employed in higher paying jobs that rendered them ineligible for the credit, and, therefore, were not accustomed to claiming the credit when they prepared their returns in the past.

The credit is determined by applying a specified percentage to a party's earned income up to a certain maximum amount. Once the larger of a taxpayer's earned income or adjusted gross income reaches a certain level, a phasing out of the credit begins and continues until it is eventually fully phased out at certain levels of income. Self-employed taxpayers with relatively moderate incomes may find it beneficial to take accelerated depreciation on assets, elect to take an I.R.C. Sec. 179 expense deduction for depreciable assets, or otherwise take a business deduction in place of an itemized deduction when the option is available. This will help to reduce their incomes to levels that would qualify them for the credit.

A married couple filing a joint return can have earned income of a little over $30,000 and still qualify for some earned income credit, if they have one qualifying child, and can have almost $35,000 in earned income and still qualify for some credit if they have two or more qualifying children. In general, to be qualifying child, the person must be either under the age of 19 at the end of the calendar year, a student under the age of 24 at the end of the calendar year, or permanently and totally disabled at any time during the calendar year. The child must also have resided with the party in the taxpayer's principal residence, located in the U.S., for over half of the taxable year.

Specific requirements concerning degree of kinship necessary for a person to be a qualifying child are provided in the instructions to Form 1040, as are general requirements that must be met by the party seeking the credit, such as his or her age and citizenship, in order to qualify for it. Rather than require taxpayers to calculate their earned income credits, the IRS supplies them with a worksheet for calculating their earned income and an earned income credit table that shows the credit available for various levels of earned income in $50 increments for each filing status.

Other Refundable Personal Credits

There are several other refundable personal tax credits that often benefit tax-payers regardless of whether or not they are self-employed. Also, there are some refundable personal tax credits that are available to such a limited group of taxpayers that they do not warrant inclusion in materials prepared for the typical taxpayer. Among the more noteworthy refundable personal tax credits are the following.

Child Tax Credit. The *Child Tax Credit* may be available to taxpayers for each qualifying child that they have. A qualifying child is one that is under the age of 17 at the end of the year, a citizen or resident of the U.S., and is claimed as a dependent on the tax return of the party claiming a *Child Tax Credit* for the child. Legislation was enacted to gradually increase the maximum credit per qualifying child from $500 in 2000 to $1,000 in 2010. However, the *Jobs and Growth Tax Relief Reconciliation Act of 2003* temporarily sped up the process and raised the maximum credit per child to $1,000 for 2003 and 2004. After this time, the credit amounts revert back to the scheduled gradual increases provided for in prior legislation. As a result, the credit per qualified child will be $700 in 2005 through 2008, $800 in 2009, and $1,000 thereafter. The *Child Tax Credit* is to be phased out at relatively high income levels, but keep in mind—a married couple filing a joint return can generally have an adjusted gross income of a little over $110,000 and still take the full credit. This may give self-employed taxpayers an opportunity to plan some of their business deductions to keep their incomes at levels that will not disqualify them for the credit.

Child and Dependent Care Expenses Credit. The *Child and Dependent Care Expenses Credit* is a credit in the amount of 35% of up to $3,000 spent for household services and care of a qualifying person. A child under the age of 13 or a disabled spouse or dependent is a qualifying person and the credit is available for qualifying expenditures for up to two qualifying people per taxable year. The percentage of the credit is reduced by one percentage point for every $2,000 increment by which a taxpayer's adjusted gross income exceeds $15,000 until the credit is reduced to 20% (which is at an adjusted gross income of over $43,000) at which time there are no further reductions in the credit rate.

Taxpayers cannot generally take a credit for child and dependent care expenses in excess of the income of a single party or the lesser of the earnings of the two spouses who file a joint return. Therefore, a self-employed taxpayer may want to time his or her deductions to avoid causing his or her income to dip below the level required to qualify for the credit. For purposes of the credit, a spouse who was disabled or a full-time student will be deemed to have earnings of $250 per month if credit for one qualifying person is claimed ($500 per month if credit for two qualifying people are claimed), even if actual earnings were less than that or the party had no earnings at all.

Credit for Taxes Withheld. The *Credit for Taxes Withheld* results from funds that actually belonged to a taxpayer but were withheld from him or her, by law or at the request of the taxpayer, either by an employer or other party, and sent to the U.S. Treasury. Self-employed taxpayers will not have such credits due to withholding by employers, unless they worked a job as an employee in addition to being self-employed. However, even self-employed parties who did not work any as an employee may still have credit coming from withholdings of taxes on unemployment benefits, gambling winnings, various types of retirement income, and investment income.

Most Common Tax Credits

- *Household and Dependent Care Credit* is a credit for expenditures for household services or care for a dependent child under the age of 13, or a spouse or other dependent of any age that is physically or mentally incapable of caring for himself or herself.
    - The credit starts at 35% and is reduced by one percentage point for each $2,000 increment or part thereof that a taxpayer's income exceeds $15,000.
    - Married taxpayers must file jointly to be eligible.
    - The maximum expenditure eligible for the credit is $3,000.
    - The credit cannot exceed the lesser of the earned income of the taxpayer or taxpayer's spouse if the party is married, unless the spouse is incapacitated or a full-time student.
- Education Credits:
    - The *Hope Scholarship Credit* is a credit for expenditures for tuition and related expenses for the first two years of a post-secondary degree program or certificate program.
        - ▲ Levels set in 2003 at 100% of the first $1,000 and 50% of the next $1,000, adjusted yearly for inflation.
        - ▲ Not available if other credits or deductions are taken for the same expense.
        - ▲ Eligible student must be enrolled at least half-time.
    - *Lifetime Learning Credit* applies to eligible education expenses for even one course incurred in behalf of the taxpayer or a dependent.
        - ▲ Credit is 20% of the first $10,000 of qualified expenditures.
        - ▲ No limit exists for the number of years that courses may be taken.
        - ▲ Not available if *Hope Credit* or a deduction is taken for the same expenditure.

(continued...)

- Both the *Hope Credit* and *Lifetime Learning Credit* are phased out at relatively high income levels.

♦ *Foreign Tax Credit* provides a credit for the lesser of tax payable to a foreign government or tax due to the U.S. government on income or profit subject to tax by a foreign government.

♦ Credit for elective deferrals and IRA contributions provides a credit to relatively moderate income earners for contributions to certain retirement plans.

- The credit is reduced from 50% to 20% for married couples filing jointly with adjusted gross incomes over $30,000 but not over $32,500 and is reduced to 10% when their adjusted gross incomes exceed $32,500 but are not over $50,000, past which the credit is no longer available. Heads of household must reduce the credit to 20% at adjusted gross income over $22,500 up to $24,375, to 10% at adjusted gross income over $24,375 up to $37,500 and lose the credit beyond that level. For everyone else the income ranges for loss of credit are exactly half of those for married couples filing jointly.

♦ Credit for estimated tax payments and overpayments from prior years allows credit for quarterly payments by the self-employed and refunds that were applied to future taxes.

♦ *Earned Income Credit* provides payments to the working poor who earn at least some income but not more than specified amounts at which a phase out begins.

♦ *Child Tax Credit* provides a $1,000 credit for each qualifying child under age 17.

- The credit will decline to $700 in 2005–2008, to go $800 in 2009 and back to $1,000 thereafter.
- The credit is phased out at relatively high income levels.

(continued...)

- *Child and Dependent Care Expenses Credit* allows a credit of 35% of up to $3,000 spent on care for a child under the age of 13 or disabled, or on a disabled spouse.
    - The credit is available for expenditures for no more than two qualifying parties.
    - The credit is reduced by one percentage point for each $2,000 increment or part thereof that a taxpayer's adjusted gross income exceeds $15,000, but will not be reduced below 20%.
- Credit for taxes withheld allows credit for taxes taken out of employees' wages as well as withholdings from retirement income, gambling winnings and investment income.

Chapter 11
Retirement Planning for the Self-Employed

Usually, a major sacrifice made by those who become self-employed is the loss of a retirement program. Some large corporations' pension plans are among the most attractive aspects of employment, and for many workers, are their largest components of the typical three-part approach to retirement funding—consisting of Social Security, company pensions, and personal savings. As a result, it will be necessary for most self-employed individual to establish some type of plan to offset their lack of an employer-provided pension plan. As previously discussed in Chapter 11, self-employed individual are allowed to take a deduction for adjusted gross income for contributions that they make to qualified retirement programs. As long as they meet certain qualifications, their contributions fall within specified limits, and their retirement plans are in compliance with I.R.C. requirements the deduction will be allowed. Following are the retirement plan options available to self-employed taxpayers that permit them to defer income taxes on contributions to them, as well as a brief summary of the specific requirements of each option.

INDIVIDUAL RETIREMENT ARRANGEMENTS

One of the most fundamental approaches available to those seeking to establish a retirement fund on their own is the *Individual Retirement Arrangement* (IRA). Under the provisions of the *Economic Growth and Tax Reconciliation Act of 2001*, taxpayers who are under 70½ years of age and are not covered by a retirement plan maintained by their employers are allowed to deposit the lesser of their adjusted gross income, or $3,000, in an IRA. They can deduct the deposit from their total income in arriving at taxable income for tax year 2004. The $3,000 limit is scheduled to increase to $4,000 for 2005 through 2007 and further increase to $5,000 for 2008 with annual adjustments for inflation in $500 increments in subsequent years. Taxpayers over 50 years of age are allowed an extra $500 in the limit for 2004 and 2005 and an extra $1,000 thereafter.

Taxpayers who file their returns as single, head of household, or widow/widower with adjusted gross income for 2004 of no more than $45,000 are still eligible to take a full IRA contribution deduction, even if they are active participants in an employer-sponsored retirement plan. If such parties have adjusted gross income above $45,000, it will result in reductions in the deduction allowed for IRA contributions, until it becomes zero at adjusted gross income levels of $55,000 or more. An increase in the adjusted gross income level that such a party may have before the deduction for an IRA contribution will be reduced is scheduled for 2005, at which time it will be $50,000 and will phase-out at $60,000.

A married taxpayer filing a joint return is permitted to have up to $65,000 in combined adjusted gross income and still take the deduction for a full allowable IRA contribution, despite actively participating in a retirement plan provided by an employer for the year 2004. Eligibility for the deduction is phased out between $65,000 and $75,000 of combined adjusted gross income for married taxpayers filing jointly. Increases in the level of combined adjusted gross income that married taxpayers filing a joint return may have and still take a full deduction for IRA contributions, despite being covered by a retirement plan provided by an employer, are scheduled until 2007, when it will reach $80,000.

Whether or not a taxpayer is eligible to make a deductible contribution to his or her IRA, the party's spouse may make a deductible contribution of up to $3,000 to his or her own IRA, even if the spouse had no income. As long as he or she is not covered by an employer retirement plan and the couple's combined adjusted gross income does not exceed $150,000—at which level there is a phasing out of the deduction, which becomes zero at $160,000—the contribution may be deducted. Not only does a deductible IRA contribution reduce the participant's amount of income upon which federal income taxes are imposed for the year in which the deposit is credited, but there is a further deferment of federal taxation on the earnings generated by cumulative IRA deposits.

When IRA deposits and earnings are withdrawn, they are subject to federal income taxation. However, there is no doubt that those who have chosen to take advantage of the IRA option will have a much larger total value in their accounts than they would have had they paid federal income taxes on those same funds and then invested what was left and paid annual federal income taxes on the earnings. Moreover, there is also a significant likelihood that when taxpayers withdraw funds from their IRAs, they will be retired, earning little or no income, and in a lower federal income tax bracket than they were when they made the IRA deposits or when the deposits generated earnings.

As with other tax provisions, there are drawbacks to investing in an IRA, as well. If an IRA participant withdraws funds from the account before he or she is 59½ years of age, the party must pay a 10% penalty on the withdrawal and must include the amount withdrawn as taxable income for the year in which it was received. However, no early withdrawal penalty will be imposed if the withdrawal is made to pay the cost of higher education for the participant, spouse, child, or grandchild of the participant. Penalty-free withdrawals are also allowed:

- for purchase of a qualified first-time home;
- for payment of medical bills that exceed 7.5% of the taxpayer's adjusted gross income;
- for payment of health insurance premiums during long-term unemployment; and,
- upon the death or disability of the participant.

But even when a premature withdrawal is penalty-free, the recipient still must include the funds received in his or her taxable income for the year in which they were obtained. Once a participant attains the age of 70½, funds must be withdrawn from the IRA at a rate that will exhaust it by the end of the participant's life expectancy, or such an amount will be imputed by the IRS as withdrawn by the party each year and be subject to federal income taxation.

ROTH IRA

A taxpayer of any age may choose to make deposits in a *Roth IRA*, regardless of whether he or she is covered under an employer-sponsored retirement plan, as long as the party's income does not exceed the statutory limits for eligibility. For the year 2004, married taxpayers who file a joint tax return may annually deposit the lesser of $3,000 each or their combined modified adjusted gross income for the year, even if only one of them had income. If their combined modified adjusted gross income exceeds $150,000, this will not be allowed. For purposes of determining eligibility for the Roth IRA, modified adjusted gross income is simply regular adjusted gross income exclusive of any income that was included that came from a regular IRA and was put into a Roth IRA through a qualified rollover. Therefore, except in extremely rare circumstances, taxpayers' modified adjusted gross incomes are the same as their regular adjusted gross incomes for purposes of determining their eligibility to make contributions to a Roth IRA.

Eligibility for participation in a Roth IRA is phased out between $150,000 and $160,000 of combined modified adjusted gross income for a married couple filing jointly. Limitations on eligibility to participate in a Roth IRA also begin at the $150,000 level of modified adjusted gross income for qualifying widows and widowers. However, single taxpayers and those filing as head of household will begin to lose eligibility when their modified adjusted gross incomes exceed $95,000, and will lose eligibility altogether at $110,000. Maximum amounts allowed for Roth IRA contributions are scheduled to increase to $4,000 for 2005 through 2007 and further increase to $5,000 for 2008 with annual adjustments for inflation in $500 increments in subsequent years.

Contributions to Roth IRA's are not tax deductible. However, if the participant waits at least five years from the beginning of the year in which the first deposit in the account was made (known as the five-year holding period) before withdrawing any funds from the account, and the participant is at least 59½ years of age, the party will be exempt from having to pay taxes on any of the earnings on it. Return of the principal is tax free since it is money that was previously taxed. If a participant dies before expiration of the five-year holding period, the party's heirs must hold the account for a sufficient time to complete the period in order to avoid paying taxes on the earnings it has generated.

If a Roth IRA participant withdraws funds from the account prior to completion of the five-year holding period, income tax will be due on the part of the distribution that consists of earnings. If the participant is under 59½ years of age, he or she will be subject to a 10% penalty for early withdrawal, unless the withdrawal was due to one of the reasons for which such penalties are waived for a standard IRA. There is no mandatory age for withdrawal from a Roth IRA, as there is for a standard IRA.

Taxpayers are not allowed separate eligibility for both the standard and the Roth IRA. However, they are allowed to divide their IRA eligibility between the two. Married taxpayers who file their tax returns as married filing separately face severe limitations on eligibility to make deposits in a standard IRA or a Roth IRA. A phase out of eligibility for a standard IRA begins with the first dollar of adjusted gross income, just as it does with the first dollar of modified adjusted gross income for the Roth IRA, with no eligibility remaining for either once the relevant income measure reaches $10,000.

SIMPLIFIED EMPLOYEE PENSION PLANS

Upon reaching stability and profitability in their business activities, self-employed taxpayers may find themselves in sufficiently high tax brackets to warrant concern over their income tax liabilities. The amount eligible for tax deductions for deposits in the standard IRA is relatively small and, therefore, offers little tax relief. Therefore, establishment of a *Simplified Employee Pension Plan* (SEP) may be a viable source of tax relief. Virtually all types of business entities, including self-employed sole proprietors, are eligible to establish a SEP.

To start a SEP, an SEP employer agreement must be completed. A signed copy of it must then be given to each employee, along with disclosures concerning details of the plan. A separate, individual SEP IRA for each eligible employee, into which the employer may then make contributions, must be established. Since self-employed individuals are considered to be their own employers, they qualify as employees for purposes of participation in a SEP and, in fact, they are eligible to establish such a plan even if there are no other employees than themselves. Qualified SEP contributions are excludable from the taxable income of self-employed taxpayers who make such contributions in their own behalves. They are also a deductible expense for self-employed parties who make qualified SEP contributions on behalf of those, other than themselves, who are their employees, but the contributions are not taxable income to the employees until they withdraw the money. Earnings generated by the account are not taxed until they are withdrawn, a 10% penalty is imposed on withdrawals before age 59½ (unless they were for a reason for which withdrawals may be made from the standard IRA without penalty), and it is mandatory that a program of withdrawal be implemented when the owner of the account reaches 70½ years of age.

The most striking advantage of the SEP is the potentially large amount that self-employed taxpayers may be eligible to put in their SEP IRAs each year. The maximum contribution that an employer may place in each participant's SEP IRA per year, or that a self-employed person may place in his or her own SEP IRA per year, is an amount equal to 25% of his or her compensation, subject to a specific dollar limitation. The dollar limitation is adjusted annually for changes in cost-of-living, but there is a $40,000 cap in the current legislation. The percentage calculation must be done in such a way that the contribution is not considered to be part of an employee's compensation when applying the percentage to calculate the allowable contribution. The *Economic Growth and Tax Reconciliation Act of 2001* favored taxpayers who had attained fifty years of age by the end of the year by allowing them to make an extra $3,000 in tax-deferred contributions to their SEP IRAs in 2004, an extra $4,000 in 2005, and an extra $5,000 for 2006 and subsequent years. These added amounts of eligibility, known as *catch-up* contributions, are to be adjusted for inflation in $500 increments after the year 2006. Publication 590 is available from the IRS to help employers calculate their eligible contributions. Most brokerage houses and financial institutions will gladly assist employers in establishing and administering their SEPs at no charge, in hopes of being chosen by their employees to administer their SEP IRAs.

Historically, owner/employees of small businesses who wanted to be able to put money in pension funds for themselves and defer taxes on it until retirement got around rules that required inclusion of all employees in the company's pension fund. They did this by either *leasing* their nonowner employees from another company or establishing a second company for which they worked that then subcontracted their services to their original company. Under the SEP rules, all eligible employees of the employer, including *leased* employees and those of affiliated companies, must be included in the plan. An *eligible* employee includes:

- an employee who is at least twenty-one years of age;
- who has worked for the employer at least three of the past five years;
- who is not a nonresident alien;
- who is not a member of a collective bargaining unit; and,
- who earned at least $450 during the year (for the year 2002, subject to cost-of-living adjustments in future years).

An eligible employee *must* be included in the employer's SEP. Employers are free to establish less stringent requirements for eligibility, such as eliminating the minimum age requirement, or reducing the required number of years of employment, but they cannot impose more burdensome requirements.

Contributions to each employee's SEP IRA *must* be proportionate to the party's compensation, up to the level for maximum contribution. Once contributions are made into an employee's SEP IRA, they are considered immediately vested, which entitles the party to retain the entire account upon voluntary or involuntary termination of employment. Therefore, it should be obvious that a SEP is best suited for small businesses in which the owners are also employees of the business and there are few, if any, nonowner employees. In such a case, adoption of a SEP simply results in a significant amount of money that would have otherwise been paid out to the owners as taxable distributions or wages and salaries being placed in tax deferred IRAs for them. Not only does the SEP offer the self-employed a way to reduce their income tax burden, but the tax savings become available to earn tax deferred returns, all of which help them fulfill their needs for a pension fund. Moreover, in situations that also involve employees of self-employed taxpayers, each participant is free to control how the money in his or her own SEP IRA is invested, rather than every participant having to make the same investment.

SIMPLE IRA

Employers who have several employees who are not owners of the company may not be willing to make the relatively large contributions to their employee's retirement plans required by a SEP. The *SIMPLE IRA* may be the preferable choice for them. For 2004, the *Economic Growth and Tax Reconciliation Act of 2001* permits company employees, whether they are owners or not, to put up to $9,000 of their own money into a SIMPLE IRA and defer taxation on that money. The employer may choose between depositing an amount equal to 2% of annual earnings on behalf of each qualified employee or merely matching employee contributions up to an amount equal to 3% of the employee's earnings. By choosing the 3% matching approach, the employer may end up making little, if any, contribution to nonowner SIMPLE IRAs. Employees with relatively modest incomes are not likely to be able to afford to significantly fund a SIMPLE IRA from their earnings and there will be nothing for the employer to match. Self-employed taxpayers are allowed to make contributions of their own into a SIMPLE IRA, up to the legal maximum, but are not allowed to deposit tax-deferred employer contributions into their own SIMPLE IRAs.

In 2005, the *Economic Growth and Tax Reconciliation Act of 2001* raises the deferral limit to $10,000, after which the deferral limit will be adjusted for inflation in $500 increments. For participants over 50 years of age by the end of the year, the Act raises the deferral limit by an extra $1,500 for 2004, an extra $2,000 for 2005, and an extra $2,500 for all subsequent years. In 2007 and beyond the catch up contribution limits will be adjusted for inflation in increments of $500.

Any type of business entity may establish a SIMPLE IRA retirement plan as long as it does not have over 100 qualified employees. As long as an employee has earned at least $5,000 in any two prior years and expects to earn $5,000 or more in the current year, the party is qualified to participate in the company's SIMPLE IRA. The maximum amount that a participant may defer taxation on by making deposits in a SIMPLE IRA is large enough that it will probably exceed the amount that most self-employed taxpayers and their employees will want to put aside for retirement. Another advantage of the SIMPLE IRA is that there is no minimum number of eligible parties that must participate in the plan in order for it to qualify for tax deferral. There are also no restrictions on having a plan that is participated in primarily be highly compensated parties, known as nondiscrimination rules, as there are in some other retirement plans. However, the rules concerning leased employees and employees of affiliated companies are the same as they are for a SEP. Also, any payments made to or on behalf of an employee to a SIMPLE IRA by an employer instantly vest and become the property of the employee, even if the employee quits or is fired soon after the payment is made.

OTHER RETIREMENT PLANS

There are still other retirement plan options available such as 401(k) plans, profit-sharing plans, and defined benefit plans. The rules and regulations governing the establishment and administration of such plans are relatively complex and require the services of experts. Many of the more complex retirement plans require minimum numbers of participants and are simply not available to self-employed individuals who have few, if any, employees. However, those who are highly profitable and who feel the need to establish a retirement program designed to build up assets rapidly may find such programs appealing and should seek the advice of qualified consultants to see if such plans can best meet their needs.

Tax-Deferred Retirement Options Available to the Self-Employed

- ◆ Individual Retirement Arrangements (IRA)
  - Taxpayers may defer taxation on deposits of up to $3,000 in 2004, up to $4,000 in 2005-2007, and up to $5,000 in 2008 and thereafter.
  - Taxpayers over 50 are allowed an extra $500 in 2004 and 2005 and an extra $1,000 thereafter.
  - Taxpayers who are not actively participating in an employer-sponsored retirement plan are eligible, as are those who are in such plans but with relatively low incomes.
- ◆ Roth IRA
  - Does not permit deferral of tax on deposits but excludes taxation of earnings on deposits left for five or more years.
  - Maximum deposit is $4,000 for 2005-2007 and $5,000 in 2008.
  - Eligibility is phased out completely at $160,000 adjusted gross income for married taxpayers filing joint returns and qualifying widows and widowers and at adjusted gross income of $110,000 for those filing as single or head of household.
  - No Roth IRA is available to the extent a taxpayer deposits funds in a traditional IRA.
- ◆ Simplified Employee Pension Plans (SEP)
  - Allow an employer to deposit an amount equal to up to 25% of each employee's wages into a tax deferred IRA for each employee and each employee has control of his or her own IRA.
  - Maximum dollar limit is $40,000 per year but for participants over 50 years of age, employers can put in up to $3,000 more in 2004, $4,000 more in 2005 and $5,000 more in 2006.

(continued...)

- All eligible employees must be included in an employer's plan and all must get the same percentage of earnings contributed to their plans for them.
- Self-employed individuals qualify since they are their own employers.
- Since employer contributions are large, these are best suited for businesses with few, if any, employees other than the owner.
- In figuring the contribution permitted, the contribution itself cannot be considered as part of an employee's earnings.

- ◆ SIMPLE IRA
  - Allows employees to put up to $9,000 of their own money into a tax deferred "SIMPLE IRA" in 2004 and up to $10,000 in 2005.
  - Participants over 50 years of age can put in an extra $1,500 in 2004, an extra $2,000 in 2005, and an extra $2,500 per year thereafter.
  - The employer may choose to contribute an amount equal to 2% of each employee's earnings to each employee's simple IRA or may choose to match the employee's contribution up to 3% of the employee's earnings per year, but must choose one or the other.

SECTION 3:
PAYING MONEY

Chapter 12
Tax Law Compliance by the Self-Employed

The self-employed are among those more likely to be audited than average. The reason that the self-employed are targets for audits is that they have more opportunities to conceal their income through underreporting and taking excess deductions for expenses than do those who worked for wages and salaries. Those whose self-employment activities normally generate significant amounts of cash receipts are among the more likely of the self-employed to be audited.

Another reason for the increased number of audits is that the burdens of tax reporting falls on the self-employed person's shoulders, as there is no other *employer* to handling these filing. Among the most basic duties of a self-employed taxpayer is the duty to make tax payments to the U.S. Treasury. Self-employed taxpayers who have employees working for them must see to it that not only their personal taxes are paid, but that taxes are properly withheld from the earnings of their employees and paid to the U.S. Treasury. There are a number of statutory provisions that govern the conduct of taxpayers and their employers that are aimed at insuring that taxpayers properly report their incomes and pay the federal taxes due on those incomes.

THE DUTY TO MAKE ESTIMATED TAX PAYMENTS

Sole proprietors, partners in the various forms of partnership, and members of limited liability companies that choose to be taxed as partnerships are all considered to be self-employed. Despite the fact that such parties may receive money from the company on a regular or irregular basis, such payments are not subject to withholding of payroll taxes. Rather, self-employed taxpayers are required to make estimated tax payments on a quarterly basis to cover their federal tax liability. That liability consists of income taxes, which are calculated at the same rate as those who are employed by others, and self-employment tax, which supplants the Social Security tax and Medicare tax that are borne equally by employers and employees.

Although estimated tax payments are said to be payable quarterly, they are actually due on April 15th, June 15th, September 15th, and January 15th, or the next business day when the due date falls on a weekend or holiday. Payments are to be made by mail to the IRS Service Center designated for the taxpayer's geographic area, and must be accompanied by a Form 1040ES voucher in order to ensure proper credit for the payment. The vouchers and an instruction booklet are available at IRS offices that assist the public, or they may be obtained by request over the telephone. Once a taxpayer obtains and sends in 1040ES forms for his or her first year of self-employment, the IRS will generally send the party some pre-printed vouchers and instructions at the beginning of each new year.

Self-employed taxpayers who do not make adequate, timely estimated tax payments will be subject to penalties and interest on their deficiencies. One who pays estimated tax payments will be considered to have paid an adequate amount if the combination of payroll taxes from any employment that the party may have held and estimated tax payments on self-employment earnings total 90% of the tax liability for the year. The remaining unpaid balance can be paid with the taxpayer's tax return without penalty. As long as a taxpayer's total tax payments for a year equal at least as much as the party's previous year's tax liability, penalties for underpayment will be waived, even if the total payments fall short of 90% of the total tax liability. The penalty for underpayment of estimated taxes is actually a form of interest on the delinquent estimated payments, calculated at the federal short-term rate, plus three percentage points.

THE DUTY TO WITHHOLD TAXES FROM WORKERS' EARNINGS

Those who hire employees are required, under the provisions of I.R.C. Sec. 3402, to withhold federal taxes from their workers' earnings. Income taxes, as well as Social Security taxes and Medicare taxes, must be deducted and withheld from each employee's earnings, and the employer must pay a matching amount of both Social Security taxes and Medicare taxes for each employee. Whether the employer is a self-employed person with a single employee or a large corporation with thousands of employees, I.R.C. Section 3402 imposes the same basic duty on the party to withhold taxes from workers' earnings. Those taxes must be paid, along with a matching employer's share of FICA taxes, to the U.S. Treasury.

Employers do not have to trouble themselves with deducting and withholding federal taxes from the compensation of non-employees, nor are they required to pay any Social Security taxes or Medicare taxes on their behalf. As a result, there is considerable incentive for employers to treat employees as if they were nonemployees. A common approach is for employers to label employees as *independent contractors*. However, the IRS will make its own determination as to whether a worker is an independent contractor or an employee, using the criteria set out in the Appendix, and will impose rather harsh sanctions when there has been a misclassification.

There is a special provision that exempts children under 18 years-of-age from Social Security and Medicare taxes when they work in the trade or business of a sole proprietor who is one of their parents, or a partnership consisting of both parents and no one else. This exception does not apply when the entity for which a minor works is a corporation or a limited liability company, even if it is owned entirely by one or both of the child's parents.

FULFILLING THE DUTY TO WITHHOLD TAXES

The amount of federal income tax, Social Security tax, and Medicare tax that an employer must withhold from an employee's earnings will depend on the tax rates in effect at the time, the employee's taxable earnings, the employee's marital status, and the number of withholding allowances that the employee has. The employer must require an employee to fill out Form W-4 in order to establish marital status and the number of withholding allowances of the employee. Otherwise, in the absence of a Form W-4, the employer must withhold taxes as if the employee were single and without any withholding allowances.

The IRS has developed charts that factor in the prevailing tax rates. There is a separate chart for each marital status and an individual column showing the tax liability on the worker's earnings at each level of withholding allowances, up to a total of ten. These charts are published by the IRS in Publication 15, which is a booklet known as *Circular E, Employer's Tax Guide*. It contains a considerable amount of information to help employers comply with their duties to deduct, withhold, and pay federal taxes on behalf of their employees. It is available at no charge from the IRS. The IRS also periodically conducts classes to instruct employers in how to comply with their duty to withhold and pay these taxes. These classes are conducted at IRS offices that serve the public and are offered free of charge.

Tax protestors have historically evaded taxes on their wages by filling out W-4 forms showing a large number of withholding allowances or claiming exemption from taxation. Therefore, although employers are not usually required to send their employees' W-4 forms to the IRS, they are required to do so in the instances when an employee claims ten or more withholding allowances, or claims exemption from taxation and is expected to earn at least $200 per week. In such cases, the employer must send the W-4 forms in question to the IRS no later than the quarter of the year following the quarter in which the form is received.

In order to be able to earn money from employment in the U.S., a worker must have a Social Security number. Employers are required to obtain each of their employee's Social Security number and to verify its accuracy.

Verification may be obtained by telephone by calling the Social Security Administration at 800-772-6270. If it is discovered that an employee has used a false Social Security number and the employer had not taken steps to verify it, the employer may be penalized.

PAYMENT OF WITHHOLDING TAXES

Once an employer deducts and withholds the appropriate taxes from each employee's earnings, they must be paid, along with the employer's portion of Social Security tax and Medicare tax, to the U.S. Treasury. In order to be able to make such payments, the employer must obtain an employer identification number (EIN). The specific details concerning application for and use of the EIN are available in the IRS Publication 1635.

Employers must deposit their share of Social Security and Medicare taxes, along with their employees' shares of those taxes, and the federal income tax withheld from their workers' wages, known collectively as *payroll taxes*, in an authorized financial institution or Federal Reserve Bank. The deposit must be made in an authorized depository institution in order for the payment to be considered to have been made at the time it was deposited. Most banks of significant size are authorized institutions for the deposit of such taxes. However, it would be advisable to verify that fact before opening a business account.

Authorized institutions are not required to take tax deposits in the form of checks drawn on other financial institutions, and even if they do, credit will not be given for such deposits until sufficient time has passed for such a check to go through the check clearing process. The simplest and most reliable way for an employer to handle the payment of withholding taxes is to write a check to the institution where he or she has the account, and, if there are sufficient funds in the account to cover the check, immediate credit will be given for the payment.

Most self-employed employers must deposit the payroll taxes by the 15th day of the month following the month in which they accrued. If the due date falls on a weekend or a holiday, the deposit will be due on the next business day. An employer may pay the payroll taxes quarterly if the liability for the quarter is less than $1,000. Otherwise, all employers start out on a monthly deposit schedule and will remain on it until being in business for a sufficient length of time to have operated for a full fiscal year, running from July 1 to June 30. At that time, each employer will apply the *lookback rule* to see if total deposits for payroll taxes exceeded $50,000. If they did, the employer will then have to deposit payroll taxes on a semi-weekly schedule, but will continue with monthly deposits if payroll taxes deposited from July 1 to June 30 of the prior lookback period did not exceed $50,000. When semi-weekly deposits are required, the employer must deposit payroll taxes withheld on Wednesday, Thursday, and/or Friday by the next Wednesday, and must deposit payroll taxes withheld on Saturday, Sunday, Monday, and/or Tuesday by the following Friday. If such payments by a semi-weekly depositor fall due on a bank holiday, they are then due on the next banking day.

Employers whose payroll taxes exceed $200,000 for a year must make their payment deposits electronically, but most self-employed parties with employees fall well short of the amount of payroll taxes requiring electronic deposits and make the deposits physically, in person or by mail, at an authorized institution. Such deposits must be accompanied by Federal Tax Deposit Coupons, which are sent to employers by the IRS a few weeks after issuance of an EIN. Replacement coupon books are sent automatically to replace the coupons as they are used up. The coupons are preprinted with the taxpayer's name, address, and EIN. A misapplication of a deposit is likely if a taxpayer makes a deposit using another entity's coupon.

CIVIL PENALTY FOR NONCOMPLIANCE

Employers who, due to willful neglect, fail to make their payroll tax deposits in a timely and proper manner will be subject to a penalty. Deposits that are made one to five days late will be subject to a 2% penalty. Deposits that are six to fifteen days late carry a 5% penalty. A 10% penalty will be imposed on deposits that are sixteen or more days late, on deposits made within ten days of the date that the IRS first sends notice asking for payment of past due payroll taxes, on deposits made other than to an authorized financial institution, and on deposits that were required to be made electronically but were not. If a taxpayer fails to make payment of delinquent payroll taxes within ten days after the date of the first notice from the IRS demanding their immediate payment, the penalty is 15%.

There are also provisions for a trust fund recovery penalty, which is the most severe penalty. The part of an employer's payroll taxes made up of withholdings from employees' earnings are what comprise the *trust fund* portion. The part of an employer's payroll tax liability that is comprised of the matching share of Social Security tax and Medicare tax is not included in the trust fund portion.

If a business or individual employer withholds payroll taxes from employees' earnings and willfully fails to pay them over to the U.S. Treasury as required, a penalty of 100% of the delinquent trust portion of the payroll tax may be imposed. The justification for such a severe penalty is that the trust fund portion of payroll taxes is made up of funds that were the employees', in the form of a part of their earnings. It then became the U.S. Treasury's funds, by virtue of law, subject to the employees' claims for refunds in the event of overpayment. Therefore, although the employer writes the check for the taxes or otherwise deposits the payroll taxes, the employer is deemed to be a mere custodian of those funds. Failure to properly pay them over is viewed as a breach of fiduciary duty, rather than a failure to pay one's own tax liability. In fact, an employee who has had payroll taxes deducted from earnings will be given credit by the IRS for having paid those taxes, even though the party's employer has failed to properly deposit them. The employee can actually get a refund, when one is due, on the basis of withheld, but unpaid, payroll taxes.

Despite the fact that the potential penalty is so severe, many employers find themselves in trouble for failure to properly deposit their payroll taxes. This is probably due to the fact that, although in theory an employer merely allocates funds from a pool made up of the employees' earnings, in reality there is no such pool. Employers calculate their employees' earnings, determine the appropriate amount of withholdings, and write each employee a check. The employers generally pay all of their other business expenses from the same account that they pay their employees. Once all the bills have been paid, there simply may not be enough money left to make the payroll tax deposit. Faced with the prospects of resignations from employees who are not paid, evictions by unpaid landlords, discontinuance of service by unpaid utility companies, and interruption of the raw materials, supplies, and inventory from unpaid suppliers, employers often view the consequences of failure to make payroll tax payments as being less imminent.

They believe it is preferable when there simply is not enough money to go around. Although the event may be a while in coming, the IRS has the authority to seize an employer's assets and liquidate them to satisfy a delinquent payroll tax liability and the penalty and interest on it. Rather than being limited only to the business entity as a source for recovery of delinquent payroll taxes, penalty, and interest, the IRS may seek recovery from the individual owner, officer, or employee of that entity who was responsible for collecting and paying those taxes, but knew that it was not being done.

The fact that individuals may be personally liable for a business entity's failure to pay its payroll taxes, that penalties of up to 100% of the tax may be assessed, and that interest will accumulate on the unpaid balance is bad enough. Matters are made even worse as neither businesses nor responsible individuals may discharge such liabilities by filing bankruptcy. Generally, if it has been more than three years since a tax liability has come due, a liable party may obtain a discharge in bankruptcy eliminating the tax obligation altogether. However, bankruptcy law simply excludes the right to discharge any liability arising from delinquency in the payment of the trust portion of payroll taxes. If an employer does get into financial trouble, payroll tax payments should be the last payment put off, rather than the first, since virtually all of an employer's other obligations may be discharged in bankruptcy.

If an employer is in the position of being unable to pay all of a payroll tax liability, yet can pay some of it, the party should clearly indicate on the check with which the partial payment is made that it is *for the trust portion of payroll taxes*. A cover letter to that effect should also accompany the payment. The IRS must observe the dictates of the taxpayer in applying credit for the payments. To the degree that an employer can pay the trust portion of the payroll tax obligation and confine the delinquency to the matching share of Social Security taxes and Medicare tax, the employer will incur no 100% penalty and will be able to discharge the liability in bankruptcy after three years from the time it first came due.

FILING APPROPRIATE RETURNS

In addition to making payroll tax deposits that are accompanied by Federal Tax Deposit Coupons on at least a monthly basis, employers must file quarterly returns in connection with those payments as well. Also, employers must report and pay Federal Unemployment Tax based on the total of the wages that they pay.

Employer's Quarterly Federal Tax Return

Employers who deduct and withhold taxes from employees' wages must file a Form 941, *Employers Quarterly Federal Tax Return*, which is due on the 15th day of the month following the last month of the quarter. Payments are not generally made along with Form 941; however, employers who accumulate less than $1,000 in payroll taxes for the quarter may forego monthly deposits and pay the taxes with their quarterly return. If an employer discovers a shortfall in required monthly payroll tax deposits for a quarter, that shortfall should be paid along with Form 941, even if it is $1,000 or more. No penalty will be assessed if the shortfall does not exceed the greater of $100 or 2% of the payroll tax liability for the quarter.

When filing Form 941, employers should use the preprinted forms supplied by the IRS in order to ensure proper credit. The forms should be automatically sent by the IRS. In the event they are not, taxpayers may obtain a blank form from the IRS and use it to timely file, and then request preprinted forms by telephone or at an IRS office.

Federal Unemployment Tax Returns

Both state and federal unemployment taxes are levied, but employers are given credit against their federal liability for most, if not all, of the state unemployment taxes that they pay. This usually results in a net federal rate of less than 1% for unemployment tax. Furthermore, the tax is applied to only a small specified amount of each employee's earnings, which results in small federal unemployment tax liability for most employers. Since the tax liability is generally modest, employers are required to deposit federal unemployment taxes only quarterly. Moreover, if the liability for a quarter is $100 or less, no immediate payment is required and the liability may be carried forward to the next quarter. Federal unemployment taxes are reported on Form 940, which is due on the last day of the month following the last month of the quarter. If the total federal unemployment tax liability of an employer does not exceed $100 for the entire year, that employer will have the option of paying the tax with the last Form 940 of the year.

TAX CRIMES AND THE SELF-EMPLOYED TAXPAYER

There are self-employed taxpayers who feel somewhat overwhelmed by the withholding and reporting requirements that go along with being an employer. Others resent having to pay the employer's share of payroll taxes. And still others conclude that the best way for them to attract the employees that they need at a wage level they can afford is to pay their workers in cash and neither withhold taxes nor report the earnings of their employees. Regardless of the employer's reasons for failure to observe the law, failure to deduct and withhold payroll taxes and report employees' earnings may have dire consequences. As previously discussed, civil liability for failure to withhold and properly pay over payroll taxes can result in substantial fines and personal liability for those taxes, but a noncomplying employer may face criminal liability as well.

Another potential tax law compliance pitfall for self-employed individuals is the simple fact that they have opportunities to violate tax laws that those who earn their livelihoods as employees do not have. Since taxes are generally withheld from the earnings of employees, and the amount of withholdings and earnings is reported to the IRS, most employees feel that they have no option other than filing their tax returns knowing they will owe only small deficiencies or even get a refund of their overpayments. Self-employed taxpayers, on the other hand, have control over whether or not they pay quarterly estimated tax payments. If they have either been unable to pay them or have chosen not to pay them, they may decide not to file their required tax returns, either in deliberate disregard of the law or out of fear of the consequences of being unable to pay their taxes. Still others file returns but understate their incomes or overstate their deductions in an effort to evade taxes. Both failure to file required tax returns and the filing of fraudulent returns may result in serious criminal sanctions.

Failure to Properly Pay Withholding Taxes

When an employer fails to meet the duties to collect and deposit payroll taxes, or file accurate, timely returns concerning those taxes, the IRS may elect to invoke the provisions of I.R.C. Sec. 7512. It provides that, in response to an employer's breach of duties regarding payroll taxes, the IRS may hand-deliver notice to the offending party. The notice will state that, due to failure to observe the law, the employer must establish a separate trust account, designated as a special fund in trust for the United States, and collect and pay all appropriate payroll taxes into that account within two banking days of collecting them. Once the proper notice is given, I.R.C. Sec. 7215 provides that failure to observe the requirements of Sec. 7512 is a misdemeanor punishable by a fine of up to $5,000, imprisonment of up to one year, or both, plus the costs incurred by the government for prosecution.

Willful Failure to Withhold Taxes

It may be determined that an employer has erroneously regarded employees as independent contractors, and thereby failed to properly withhold payroll taxes. If the failure to collect and pay over payroll taxes was due to a reasonable doubt as to whether a worker was an employee, a negotiated agreement with the taxpayer to begin properly withholding payroll taxes, or the use of I.R.C. Sec. 7512 (with the threat of the sanctions provided in I.R.C. Sec. 7215), are the government's likely responses. However, if a party willfully fails to collect payroll taxes, truthfully account for them, and pay them to the U.S.

Treasury, the employer will be guilty of a felony as provided in I.R.C. Sec. 7202. The consequences of such a violation are fines of up to $10,000, imprisonment of up to five years, or both, plus the costs incurred by the government for prosecution.

False Statements

There are several other federal criminal statutes that an employer may run afoul of due to failure to properly report employees' earnings, and then withhold and pay over the appropriate payroll taxes on them. The employer who surrenders to an employee's demand to be paid in cash without disclosure of those earnings to the IRS will have committed a felony under the provisions of I.R.C. Sec. 7206(1). They will have willfully and knowingly made a false statement (when the party files Form 941 understating total wage payments for the prior quarter). Such an employer will also violate Sec. 7206(2) by sending the employee a W-2 form showing an understatement of earnings—or no W-2 form at all—and the employee then files a false income tax return with the aid of the employer's understatement of the employee's earnings.

A person who presents the false information to a federal employee or agent is guilty of a felony punishable by up to five years in prison, fines of up to $10,000, or both. Written statements do not have to be signed under the penalty of perjury provision, nor do they have to be signed at all, as long as they can be otherwise attributed to the defendant. False oral statements that are material are also a violation. Therefore, the employer who has otherwise done nothing wrong, but attempts to help an employee or independent contractor by supplying the IRS or Department of Justice with false information, will then have his or her own violation to deal with. The employer who has already engaged in illegal conduct and then attempts to conceal that fact by providing investigators with false information will then be guilty of an additional offense. Silence would be preferable to making false statements.

Aiding and Abetting Evasion

Section 7206(2) of the I.R.C. prohibits anyone from aiding or assisting someone in preparation or presentment of a false tax return or tax document. The penalty for violating I.R.C. Sec. 7206 is a fine of up to $100,000 ($500,000 for a corporation), imprisonment for up to three years, or both, plus the costs incurred by the government for prosecution. Title 18 of the United States Code (USC) has provisions for substantial increases in the fines for this and several other criminal sections of the I.R.C.

As an alternative to prosecution under I.R.C. Sec. 7206(2), when an employer assists an employee in evading a tax liability, the Department of Justice may elect to prosecute the employer under 18 USC Sec. 2. This provides that anyone who *aids, abets, counsels, commands, induces or procures* the commission of an offense against the United States may be punished as if the party had committed the actual offense itself.

This is a broader statute than its I.R.C. counterpart, Sec. 7206(2), as evidenced by the fact that neither preparation nor presentment of a false document is required to sustain a case under 18 USC Sec. 2. Therefore, the employer who facilitates an employee's willful *failure* to file a tax return, a violation of I.R.C. Sec. 7203, may be prosecuted under 18 USC Sec. 2, to the same extent as if the party had aided the employee in the filing of a fraudulent return. Prosecution of the employer under Sec. 7206(2) would be doomed to failure if the employee, with the employer's assistance, had chosen to file no return at all, despite being legally required to do so. The penalty for violation of 18 USC Sec. 2 is determined by the sanctions provided in the statute that the offender aids someone else in violating.

Tax Evasion

The broadest criminal provision in the Internal Revenue Code is Sec. 7201. It provides for up to five years in prison, up to a $100,000 fine ($500,000 for corporations), or both for *any person who willfully attempts in any manner to evade or defeat any tax imposed by this title or the payment thereof.* The fines for violations of this section of the Code are subject to being increased by Title 18 of the USC. Any act that constitutes an attempt to evade federal taxation is sufficient to constitute a violation of Sec. 7201 as long as it was done willfully. Employers can be prosecuted under this provision for filing false returns pertaining to the wages they pay their employees. The employer who offers to pay workers in cash and suggests that they will then be able to escape payment of taxes on those earnings by not reporting them will probably be guilty of violating I.R.C. 7206(2) and 18 USC Sec. 2 by aiding and abetting violation of I.R.C. Sec. 7201.

Not only does I.R.C. Sec. 7201 serve as a basis for prosecution for false returns, but it also can be used to prosecute those who willfully evade payment of taxes. Employers are vulnerable to prosecution for evasion of payment of their own tax liabilities when it can be shown that they took steps to conceal money and assets from the IRS in order to avoid collection attempts. They can also be prosecuted for aiding and abetting an employee's attempt to evade payment of taxes by doing things to conceal the party's employment from the IRS.

EXAMPLE: Fred is the top salesman at the small company where he works. Late in the year, he closed a large sale entitling him to a $12,000 commission. He was concerned because the additional commission would be taxed at a higher rate than his other income and would also cause him to lose certain credits and part of his exemption deduction and standard deduction. Fred has a sister, Ethel, who lives with their retired parents and does not work. The parents do not even have enough income to benefit from claiming Ethel as a dependent. Fred tells his employer that he wants the $12,000 bonus paid to Ethel as if she had earned it rather than the bonus being paid to him. If this were done, scarcely any income tax would be due on the money and the only tax imposed would be Social Security tax and Medicare tax. If the employer agrees to Fred's request, he or she will be subject to prosecution for aiding and abetting Fred in his attempt to evade federal income tax.

Assigning Income

Some taxpayers attempt to evade taxation of their income by assigning their right to receive income to someone else. Typically, this practice involves a taxpayer who is in a relatively high marginal tax bracket causing his or her own income to be paid to someone else, who is in a relatively low tax bracket. The result would be that the income would be taxed at a lower rate than it would be had the income been properly reported by the party that earned it. Schemes such as these are illegal and likely to result in the imposition of penalties and interest, if not prosecution.

EXAMPLE: Mark, a self-employed structural engineer, did a consulting job for homeowners who were restoring an old house. When it came time to collect his fee of $5,000, Mark had the homeowners write the check to his daughter, Elle Mae, who is a college student and does not have a job. As a result of his assigning the $5,000 fee to Elle Mae, Mark plans on excluding the income from his taxable earnings and having Elle Mae report the income on her tax return. If Elle Mae had no other income, her reported earnings would be so low that she would pay no federal income tax on the earnings that were assigned to her. However, since Elle Mae did not perform work to earn the fee, the IRS would consider Mark to have constructively received the $5,000 and have then made a gift of it to his daughter.

In addition to the deliberate attempts to assign income and escape taxation, there are also instances in which taxpayers assign income without realizing that they have done so. This is particularly common in situations involving the purchase of a business by means of payments to the seller out of future earnings. Since a certain percentage of business earnings are to be paid to the former owner of the business in order to complete the purchase, it is common for those payments to be made to the former owner as if they were a salary. This form of payment is taxable to the recipient, but deductible as a salary expense by the party that paid him. However, it is inappropriate to characterize the payments in such a manner. Payments from profits by a buyer to a seller as payment for a business should be treated first as income to the new owner. The IRS will regard such payments that are made directly from a business to a former owner as having initially been constructively received by the new owner. The result will be additional income from the business to the buyer and proceeds from the sale of the business to the seller, rather than earned income for the seller. (see Chapter 3.)

EXAMPLE: Jessica agreed to sell her auto repair shop to Spike for $250,000. At the closing of the sale, Spike paid Jessica $100,000 and agreed to pay the remaining $150,000 by giving Jessica 20% of the profits each year until the balance was fully paid. At the conclusion of his first year of operation, Spike determined that he had made a profit of $85,000 and wrote a check to Jessica for $17,000, which he deducted as a labor expense and sent a form to the IRS indicating that Jessica had been paid $17,000 by his business. Spike's treatment of the $17,000 payment to Jessica is improper. Spike has essentially assigned $17,000 of his own income to Jessica.

Proper tax treatment would require Spike to report his full $85,000 profit as income and Jessica would be required to report the $17,000 as part of the proceeds from the sale of her business. Spike would not be allowed to deduct the $17,000 as an expense of operating his business, but would regard it as a part of his investment in the business (known as basis). He will subtract this from the proceeds he receives if he ever sells the business in order to determine his gain or loss from the sale.

Conspiracy to Evade Taxes

Any scheme that an employer enters into with an employee for the purpose of evading federal taxes may leave the parties subject to conviction under 18 USC Sec. 371. It makes it a felony when at least two parties *conspire to either commit any offense against the United States, or to defraud the United States, or any agency thereof in any manner or for any purpose.* All that is required for conviction is proof of an agreement and at least one overt act to put the agreed conspiracy into effect. The Department of Justice has successfully used 18 USC Sec. 371, which carries a penalty of up to five years imprisonment and substantial fines for its violation, to prosecute parties who, in perpetration of a conspiracy, have:

- filed false returns;
- shifted money from one account or corporation to another to conceal it;
- categorized payments of taxable earnings as nontaxable *loans* (knowing that they would never be repaid); or,
- made false statements to IRS agents.

SUMMARY OF AN EMPLOYER'S DUTIES REGARDING FEDERAL TAXES

With all of the statutory provisions for prosecuting tax fraud that are at the disposal of the IRS and Department of Justice, employers really have no choice but to properly deduct, withhold, and pay appropriate payroll taxes and truthfully report the wages and salaries that they pay their employees. Those who use the services of bona fide independent contractors have no duty to withhold taxes from payments made to them, but they do have a duty to report the payments made to such parties on an annual basis using a Form 1099. Failure to comply with this requirement could result in disallowance of a deduction for payments made to independent contractors, as well as a $50 penalty for each omitted form. However, if the failure to send someone a Form 1099 is part of a conspiracy to enable them to evade their federal tax liability, this would be a violation of 18 USC Sec. 371, and the parties would face the onerous penalties that go with it.

Admittedly, prosecution for tax crimes is relatively uncommon. The decision to prosecute is not made for the purpose of collecting revenue from the offenders; this is done by audits. The purpose behind prosecutions for tax crimes is to set an example to motivate others to comply with the tax laws. Therefore, since employers are the ones who collect most of the taxes that the U.S. Treasury receives, it is only logical that an errant employer is much more likely to be singled out for prosecution than an individual who fails to comply with the tax laws.

Checklist of a Self-Employed Party's Duties Regarding Federal Taxes

- ◆ Pay quarterly estimated taxes on April 15th, June 15th, September 15th, and January 15th
- ◆ Withhold and pay income taxes and FICA taxes from employee's wages, and pay employer's share of FICA
  - • Payments must be made at least monthly
  - • Payments can usually be made at the employer's bank
  - • There is no withholding duty or duty to pay FICA for independent contractors
- ◆ File a Form 941 regarding withholding taxes every quarter
- ◆ File a Form 940 reporting federal unemployment taxes due each quarter and pay the taxes if a sufficient amount is due
- ◆ Refuse to aid employees in evading their income taxes
  - • Fully report employees' incomes on W-2 forms
  - • Fully report income of independent contractors on 1099 forms
  - • Supply only accurate information to employees and I.R.S. regarding employees' employment and earnings

Glossary

A

accounts receivable. Monies owed to a party for goods or services that were provided, but were not paid for at the time they were provided.

accrual method of accounting. A system of income reporting that recognizes the right to receive it, rather than when it is actually received. Expenses are recognized when they are incurred, rather than when they are actually paid.

adjusted gross income. A taxpayer's gross income, less various deductions that are provided for by law (such as educator expenses, student loan interest, and alimony payments). The deductions are shown on the lower fourth of the front of *Form 1040* and adjusted gross income is the last figure at the bottom of *Form 1040*.

B

basis. The value assigned to property in the hands of a taxpayer, upon which depreciation and gain or loss from sale or deemed sale are calculated. (The starting point for calculating a taxpayer's basis in his or her property is usually its original cost plus capital improvements less depreciation and insurance proceeds received for losses that are not repaired or replaced.)

bonus. Compensation over and above a party's base salary or wages. (Such payments are often based on performance, but are also sometimes used by small business owners as a method for reducing profits that will be realized by their companies.)

C

capital gain. Income that a taxpayer realizes when a capital asset is sold or exchanged for more than the taxpayer's basis in the asset.

capital loss. The difference between the value that a taxpayer receives in the sale or exchange of a capital asset and the taxpayer's basis in that asset when the sale or exchange occurs at a value that is less than the taxpayer's basis in the asset.

cash method of accounting. A system of income reporting that does not recognize income until receipts from a sale are actually received. Expenses incurred in connection with such sales are not recognized until they are actually paid.

commission. Compensation paid to a party for services rendered that is generally calculated on the basis of the party's performance. This commonly occurs in the form of a percentage of either the gross sale price or profit generated from the sale of a good or service.

cost of doing business. A term used to refer to the price incurred as a consequence of carrying on a given business enterprise. (Although it usually refers to the price in money, it may also include the sacrifice of alternative choices that must be made when one enterprise is chosen over others.)

D

deduction. A tax term used to refer to an amount of money that may be subtracted from a taxpayer's gross income in arriving at the party's taxable income.

deficit. A shortage in the amount of money that is required for some purpose.

dependency exemption. The right to take a prescribed amount of money as a tax deduction for purposes of arriving at taxable income due to having provided support for a party who is considered to be the taxpayer's dependent as provided by tax law.

dependent. A party for whom a taxpayer is entitled to take a dependency exemption, generally due to having provided more than half of the person's support for the tax year. The person may be deemed to be a taxpayer's dependent by agreement between divorced parents or among multiple parties who provide support for a person.

direct expense. Costs that are readily traceable to a particular activity or business venture.

direct tax. A levy specifically imposed on a given source of revenue or income.

dividends. Distributions of property or money made by corporations out of earnings and profits to their shareholders.

E

earned income. A taxpayer's total income from wages, salaries and tips; net earnings from self-employment; or, gross income received as a *statutory employee*.

earned income credit. A type of welfare payment for those taxpayers whose earned incomes are beneath certain statutorily prescribed amounts. The purpose of the credit is to keep moderate income earners working since they must have earned income in order to qualify for the credit.

employee. One who labors under the direction and control of another in exchange for wages, salary, and/or other compensation.

excise tax. A levy imposed by a governmental entity upon the sale or use of a good or service or upon the right to engage in certain occupations or activities.

exemptions. Allowances that entitle a taxpayer to exclude some statutorily prescribed amount of income from taxation. The allowances are generally based on the number of parties that the taxpayer provides support to including the taxpayer.

F

fair market value. The amount of money at which property or services would change hands in an arms length transaction between unrelated parties.

federal income tax. A levy imposed by the federal government on earnings.

Federal Insurance Contributions Act (FICA) Tax. The combination *of Old Age Security and Disability Income* (OASDI) taxes and *Medicare* taxes that are assessed on the earnings of employees in the U.S. These must be withheld from workers' earnings by their employers and paid to the U.S. Treasury along with a matching share paid by the employer.

filing status. One of five categories of individual taxpayers (single, married filing jointly, married filing separately, head of household, and qualifying widow or widower) that determine the level of income at which a taxpayer will be required and at what rate.

financial records. Written records which pertain to a party's money matters.

flat tax. A levy by a governmental entity on income or revenue whereby a single rate of taxation is applied on the entire amount that is subject to the levy.

form W-4 (Employee's Withholding Allowance Certificate). A federal tax form that employers must require their employees to complete indicating their number of dependents and basis for other withholding allowances thereby enabling the employer to determine how much income tax to withhold from each employee's earnings.

fringe benefits. Nonmonetary compensation provided to employees in addition to wages or salary. (Among the most common fringe benefits are health insurance, life insurance, and pension plans.)

G

gasoline excise tax. A levy by a governmental unit on gasoline used as fuel. The tax is usually imposed upon a party in the distribution chain and the tax is then added to the price of the gasoline as part of the sale price paid by the consumer, rather than as a direct tax paid by the consumer.

gross income. A party's total income from all sources before any allowances for exemptions or deductions from adjusted gross income.

H

head of household filing status. A taxpayer who is single and who provides a home and over half of the support for over half of the year to his or her child or to any relative (other than a cousin). Also, a taxpayer who is married, but has lived apart from his or her spouse for the last six months of the tax year and who has provided over half of the cost of maintaining a home for him- or herself and a dependent child for whom the party is entitled to claim a deduction as an exemption.

I

income taxes. A levy imposed by a governmental entity upon what it defines as the *income*. Generally, such entities define income to include wages, salaries, profits, gains from the sale of assets, and returns from investments.

independent contractor. One who performs work for others but retains the right of control over how the work will be performed.

indirect expense. Costs that are not specifically related to a given transaction or venture, but which must be incurred to support the activity.

indirect tax. A levy by a governmental entity upon a good, service, or privilege that is imposed upon a party in the chain of distribution but which is then passed on to the consumer as a part of the price of what is sold.

inflation. A general increase in prices throughout a particular economy.

interest. A form of income that is payment by one party to another for the use of money.

interest income. Money received as compensation for the right to use ones money.

Internal Revenue Service (IRS). An agency within the U.S. Treasury Department that is charged with administration of the U.S. Internal Revenue Code.

investment income. Revenue generated as a result of ownership of assets that promise such payments as a reward for ownership. The most common types of investment income include interest and dividends.

K

key-man insurance. Life insurance and/or disability insurance taken out by an employer on employees who are of critical importance to the employer. The benefits of the policy accrue to the employer in order to provide the employer with funds to help offset the disruption caused by the death or disability of such an employee.

L

luxury tax. A levy imposed on the sale and/or purchase of goods or services that are considered frivolous. The tax may be imposed on the full sale price or merely on the part of the price that exceeds a certain exempt amount. The tax is often imposed to discourage consumption of a good or service.

M

married filing joint filing status. A category for filing a tax return that is available to married couples as long as they were married on the last day of the tax year and both elect such status. The filing status will determine whether or not the parties must file a return and their rates of taxation if they do file.

married filing separate filing status. A category for filing a tax return that is available to married couples. If either party of a married couple residing together chooses to file separately, both must. The status will determine if the parties must file a return and their rates of taxation if they do file.

Medicare tax. The portion of *Federal Insurance Contributions Act* (FICA) tax that is used to provide medical care primarily to the elderly. Unlike the Social Security part of FICA taxes, there is no limit to the amount of a party's income to which the Medicare part of FICA taxes applies.

modified adjusted gross income. A taxpayer's income remaining after certain additions are made to his or her adjusted gross income. Such adjustments will be prescribed for purposes of calculating a particular credit, deduction, or tax liability and they will be provided for in the instructions for making such calculations.

N

net operating loss (NOL). The degree to which a business operation's expenses exceed its business income for the tax year.

P

payroll taxes. Income taxes and *Federal Insurance Contributions Act* (FICA) tax withheld from the earnings of employees by their employers as well as the matching share of FICA taxes that are paid by employers.

personal exemption. A statutorily provided allowance that a taxpayer is permitted to exclude from taxation. Personal exemptions are usually available to taxpayers for the parties for whom they provide support including themselves.

personal identification number (PIN). A series of numbers, letters, or characters selected by a party that must be entered in able to access certain information or an account or in order to conduct certain business transactions.

phantom income. An amount of money that a party is deemed to have earned according to standard accounting practices, but which the party has not yet actually received.

progressive tax. A levy imposed upon income, revenue, or spending that is structured such that as the amount of money that is being taxed increases, the rate at which it is being taxed is increased at certain intervals.

property taxes. A levy imposed upon the realty or personal property that is owned, leased, or used by parties.

proportional tax. *See flat tax.*

Q

qualifying child. A party who, by virtue of his or her age, relationship, income, and dependency, enables another party to qualify for certain tax advantages such as a dependency exemption, child credit, or earned income credit.

qualifying person. A party—other than a taxpayer's child—who, due to their relationship with or dependency upon a taxpayer, enables the taxpayer to be eligible for certain tax advantages.

qualifying widow(er) filing status. A category for filing a tax return available to a surviving spouse that permits him or her to use the married filing jointly rates for the year of the deceased spouse's death, and even the next two years if the surviving spouse has provided over half support for a qualifying child.

R

refund. Money paid to a taxpayer by a taxing authority due to overpayment of the party's tax obligation.

regressive tax. A levy imposed upon the income, revenue, or spending that is structured such that as the taxpayer's taxable base increases, the rate of tax levied on that base decreases.

rents. Payments made to the owner of rights in realty or personal property for the right to use that property.

resources. Assets of virtually any kind, including, but not limited to, money as well as the ability to meet future needs.

revenue. Income received.

S

salary. Payment to an employee as compensation for his or her employment that is often calculated without regard to hours spent on the job or actual work performed during the payment period but, rather, is calculated at a fixed rate.

sales tax. A levy imposed on the sale of goods and/or services. (Such taxes are usually calculated as a fixed percentage of the amount of the sale and are generally paid directly by the buyer.)

Section 1244 stock. Stock issued by a U.S. corporation whose capital and paid-in surplus at its inception did not exceed $1 million; has not derived over 50% of its gross receipts of the past five years from passive income sources; and, whose stock is owned by either an individual or partnership to whom it was issued at its inception.

self-employment tax. A levy imposed upon those who earn income through self-employment as a replacement for the *Federal Insurance Contributions Act* (FICA) tax that is paid by employees and their employers.

single filing status. A category for filing a tax return available to those who are unmarried on the last day of the tax year.

Social Security tax. The portion of *Federal Insurance Contributions Act* (FICA) tax that is used to finance retirement benefits for the aged, disability benefits for the disabled, and survivors benefits for dependent children of deceased taxpayers. (It is also referred to as *Old Age Security and Disability Income* (OASDI) tax.)

standard deduction. An amount set by Congress that taxpayers may exclude from taxation without having to offer any proof as to the amount of expenditures to support the deduction. (The standard deduction is a simplified alternative to itemizing deductions.)

T

tax code. A compilation of laws by a governmental entity that mandate the payment of levies to that entity by those over whom it has jurisdiction.

tax credit. An allowance that can be used to offset tax liability on a dollar-for-dollar basis.

tax credits. The sum total of each tax credit that a taxpayer is allowed to take. Some tax credits are permitted to generate tax refunds (refundable credits) whereas others can be used only to the extent that they offset tax liability (nonrefundable credits). Some can be carried to other years and some cannot.

tax liability. The amount of money that a party owes as the result of the levy of some tax upon him or her.

tax shelters. Activities that are designed to produce tax deductions and credits that may be used to offset regular taxable income.

taxable interest income. The portion of money received for allowing another party to use ones money that is subject to taxation.

taxes. Mandatory levies imposed by a governmental entity upon those over which it has jurisdiction.

tax-exempt interest income. That portion of funds received for allowing another party to use ones money that is not subject to taxation.

telefile. A paperless method of filing a tax return by telephone.

tentative minimum tax. An intermediate figure arrived at in the process of calculating a taxpayer's alternative minimum tax. It consists of his or her alternative minimum tax before deducting the party's federal tax liability, less foreign tax credits and taxes paid on lump sum distributions from qualified plans.

tip income. Payment given to a party for personal services that were rendered. Typical of such payments are those made to waiters and waitresses.

W

wages. Payments made to an employee as compensation for his or her employment. (Such payments are generally made on the basis of the number of hours that the employee has spent on the job during the pay period.)

withholding. Money held out of an employee's compensation by his or her employer that are to be paid to the U.S. Treasury by the employer in order to enable the employee to meet his or her obligation to pay income taxes and the *Federal Insurance Contributions Act* (**FICA**) tax.

Appendix:
Distinguishing between Employees and Self-Employed Independent Contractors

It is not always clear-cut as to whether a worker is an employee or a self-employed independent contractor. This is a particularly important issue for workers and employers alike. An employer is required to do certain things in regards to employees. It must:

- deduct income taxes;
- deduct FICA taxes;
- pay the taxes deducted to the U.S. Treasury;
- pay the federal unemployment tax;
- file a quarterly Form 941 to report the income and FICA taxes withheld and paid;
- file a quarterly Form 940 to report the unemployment taxes paid;
- maintain worker's compensation insurance coverage (once some minimum number of employees are hired) on employees; and,
- pay a matching share of the FICA tax.

The paperwork required of an employer to withhold, pay, and report income and FICA taxes from employees' earnings, and the financial burden of having to pay unemployment taxes, workers' compensation insurance premiums, and a matching amount of FICA taxes, causes many employers to attempt to pass employees off as independent contractors. As a result, the worker, who is treated as if he or she were an independent contractor, will likely be uncovered by workers' compensation insurance and will be required to pay self-employment tax at the nominal rate of 15.3%. That is twice the 7.65% combined OASDI and Medicare rates of an employee's share of FICA taxes. Moreover, the worker will be saddled with the burden of calculating the amount of his or her estimated income tax and self-employment tax liabilities and sending estimated quarterly payments for the taxes to the U.S. Treasury.

Being misclassified as an independent contractor will often cost the worker several thousand dollars in self-employment taxes that should rightfully have been paid by the party's employer in the form of FICA taxes. An employee who is faced with this prospect should raise the issue with his or her employer in order to avoid this extra tax burden. Employees who have already worked in a situation in which they were misclassified as in independent contractor and are faced with large tax deficits due to their employer's failure to withhold taxes and pay in the employer's share of FICA taxes can file a Form SS-8 with the IRS requesting that a determination of their employment status be made. They can also go to a local IRS office and report the misclassification, and the employer's practices will be investigated. If an employer treats a worker as a nonemployee when he or she is determined to be an employee, I.R.C. Sec. 3509 provides that the employer may be held liable for the taxes that it should have withheld.

Section 7202 of the I.R.C. makes proper classification of workers as employees, when it is appropriate, even more important. It provides that if an employer is found to have willfully failed to withhold the appropriate taxes from employees' earnings, truthfully accounted for these payroll tax deductions, and properly pay them to the U.S. Treasury, the employer will be guilty of a felony. The felony is punishable by imprisonment of up to five years, fines up to $10,000, or both, plus the costs of prosecution incurred by the government. Even workers who are clearly independent contractors need to be familiar with the factors that distinguish employees from nonemployees since it is common for them to hire helpers to assist them or to further subcontract the work that they have agreed to do.

GUIDES FOR DISTINGUISHING BETWEEN INDEPENDENT CONTRACTORS AND EMPLOYEES

The analysis in determining whether or not a worker is an employee or an independent contractor may seem tedious, but it is worth the effort. From the worker's perspective, a determination that he or she is an employee will free him or her from the requirements regarding taxes that self-employed parties must meet. Also, at a minimum, when a worker who was wrongfully treated as if he or she were an independent contractor is reclassified as an employee, the worker will then be required to pay only his or her 7.65% share of FICA taxes with a matching rate of taxation being shifted to the employer.

It is also important for *bona fide* self-employed workers to have an understanding of the factors that determine whether a worker is an employee or an independent contractor. For example, a self-employed worker is likely to at least occasionally, if not regularly, have need of assistants. If so, and they want to avoid the consequence of having hired an employee, it will be imperative that they know how to structure their arrangements with workers they retain so that they, too, are self-employed independent contractors rather than employees.

In order to assist taxpayers and tax practitioners in interpreting the Internal Revenue Code or dealing with complex tax issues, the U.S. Treasury Department publishes *regulations* that supplement the Code or offer guidance in interpreting and complying with the law. Treasury Regulation Sec. 31.3401(c)-1, which describes the characteristics that the IRS looks for in determining whether or not a worker is an employee. In addition to Treasury Regulations, which offer general guidance in interpreting and applying the U.S. Tax Code, the IRS also issues Revenue Rulings in response to requests involving specific details.

Revenue Ruling (Rev. Rul.) 87-41, 1987-1 C.B. 296 addressed the specific issue of whether workers who were rendering services to firms in each of three different employment relationships were employees or independent contractors. The ruling went beyond merely making the determinations requested and set forth twenty factors for consideration in determining whether a worker is an employee or an independent contractor. For the most part, the twenty factors are a summary of the most important common law principles used in various cases to decide the issue of whether a worker was an employee or an independent contractor.

Among the twenty factors set forth in Rev. Rul. 87-41 that, if answered in the affirmative, indicate that a worker is an employee are as follows.

- ◆ The party for whom a worker is performing services has the right to instruct the worker concerning the details of how the work is performed.
- ◆ The employer provides training for the worker.
- ◆ The worker's services are integrated into the employer's operation.
- ◆ The worker must personally render the services.
- ◆ The employer hires, supervises, and pays any workers who assist the worker whose employment status is in question.
- ◆ The relationship between the worker and employer is continuing.
- ◆ The worker must work set hours.
- ◆ The worker must work full-time for the employer.
- ◆ The worker must perform the services provided on the premises for the employer.
- ◆ The work performed must be done in an order or sequence set by the party for whom the services are done.
- ◆ The worker must submit regular oral or written reports.
- ◆ The worker is paid on an hourly, weekly, or monthly basis, rather than by the job or on commission.
- ◆ The employer pays the worker's business and/or travel expenses.
- ◆ The employer provides the worker with tools and materials necessary to do the work.
- ◆ Either the worker or employee is free to terminate the relationship between them at any time.

Among the twenty factors to which an affirmative answer indicates that the worker is an independent contractor include the following.

◆ The worker has had to make a significant investment in the facilities used in performing the agreed on work.

◆ The worker can either realize a profit or suffer a loss as a result of the performance of the services as agreed.

◆ The worker performs services for multiple parties that are not related to one another.

◆ The worker's services are made available to the general public.

Rev. Rul. 87-41 cautions that the twenty factors are *designed only as guides for determining whether an individual is an employee.* The Ruling further points out that the importance of each factor depends on the particular occupation involved, as well as the facts in each situation.

FORM SS-8

Among the most useful tools in applying the twenty factors is the previously mentioned Form SS-8, which may be used not only by employees to request an IRS ruling concerning their employment status, but may also be used by employers to request such a determination in order to avoid the consequences of misclassifying workers. Form SS-8 uses a variety of questions to seek information concerning the working relationship between a worker or workers and the party for whom services are performed. The information sought by the form supplies the IRS with the data necessary to apply the twenty factors of Rev. Rul. 87-41 to the specific case for consideration.

Form SS-8 initially requires disclosure of information identifying the employer and, if the request is submitted by an employee, information identifying the worker, as well. The form asks for an explanation as to why the form is being submitted and suggests such reasons as having received a tax bill from the IRS, having erroneously received a Form 1099 or Form W-2, having been audited, or having been unable to obtain workers' compensation benefits. An employer could indicate that it is seeking an advisory opinion in order to avoid misclassifying workers.

Throughout the form, the employer is referred to as the *firm*, although the instructions that accompany Form SS-8 make it clear that the word "firm" in this situation includes individuals, all types of business organizations, and even state entities. Those filing Form SS-8 are required to provide a description of the firm's business, a description of the work done by the worker and his or her job title, and any written documentation (such as contracts, memos, invoices for services, or IRS rulings) that have a bearing on the terms and conditions of the work arrangement between the firm and the worker or workers in question.

There are questions pertaining to how a worker got the job in question and whether the worker had previously been an employee of the firm before becoming an independent contractor and, if so, how the worker's duties as an independent contractor differ from the duties performed as an employee. If a worker got the job by filling out an application or through and employment agency, this is typical for an employee, whereas, if the worker got the job by submitting a bid for it, this is more common for independent contractors. Also, an employee who is suddenly labeled as an independent contractor, but whose duties have not changed, is likely to still be considered an employee who has simply been misclassified for the benefit of the employer. The party submitting Form SS-8 is also asked specifically to explain why he or she believes that the worker is an employee or an independent contractor.

Form SS-8 also solicits various types of information from which IRS personnel can make a determination as to a worker's employment status. The information sought is divided into the following four general categories:
- behavior control;
- financial control;
- relationship of the worker and firm; and,
- service providers or salespersons.

Each of the sections contains between ten and thirteen requests for specific information, which are stated primarily in the form of questions.

Behavior control

The right of behavioral control of a worker by a firm is generally considered to be the most important determinant in ascertaining the worker's employment status. Regulation Sec. 31.3401 (c)-1 clearly states that *it is not necessary that the employer actually direct or control the manner in which the services are performed; it is sufficient if he has the right to do so.* Therefore, the employer who simply avoids exercising control over its employee's behavior, despite having the right to exercise such control, will not, thereby, transform its employees into independent contractors. The information sought by Form SS-8 for use in making the determination as to whether a firm has behavioral control over a worker is as follows.

Is there specific training or instruction that the worker is given by the firm?

Typically, employees are given training or instructions as to how to specifically perform the jobs they are assigned. Independent contractors are usually expected to already be trained and their instructions are generally focused on the outcome desired and deadline for completion, rather than how to specifically perform the work to be done.

How does the worker receive work assignments?

Usually, employees get their work assignments from a foreman or manager of the firm for which they work, but independent contractors are given their assignments by means of a contract between the firm and themselves.

Which party determines the methods used to perform the assignments?

Independent contractors are generally free to choose their own method for performing the assignments that they have agreed to do, while employees must generally use the methods dictated to them by their employers in carrying out their assignments.

Is there a party the worker must contact if problems or complaints arise, who is also responsible for resolving them?

There is generally a protocol that employees must follow in response to problems and complaints. Resolution of the problems is often the responsibility of some other employee, such as a customer relations department or manager. Independent contractors must generally deal with their problems and complaints themselves.

What types of reports are required from the worker?

Employees are often required to submit regular detailed reports on forms provided by the firm. Independent contractors generally submit few, if any, progress reports and use their own forms for what reports they submit. Form SS-8 requests that examples of the types of reports required be attached to the form and submitted along with it.

Does the firm determine the worker's schedule?

In particular, the description should include the worker's schedule and work hours. If the hours are scheduled to start and end at specific times each day, and especially if the firm schedules those times for the worker, then the worker would appear to be an employee rather than an independent contractor.

Where does the worker perform the services?

Independent contractors typically work from their own shop or office, or even from their homes, whereas employees are more likely to be required to perform services on the premises of the firm. When services are to be performed on a customer's premises, typical of a service call by a repairman, little guidance is offered in making the determination, since both employees and independent contractors have no choice as to where the services must be performed. However, if a worker must pick up his or her service truck each day at the firm's place of business and return it at the end of the day, he or she will likely be considered to have performed services from the firm's business location.

What types of meetings must the worker attend and is there a penalty for failure to attend?

A worker who is required to attend regular sales meetings, staff meetings, or routine weekly or monthly meetings of the firm is more likely to be regarded as an employee of the firm. A worker whose meetings with managers of the firm are set by special request and are generally for a specific purpose, such as reviewing the worker's progress or making changes to the work is less likely to be regarded as an employee. Also, employees who miss regularly scheduled meetings are usually subject to disciplinary action or even dismissal. Independent contractors are generally allowed input in scheduling what meetings they have with managers of the firm they perform work for and often must reschedule meetings when unexpected developments occur.

Must the worker provide service personally or can he or she use substitutes or helpers? If permitted to use substitutes or helpers, does the worker or the firm select them, hire them, and pay them?

Employees are almost never allowed to hire someone else to do their work for them, a practice known as *delegation*. An employee who performs work that requires a helper will generally be assigned such a helper by his or her firm and that helper will generally be an employee of that firm. If the work that an independent contractor has agreed to do is of the type that personal work or supervision is an important element of the agreement, such as when an artist is retained to paint someone's portrait, he or she will not usually be permitted to delegate the work to a substitute or an assistant unless the parties involved have all agreed to such a delegation.

However, in most cases, it is expected that independent contractors will hire assistants of their choosing to help them carry out their duties and will be responsible for compensating them. Also, independent contractors will almost always be personally responsible for the inadequacies in their helpers' performances, but employees are not usually responsible for their fellow employee's shortcomings.

Financial control

The next general determinant as to whether a worker is an employee or an independent contractor is the issue of which party has financial control. This focuses largely on whether the firm, in whose behalf a worker is performing services, directly pays all of the expenses incidental to the worker's activity or simply pays a lump sum to the worker from which the worker must then pay the expenses associated with his or her work. It is far more common for independent contractors to be paid an agreed-on sum from which they must pay all their expenses, rather than for the firm that they have contracted with to pay the expenses directly. However, direct payment of various expenses associated with a worker's performance is quite common in an employer/employee relationship. A situation in which a worker pays expenses and is then reimbursed for those exact payments will likely be viewed no differently than if the employer had paid the expenses directly.

The information sought by Form SS-8 for use in making the determination as to whether the worker or the firm has financial control for the work being performed is as follows.

Which party supplies the equipment, materials, and property that are used in connection with the work that is performed?

Employers typically supply most of the equipment, supplies, and materials used by their employees in performing their work or they directly reimburse their employees for expenditures that they have made for such items. Independent contractors will need to figure such costs into their bids when contracting for work, but, rather than a direct dollar-for-dollar reimbursement, the independent contractor will have to allocate some of his or her total compensation package to cover the costs of equipment, supplies, and materials. Occasionally, equipment or supplies and materials will be furnished by some other party, such as a customer for whom work is being done. This type of arrangement is used in situations involving both employees and nonemployees and may not offer much guidance in determining a worker's employment status.

Does the worker lease any equipment that he or she uses for the particular work in question and, if so, what are the terms of the lease?

It would be rare for an employee to be expected to lease the equipment that he or she uses in performing his or her job and have to pay the lease payments without being reimbursed. It is quite common for independent contractors to lease equipment that they need in order to do their work. Moreover, it is not altogether uncommon for independent contractors to be required to pay a firm for the use of equipment that it provides or to even be required to reimburse a firm for equipment that it leases for the independent contractor. Such an arrangement would clearly demonstrate that although the equipment used by the independent contractor may belong to the firm, it is not being *furnished* to the worker, since payment for its use is required. Therefore, firms negotiating with an independent contractor are well advised to insist that a separate provision be made for the specific payment for equipment obtained by the firm or that belongs to the firm but that the worker is allowed to use, rather than reducing his or her bid to allow for the use of the equipment.

Are the expenses personally incurred by the worker in the performance of his or her services for the firm?

Employees incur the cost of commuting to and from work and may have to buy work clothes, but incur few, if any, other work related expenses. Independent contractors are commonly confronted with what seems to be an unlimited array of work related expenses that include not only supplies, materials, and equipment used to complete their work, but also a host of indirect expenses such as office supplies, telephone and utility expenses, insurance premiums, and licensing fees.

To what degree are the worker's expenses reimbursed by the firm?

It is typical for employees to receive reimbursement for their work related expenses. However, some independent contractors customarily pass certain expenses on to the parties for which they work. For example, attorneys often charge for the services of court reporters, private investigators, and the cost for copying documents. Also, some independent contractors, such as home builders, routinely enter into what are referred to as *cost plus* contracts in which the contractor is reimbursed for the costs that he or she incurs for materials, labor, and incidental expenses, plus a percentage of those costs, as his or her compensation for overseeing the work.

What is the method for calculating the worker's pay?

Independent contractors are likely to be paid in a lump sum at the conclusion of their work or in periodic installments at various stages of the work. On the other hand, employees are typically paid at a set interval, such as weekly, on the basis of hours worked or as a portion of each worker's annual salary. However, analyzing the method of calculating a worker's compensation to determine employment status can prove frustrating. There are independent contractors, such as private consultants and engineers, who base their charges on an hourly rate, and there are employees who are paid based on their productivity, such as sales representatives who are paid on commission. Form SS-8 specifically asks whether workers who are paid on commission are guaranteed a minimum amount of pay and, if so, how much. Such payments will likely be viewed as a form of salary, if the amount is significant, and tend to cause the worker to be viewed as an employee, despite the fact that his or her earnings vary on the basis of his or her performance.

What is the identity of the party who pays the worker?

In order to avoid the burdens of withholding and paying taxes, in order to qualify for group insurance rates, or for various other reasons, many firms find it advantageous to have a relatively large company hire their workers and *lease* the workers from that company. In such cases, those workers will probably not be considered to be employees of the firm that they actually perform work for, but will be employees of the company that formally hired them. Even if the workers are not employed by the firm for which they actually work, the company that is their formal employer of record would still be required to withhold payroll taxes, pay those taxes—along with the employer's share of FICA taxes and unemployment taxes—to the U.S. Treasury, and maintain the appropriate workers' compensation insurance on the workers.

As a result, if workers are being paid by a company other than the one that they actually perform work for, Form SS-8 requires that the party submitting Form SS-8 supply the name, address, and employer identification number of the party that actually pays the workers. Accordingly, if it is determined that the employer has failed to meet its financial duties regarding its employees, but the workers are really employees of a firm other than the one for which they actually perform services, the IRS will then know the identity of the party it should hold responsible.

Is the worker allowed a drawing account for advances and if so, what are the restrictions?

Both independent contractors and employees may find themselves in arrangements that permit them to draw money from the firm for which they perform work. Employees draw money as advances of salary or commission, or in anticipation of reimbursable business expenses. Independent contractors draw money from the firms that they do work for as incremental payments on their contracts. In an effort to help in making the determination as to which kind of draw is involved in a given case, Form SS-8 requires disclosure of the frequency of such draws as well as any specific restrictions that must be met by a worker in order to receive such a draw.

Is the worker who is sent to do work for a customer paid directly by that customer

When workers are employees who are sent by their firms to do work for customers, those customers are generally expected to pay the firm, who then pays the worker. Independent contractors who perform work for customers that are supplied to them by another firm are likely to collect for their services themselves and may then be required to pay a fee to the firm for having secured the work for them. However, there are instances when *bona fide* independent contractors are paid from the proceeds of a firm's sale in order to enable a customer to more easily arrange credit terms for the entire purchase. Typical of this approach would be when sellers of goods, such as siding or satellite television antennas, contract to sell their products on an installed basis but then subcontract the installation to an independent contractor who is paid by the firm.

Does the firm carry workers' compensation insurance on the worker?

All states require employers to carry worker's compensation insurance on their employees if they have some minimum number of employees or they are involved in an activity that the state considers to be particularly hazardous. Independent contractors are either not covered by a firm's worker's compensation insurance or must request that the coverage be extended to them and pay for it.

What is the economic loss or financial risk (beyond loss of normal salary) that a worker can incur in connection with the work performed?

This is, unquestionably, the most revealing information available for use in determining a worker's employment status. For the most part, independent contractors bid on, or negotiate for, jobs for a set price. If the contractor is unable to complete the work for the price that was agreed on, he or she will be obligated to make up the shortfall from his or her own funds, thereby suffering a loss on the contract. By contrast, employees expect to be paid whether their employers are profitable or not. They certainly do not ever expect to be required to share in the losses that the employer suffers. At worst, an employee may be unable to collect his or her salary or wages for work performed for an insolvent employer.

The fact that an employer has a profit sharing plan will not alter the employment status of a worker who is an employee. The key issue is not how much profit a worker might get from a job, but whether he or she is faced with the possibility of suffering an out-of-pocket loss should the job prove unprofitable.

Relationship of the Worker and Firm

Part III of Form SS-8 is the section that addresses the relationship between the worker and the firm as a factor in determining the worker's employment status. The information required by the form focuses on the working relationship between the parties. Not only is the actual working arrangement between the parties considered, but attention is also given to the appearance of the relationship between them. The following specific information is required by Form SS-8 for use in evaluating the relationship between a worker and the firm for which he or she performs work.

Are there fringe benefits available to the worker?

Such benefits as paid vacations, sick leave, paid maternity leave, and pensions are often among the fringe benefits available to employees but are virtually never provided by firms to their independent contractors.

Can the relationship between the firm and the worker be terminated by either party, without cause, without resulting in liability or penalty?

Most states subscribe to the *employment at will* doctrine that entitles either an employer or an employee to terminate an employment relationship, for no reason at all, without any liability or penalty for having done so. Independent contractors usually enter into contracts that obligate both the firm and the worker for a particular period of time. Such agreements often spell out particular aspects of the agreement between the parties, including events, that could give either party the right to terminate the contract early and penalty provisions for wrongful termination. It would be very rare for either a firm or an independent contractor to have the right to terminate a contract without cause during the course of its performance, but before completion.

Does the worker perform similar services for a variety of customers?

Independent contractors typically perform services for a variety of firms, but employees usually work for only one employer. However, this can become a somewhat complicated analysis in situations in which employees are sent by their employer to various customer's sites to perform work. This may give the appearance of the workers performing services for a variety of firms when they are actually performing services for a single employer who has a variety of customers to which it renders services.

There are instances in which a *bona fide* independent contractor enters into a contract of such magnitude with a firm that he or she simply has no time to perform services for anyone else. In such instances, the key issue then often becomes a matter of whether the worker had the right to perform similar services for others, despite having decided to voluntarily forego the right. Likewise, if an employee does perform similar services for others, but must get the employer's permission before doing so (even though those services are performed on his or her own time), this lack of freedom to choose to work for others will prevent him or her from being regarded as an independent contractor.

Adding to the confusion is the fact that many workers who are clearly employees work additional jobs, often as independent contractors, a practice known as *moonlighting*, and their activity as independent contractors should have no bearing on their employment status with their primary employer. For example, if a carpenter who was employed by as an hourly employee of a construction company were to do small carpentry jobs for individuals after getting off from his or her primary job and on weekends, he or she would be a self-employed, independent contractor as far as the work done on his or her own time is concerned. He or she would still be an employee of the construction company that is his or her primary employer.

Is there is a noncompetition agreement between the worker and the firm?

Independent contractors simply could not function if they agreed to refrain from doing business with other firms. On the other hand, employees are often required to execute noncompetition agreements as a prerequisite to employment since employers, in the course of training their workers, reveal processes, production techniques, trade secrets, and customer lists to their employees.

Is the worker a member of a union?

Some employees, in an effort to increase their bargaining strength in dealing with their employers, have joined unions that represent them in negotiations concerning employment. Independent contractors negotiate their own contracts with the firm for whom they perform services, rather than bargaining on a collective basis.

However, it is common for independent contractors to belong to trade associations that may engage in lobbying efforts, sponsor advertising campaigns, or otherwise promote their collective interests.

What type of advertising is done by the worker?

Among the types of promotion efforts typical of independent contractors are business listings in telephone and business directories, newspapers, television, radio, and Web advertising, and direct solicitations through sales calls or mail. When these types of activities are carried out by a party to obtain business for him- or herself, they are an indication that the worker is an independent contractor. Employees sometimes engage in promotional efforts, as well, but they are intended to obtain business for their employers.

If working from home, is the worker provided with materials and instructions or patterns?

The fact that a worker processes or assembles products at home, rather than on the premises of a firm, is an indicator that the worker is an independent contractor. However, if a firm is still able to control the worker's activities, even though they are conducted away from the firm's business site, by supplying the materials needed to produce a product, as well as patterns or instructions, the importance of the location of the performance of the work will be overshadowed by the degree of control exercised by the firm. The relationship between the firm and the worker will likely be viewed as that of employer and employee.

What do workers do with their completed products?

Workers who assemble goods or further process goods from materials supplied to them, and must return those goods to the firm that supplied the materials, are likely to be regarded as employees, even when they work at home or otherwise away from their employer's premises. If a worker assembles goods and is also responsible for marketing them, he or she is likely to be considered to be an independent contractor.

Arrangements in which workers must deliver the goods that they process to a party other than the firm are less revealing and require further analysis. If the third party to whom finished goods are delivered is a customer or a part of the firm, such an arrangement is actually no different than one in which the goods are returned to the firm. If the third party to whom the goods are delivered is a customer or agent of the worker, it is merely a method whereby the worker is marketing the product.

How does the firm represent the worker to its customers?

If a firm chooses to represent a worker as its employee, representative, or associate, the firm must be prepared to deal with the consequences of the worker being regarded as an employee, rather than an independent contractor. Those consequences include not only tax ramifications, but also potential liability for the worker's negligence or intentional misconduct. Those problems can be avoided by identifying independent contractors as such to customers and the general public.

However, if a relationship—as determined by the various tests used by the IRS—is actually one of employer and employee, the fact that the employer represents the employee as an independent contractor will not alter the character of that relationship. In essence, improperly representing an independent contractor as an employee can result in that bona fide independent contractor being reclassified as an employee, whereas improperly classifying an employee as an independent contractor will not cause the employee to be reclassified.

How was the worker's relationship with the firm terminated?

If a worker has quit his or her job or was terminated by the firm, this is an indicator that the worker was an employee, since most employees work under an employment at will arrangement. Conversely, the relationship between independent contractors and the firms that engage them are usually concluded due to the worker having fully performed the contract as agreed. However, the results of this type of analysis are not always reliable.

Some agreements between firms and independent contractors permit either of the parties to terminate the relationship without cause by merely giving reasonable notice of the termination to the other party. Most agreements between firms and independent contractors provide for termination for specified causes. Also, rather than working under an employment at will arrangement, a significant number of workers labor under the terms of employment contracts that expire after a definite time, much as do the agreements of independent contractors. Therefore, an analysis of the issue of how a worker's relationship with a firm was terminated requires closer scrutiny than merely determining whether it was terminated by one of the parties or ended due to the expiration of an agreement.

Service Providers or Salespersons

In addition to including workers under the definition of *employees* if they would be regarded as such by common law rules used in making such determinations, I.R.C. Sec. 3121(d)(3)(A) specifically defines employees as *those who perform services for pay for another as an agent-driver or commission-driver engaged in distributing meat products, vegetable products, fruit products, bakery products, beverages (other than milk), or laundry or dry cleaning services for his principal.*

As a result of this specific provision, Part IV of Form SS-8 requires those submitting the form in regard to workers who are involved in the distribution of goods and services to list the type distributed, and in particular, to state which product or service is the principal one distributed.

Full-time life insurance salesmen are singled out as employees under the provisions of I.R.C. Sec. 3121(d)(3)(B). Form SS-8 addresses the issue of whether a worker who sells life insurance does so on a full-time basis by specifically asking whether the worker is classified as a full-time life insurance salesman, whether the worker also sells other types of insurance, and, if so, what percentage of the worker's time is spent doing so. Revenue Ruling 59-103 offers guidance by stating that for a party to be considered employed as a full-time life insurance salesman, his or her *principal business activity* should be the solicitation of life insurance or annuity contracts for one life insurance company.

Still another type of worker that is specifically defined as an employee is a *traveling or city salesman* who works full-time soliciting orders from wholesalers, retailers, contractors, or hotel or restaurant operators for merchandise for resale or supplies for use in business operations. The solicitations must be primarily on behalf of one principal and Rev. Rul. 55-31 provides that if the worker spends 80% or more of his or her time soliciting orders on behalf of one principal, he or she will be considered to have met that requirement. However, if a traveling salesman or city salesman *has a substantial investment in facilities used in connection with the performance of such services (other than in facilities for transportation), or if the services are in the nature of a single transaction not part of a continuing relationship with the person for whom services are performed,* I.R.C. Sec. 3121(d)(3)(D) provides that the worker will not be automatically included within the statutory definition as an employee. Instead, the worker would be categorized on the basis of the various factors used by the IRS in making such determinations.

EXAMPLE: Joe is a manufacturer's representative for several companies that manufacture cutlery and kitchen gadgets. He entered into an agreement to represent the largest pocket knife manufacturer in the country in a territory that covers the southeastern part of the U.S. Joe has begun to devote most of his time to the pocket knife line. He has a showroom where he holds sales meetings with prospective customers and with members of his staff. He also stocks samples and displays in a small attached warehouse.

Joe would not be included under the definition of an employee under I.R.C. Sec. 3121(d)(3)(D) since he has a substantial investment in facilities used in connection with his sales activities. Also, Sec. 3121(d)(3)(D) requires that the sales services be performed personally by the salesman in order for him to be labeled as an employee by the statute and, since Joe has staff members who make sales calls, this will also prevent him from being considered an employee.

In order to assist the IRS in making the determination as to whether a salesman's activities fit the parameters of I.R.C. Sec. 3121(d)(3)(D) resulting in an automatic classification as an employee, Form SS-8 in Part IV specifically asks, in determinations involving a salesman, who the worker solicits and whether the merchandise being marketed is being resold by the buyers or used by them in their business operations. If a salesperson does not fit the criteria of I.R.C. Sec. 3121(d)(3)(D) to be automatically considered an employee, he or she may still be determined to be an employee on the basis of the relationship between the worker and the firm whose products the worker sells. Therefore, when a determination is being made regarding salespersons, Form SS-8 requires disclosure of a substantial amount of information concerning the relationship between the salesperson and the firm whose goods or services he or she is selling. The specific information sought in such instances includes the following.

What is the worker's responsibility for soliciting new customers?

If a worker merely takes or processes orders from existing customers, he or she is very likely to be classified as an employee. Workers who are responsible for soliciting new customers will not necessarily be considered to be independent contractors, since there are working relationships for both employees and independent contractors that involve the solicitation of new customers. However, such responsibility will prevent the presumption of an employment relationship and open the matter up for further analysis in making a determination of the relationship between the parties.

How does the worker get leads for prospective customers?

Employees commonly are supplied leads to customers by their employers as a result of advertising campaigns undertaken by the firm. Independent contractors are generally expected to generate their own leads and it is much less likely that they will be supplied with leads on a regular basis by the firms whose goods and services they sell, although occasional referrals from the firm are common, even for independent contractors.

What are the reporting requirements that must be met by workers regarding leads supplied by the firm?

Detailed reports of the results of contacts with potential customers from leads supplied by the firm are typically required of employees by their employers. Such requirements are a basic method for maintaining the degree of control over the salesperson that employers generally seek. Leads supplied by a firm to an independent contractor are often merely the result of an unsolicited inquiry from a potential customer and are referred to the salesperson to avoid having to deal with the customer. Firms who have contracted with independent contractors to sell their goods and services are usually much more interested in the overall results of the salesperson, rather than the dealings with a specific customer, than are firms who use their own employees to sell their goods and services.

Are the sale terms and conditions dictated by the firm?

A salesperson who buys goods from a producer or distributor and then resells them on his or her own terms in hopes of making a profit is clearly not an employee of the producer or distributor. On the other hand, a salesperson who must follow the dictates of the producer or distributor in marketing goods or services for the party and, especially if orders must be submitted to the producer or distributor for approval, is likely to be considered to be an employee of the firm. That is unless he has a substantial investment in facilities, other than a mere vehicle, used in connection with the sales effort. Often salespeople fall between the two extremes causing it to become necessary to consider a number of factors in order to properly classify the workers.

Factors that Indicate a Worker is an Independent Contractor

- ◆ Worker has a significant investment in facilities in which work is performed
- ◆ Worker has potential to suffer loss as well as make profit from work performed
- ◆ Worker is employed by a variety of employers
- ◆ Worker's services are available to the general public
- ◆ Worker is paid by the job
- ◆ Worker obtained the job by bidding on it
- ◆ Payment at erratic intervals depending on how work is progressing
- ◆ Lack of fringe benefits such as paid vacation, paid holidays or employer-provided health insurance
- ◆ Employer reports worker's earnings on a Form 1099

Factors that Indicate a Worker is an Employee

- Employer has the right to instruct employee as to details of how to perform job
- Employer provides training
- Integration of worker's activity into employer's operation
- Services must be personally rendered by worker
- Employer hires and pays those who assist worker
- Continuing relationship between worker and employer
- Worker must work set hours
- Worker works full-time for employer
- Worker must work on employer's premises
- Employer sets sequence in which work must be done
- Worker must submit regular reports
- Worker is paid hourly or on salary
- Employer pays worker's business and travel expenses
- Employer provides tools used by worker
- Worker and employer may terminate the relationship any time
- Worker obtained the job by applying for it or through an employment agency
- Payment at regular intervals such as weekly or monthly
- Employer provides fringe benefits
- Earnings are reported on Form W-2

Index

J

About the Author

James O. Parker has repeatedly encountered clients who were somewhat bewildered by our country's tax laws, having been a practicing attorney for over twenty-five years. Calling upon his twenty-nine years as an educator at Christian Brothers University in Memphis Tennessee and being a small business owner himself for over forty years, he set out to take some of the mystery out of the tax code. His first book, *Tax Smarts for Small Business,* was written with the over seven million owners of small businesses in the U.S. who operate through formal business entities in mind. His latest effort, *Tax Power for the Self-Employed,* was written to offer tax guidance to self-employed individuals, a group that now exceeds fifteen million in the U.S.

A former U.S. Marine and community advocate, he possesses both a Masters of Arts in Economics and J.D. from the University of Memphis, as well as an LL.M. from Emory University in Atlanta, Georgia.

A frequent speaker on tax topics, business succession planning, and small business development, he continues to advise others on the importance of tax planning.

Mr. Parker lives with his wife, Linda, in Germantown, Tennessee.